THE SIMON AND SCHUSTER POCKET GUIDE TO BEER

MICHAEL JACKSON

A FIRESIDE BOOK
PUBLISHED BY
SIMON & SCHUSTER, INC.
NEW YORK

Key to symbols

This book attempts to review not only the principal names in each important brewing region but also a selection of especially interesting smaller houses. Star ratings are intended merely as a guide, and assess beers against others from the same country.

    * Typical of its country and style
   ** Above average
  *** Worth seeking out
 **** World Classic
  ☎ Telephone

Dedication

To my late father, Jack Jackson,
born Isaac Jakowitz, Yorkshire, 1909–84.

Acknowledgments

Brewers and importers of beer all over the world, and their trade organizations, have gone to trouble and expense far beyond their self-interest to help me research this book. My heartfelt thanks to all of them. Many friends and professional colleagues have also helped, and I owe a special debt of gratitude to Johannes Schulters, of Bamberg, Germany; Antoine Denooze, of the Hopduvel, Ghent, Belgium; Denis Palmer, of Anglo-Dutch Ales, and Henk Eggens, of Café Gollem, Amsterdam, The Netherlands; Brian Glover and Danny Blyth, of the Campaign for Real Ale, in Britain; Elisabeth Baker, at The Grist; friends at CAMRA Canada and the Canadian Amateur Brewers' Association; Alan Dikty, of The New Brewer; Charlie Papazian and friends, at the American Homebrewers' Association, in Boulder, Colorado; and – especially – Vince Cottone, of Seattle; and to friends at Suntory, in Tokyo and Osaka, Japan.

Editor Alison Franks
Designer Jill Raphaeline
Proofreader and Indexer Rosamond Cocks
Research Assistant Sonia Abeliuk
Production Androulla Pavlou

Senior Editor Dian Taylor
Senior Executive Editor Chris Foulkes
Senior Executive Art Editor Roger Walton

CONTENTS

MAPS

INTRODUCTION

THE NEW APPRECIATION OF BEER

The *hauteur* that rightly attends wine has for too long overshadowed beer, but that is changing. It is increasingly being appreciated that the two are companions of honour as the principal types of fermented drink: part of the gastronomic heritage of the warm and cool climates that grow the grape and the grain respectively.

The spread in travel and leisure has made for a more universal interest in wine, and the same is true in respect of beer. There is an international wave of serious interest in beer, from Italy (where it is the most chic of drinks), through Germany and Belgium (where speciality styles are in ever-greater demand) to Britain (first came the "real ale" renaissance; now the surge of "foreign" lagers) and to the United States (where imported beers arrive in bewildering profusion). In all of these countries, there has also been in recent years a blessing of new, tiny *boutique* or *micro* breweries, often producing speciality styles of beer.

Most varieties of wine are understood outside their regions of production, but the stylistic diversity of beer is only now beginning to confront the consumer. From the Pilseners, Mucheners and Dortmunders to the different wheat beers of north and south Germany, to the spontaneously fermenting specialities and Trappist monastery ales of Belgium, to the ales of England and Scotland, the sweet and dry stouts of the British Isles, there are between 20 and 30 classic styles of beer, and yet more sub-categories.

Just as a Chablis or a champagne, a claret or a Zinfandel, each has a different purpose in life, so does each style of beer. An everyday, mass-market lager might do nothing more ambitious than quench the thirst, but some styles of beer are best served as aperitifs, others as digestifs; this with crustaceans, that with red meat; one as a restorative, another in a moment of reflection, a third as a nightcap.

An intensely dry aperitif beer will not necessarily quench the thirst. Nor will a big, warming brew. A tart, quenching beer may not be the one to sip in front of an open fire. The wrong beer for the occasion will at best disappoint and at worst confuse. The same is true if the beer is not served in the manner, or at the temperature, at which it best expresses its qualities of aroma, palate and character.

Whether the beer-fancier carries out his (or her)

explorations in the local pub or restaurant, or by trains and boats and planes, this Pocket Guide may be of assistance.

WHAT MAKES A GREAT BEER

Wine is more vulnerable to the mercies of soil and weather, but beer is the more complicated drink to make. The barley must first be malted and made into an infusion or decoction, the enigmatic (and none too hardy) hop added as a seasoning, and the whole brewed before it can be fermented, matured and conditioned.

In carrying out these procedures, the brewer is seeking to impart (in aroma, palate and finish) his own balance between the sweetness of the barley malt, the herby dryness of the hop, and the background fruitiness of the yeast used in fermentation. These characteristics are immediately evident in a fresh beer, especially one that has not been pasteurized (this process, unless it is carried out with the greatest of care, may merely deaden the beer to the ravages of travel and time).

The balance will be weighted differently according to the style of the beer, but it must always be achieved. A chef may intend one dish to be delicate, another to be robust, but each must have its own balance. After balance comes complexity. A winemaker knows that each style is expected to have certain features, but beyond those there should be the individuality of its own character. Each time the drinker raises a glass of fine wine, new dimensions of aroma and palate should become apparent. So it is with a fine beer.

Any fine food or drink is enjoyed with the eyes and nose as well as the palate. The more individualistic beers, especially of the darker styles, can have a great subtlety of colour; most styles will present a dense, uneven "rocky" head if they have been naturally carbonated in fermentation, rather than having been injected with carbon dixoide; a properly carbonated beer will leave "Brussels lace" down the sides of the glass after each swallow. A good beer should be poured gently down the side of a tilted glass. A final, upright, flourish may contribute to its appearance, but the formation of a good head should not rest on the beers being dumped violently into the glass.

Conventional beers are intended to be clear though excessive refrigeration can cause a "chill haze" in a good-quality, all-malt brew. The haze should subside once the beer reaches about 7°C (45°F). Conventional beers are also at risk of general deterioration (though they will not necessarily succumb to it) from the moment they leave the brewery. They are intended for immediate drinking, and not for keeping.

Brews indicated to be conditioned in the cask or bottle will contain living yeast. Unless the beer is poured carefully, the palate will have a "yeast bite", but the sediment is not harmful (in fact, its health benefits are quickly apparent). Very strong bottle-conditioned brews will improve with age.

Bottle-conditioned ales naturally have a very fruity aroma. In any beer, an unpleasant aroma reminiscent of damp paper or cardboard indicates oxidation (quite simply, the beer has gone stale). A cabbagey or skunky aroma means that the beer has been damaged by supermarket lighting or by being left in the sun. Beer is a natural product, and does not enjoy rough treatment.

Strength

This is not a measure of quality. The ideal strength for a beer depends upon the purpose for which it is intended. A beer that is meant to be quenching, and to be consumed in quantity, should not be high in alcohol. The classic example, the *Berliner Weisse* style, has around 3 percent alcohol by volume. A typical premium beer, whether in Germany, Britain or the United States, might have between 4 and 5 percent by volume. A strong "winter warmer" may typically have between 6 and 8 percent. Although there are specialities exceeding 13 percent, beers of this strength are hard to brew, and to drink in any quantity. At these levels, alcohol stuns beer yeasts to a point where they can no longer work, and the residual sugars make for heavy, cloying brews. There are, of course, wines of this strength, but they are not drunk by the half-pint.

Alcohol by volume is the system most commonly used to describe the strength of wine, and it is the simplest rating to understand. However, this system is rarely employed in respect of beer. The Canadians use it, but American brewers usually quote alcohol by weight. Since water is heavier than alcohol, this produces lower figures. In many countries, a measure of alcohol content is not required by law. In those countries, the authorities are more concerned to tax what goes into the beer: the malt, wheat or other fermentable sugars. This is variously described as density or original gravity. Each of the older brewing nations developed its own scale for measuring this, the German Plato and similar Czechoslovakian Balling systems being the most commonly used. In those countries, drinkers are inclined to be less familiar with alcohol content than with gravity.

The two do not have a direct relationship, since

alcohol content is also a function of the degree of fermentation. The more thorough the fermentation, the higher the level of alcohol produced from a given gravity. The less thorough the fermentation, the fuller the body. Alcohol content and body are quite different, and in this respect opposed, elements of a beer.

The Malts

As grapes are to wine, so barley malt is to beer the classic source of fermentable sugars. The barley is malted (steeped in water until it partially germinates, then dried in a kiln) to release the starches that are then turned into fermentable sugars by infusion or decoction in water in a mashing vessel. This process is parallel to that carried out in the first stages of production of malt whiskies.

In addition to deciding the proportion of malts to be used to achieve the desired density, the brewer is also concerned with their origin.

Certain varieties of barley are grown especially to be malted for the brewing industry. Among them, those that are grown in summer are held to produce cleaner-tasting, sweeter malts, though there is some debate on this. Some brewers also feel that inland, "continental" barleys produce better results than those grown in maritime climates. With varying harvests, there are differences in the quality and availability of barley, and the brewer has to account for this in the fine detail of his mashing procedure, its durations and temperatures. He will also adjust these according to the precise character he is seeking in his beer. They are among the hundreds of variables, and thousands of permutations, that contribute to the final character of every beer.

The traditional malting barleys are of varieties that have two rows of grain in each ear. Six-rowed barley is also used, though it produces a huskier, sharper character in the beer. Traditionalists stick to two-row barley but some brewers claim to seek the character they find in six-row varieties.

To the consumer, the more immediately obvious influence is the way in which the barley has been malted. There are many different standard malting specifications, each intended to produce a different result in terms of both colour and palate. As to colour, the more intense the kilning of the malt, the darker the beer. In palate, the character of the barley and the way in which it is malted can impart tones that are reminiscent, for example, of nuts, caramel, chocolate, espresso or licorice. These variations in malting differ in the moisture of the grains at the time of the kilning, as well as in the cycles of temperature and duration.

Depending upon the style of beer being produced, the brewer may use only one or two different types of malt, or as many as seven or eight. He may also use a proportion of unmalted barley, sometimes highly roasted, as in the case of dry stouts like Guinness. German and Belgian *Weisse* beers are made with a proportion of malted wheat. So, naturally enough, are *Weizen* beers (it means wheat, after all). Belgian *lambic* beers use a proportion of unmalted wheat. One or two highly specialized beers use a small quantity of oats. Less traditional grains include proportions of rice and corn, both used to lighten beers, and the latter especially for its low cost. Also for reasons of cost, and to boost alcohol in inexpensive strong beers like American malt liquors, cane sugar may be used. In Belgium, candy sugar is used in strong Trappist monastery beers. In Britain, milk sugars are used in sweet stouts.

In a cheap beer, barley malt may represent 60 percent of the mash, and corn or other adjuncts the rest. In Bavaria, barley malt and wheat are the only fermentable materials allowed. Elsewhere in West Germany, the same goes for domestic beers but not for exports. One or two other countries have similar laws, the closest being those of Norway and Greece.

The Hops

Early wine-makers lacked the knowledge to produce by fermentation alone products of the quality they sought, so they employed seasonings of herbs and spices, creating the forerunners of today's vermouths and of patent aperitifs like Campari. Distillers, faced with similar difficulties, used a spicing of juniper and coriander to dry the palate of their product, thus creating gin. Liqueurs like Chartreuse have a similar history of development. In the same tradition, early brewers used tree-barks, herbs and berries.

Juniper and coriander are still used in a handful of highly specialized beers, but the hop eventually became the normal choice. The hop is a climbing plant, a vine, that is a member of the same family as cannabis. In ancient times, its shoots were eaten as a salad, and in Belgium they still are. Its cone-like blossoms can have a sedative effect, and are used in hop pillows. The cones also produce tannins that help clarify and preserve beer, and resins and essential oils that are the principal sources of aroma and dryness.

Not to mince words, this is not so much a dryness as a bitterness, a quality that is greatly enjoyed by connoisseurs of good beer, but one that seems to frighten less devoted drinkers. Perhaps it is the negative connotations of the word "bitter". People who enjoy a Campari before dinner, or a coffee afterwards, complain that beer is too "bitter". Of course it is bitter; that is why the hops are there. That is why the British ask for "a pint of bitter". That is why some beers are such marvellous aperitifs; their bitterness arouses the gastric juices. Contrary to some opinions, there is also much more than bitterness to the hop; it has a tangle of fresh, earthy, arousing flavours that blossom like a herb garden. It is too adult a taste for people who have not yet grown out of doughnuts and Coca-Cola.

Since all hops contain elements of both bitterness and aroma, the same variety may be used for both purposes, but this is not generally done. Each variety of hop is usually identified as being ideal either for bitterness or aroma. A brewer may, indeed, use just one variety, but he is more likely to use two or three, occasionally even seven or eight. He may put hops into the kettle once, twice or three times. The early additions are to provide bitterness, the later ones to confer aroma. To heighten aroma, he may even add blossoms to the hop strainer, or to the conditioning vessel. This last technique is known as "dry hopping". At each addition, he may use only one variety, or a different blend of several. He may use hop oils or extracts, or the whole blossom, in its natural form or compacted into pellets.

There are many varieties of bittering hop, but few that enjoy special renown. Aroma hops are the aristocrats.

In continental Europe, the classic is the Saaz hop, grown in the area around the small town of Žatec, in Bohemia, Czechoslovakia. In Germany, considerable reputations are enjoyed by the Hallertau Mittelfrüh and Tettnang aroma hops, named after areas near Munich and Lake Constance respectively.

In Britain, the delightfully named Fuggles are often used for their gentle, rounded, bitterness, though they are also regarded as aroma hops. The counties of Hereford and Kent are known for their hops, and the latter especially for a slightly more bitter and hugely aromatic variety called Goldings. These are at their finest in east Kent, near Faversham, allegedly in a strip of countryside a mile wide.

In North America, the Cascade is the classic aroma hop, grown especially in the Yakima Valley of Washington State. There are hop-growing areas in British Columbia, Canada, too, and in not dissimilar latitudes of the southern hemisphere, in Tasmania.

The Yeast

Among wines, it might be argued – perhaps simplistically – that there is a central division along lines of colour, between the reds and the whites. Among beers such a division concerns not colour but the type of yeast used.

For centuries, all brewing employed what we now know as top-fermenting, or "ale", yeasts. In those days yeast was barely understood, except as the foam which, when scooped from the top of one brew, acted as a "starter" for the fementation of the next. In this primitive method of brewing, the yeasts naturally rose to the top of the vessel, and were able to cross breed with wild micro-organisms in the atmosphere. In the summer, they did so to a degree where beer spoilage made brewing impossible.

Brewers in the Bavarian Alps first discovered empirically, that beer stabilized if it was stored (in German, *lagered*) in icy, mountain caves during the summer. Not only was it less vulnerable to cross breeding; the yeast sank to the bottom of the vessel out of harm's way. As scientists began to understand the behaviour of yeast in the 19th century, "bottom fermenting" strains were methodically bred.

Today, all of the older brewing styles — ales porters, stouts, German *Altbier* and *Kölsch* and all wheat beers — are (or should be) made with top fermenting yeasts. All of the *lager* styles — Pilseners Muncheners, Dortmunders, *Märzen*, Bock and double Bock and American malt liquors — are made with bottom-fermenting yeasts.

"Top" yeasts ferment at warm temperatures (classically $15-25°C/59-77°F$), after which the beer may be matured for only a few days, or a couple of weeks, at warm temperatures. With modern means of temperature control, brewing in summer no longer poses a problem. A beer that has been "warm conditioned" will most fully express its palate if it is served at natural cellar temperature, ideally not less than $12°C$ ($55°F$). This is why a well-run British pub will serve ales at such a temperature. British ale can be rendered worthless by refrigeration.

"Bottom" yeasts ferment at cooler temperatures (classically $5-12°C/41-54°F$), and the beer is then matured by being stored (*lagered*) at around $0°C$ ($32°F$). Many mass-market beers are lagered for barely three weeks. Even in Germany, many brewers are content with four weeks, but traditionalists argue for three months. Bottom-fermenting beers taste best if they are chilled to between $7°C$ ($45°F$) and $10°C$ ($50°F$), the lighter their body, the lower the temperature and vice-versa.

In both techniques, very strong ales and lagers are matured for longer periods, sometimes for nine, or even 12, months. For whatever duration, this is a period in which the remaining yeast settles, harsh flavour compounds mellow out, and the beer gains its natural texture and carbonation (its "condition").

In top-fermenting ales that have a short period of maturation, the yeast may be settled with the aid of finings, usually isinglass. In Britain the classic ales are delivered to the pub with some working yeast still in the cask, so that they may reach the prime of condition in the cellar. This is known as *cask-conditioning*. Some speciality ales are bottled without filtration, or with an added dosage of yeast, as in the *méthode champenoise*. This is known as *bottle-conditioning*.

Because they pre-date the true understanding of yeasts, some top-fermenting strains are hybrids. Others have picked up some "house character" from the micro-organisms resident in the brewery. Some brewers of top-fermenting specialities intentionally use a blend of yeast, or employ different strains at different stages. Many, of course, use single-cell pure cultures, as do almost all brewers of bottom-fermenting beers. Bottom-fermentation has its origins in a more methodical, scientific, approach to brewing.

Beers made with top-fermenting yeasts are inclined to have more individualistic and expressive palates, often with elements of fruitiness and acidity. Bottom-fermenting beers tend to be cleaner and rounder but the trade-off is that they may be less individualistic.

The Water

Claims about the water used in brewing were probably the most common feature of beer advertizing in the Victorian and Edwardian periods, and they are still to be heard.

In the 18th and 19th centuries, sources of pure water were not always easy to find. That is why towns or cities with good sources – among them, Pilsen and Munich in continental Europe; Burton and Tadcaster in England – became centres of brewing.

Even today, a source of water that requires little or no treatment is an asset to a brewery. A great many breweries have their own springs or wells (this may not be the rule, but it is by no means the exception). In a good few instances, the town supply is adequate once the chlorine has been removed. Only in isolated cases is a water supply a problem. There is at least one island brewery that has to de-salinate sea water, and one in New Orleans has been known to truck in water, but they certainly are exceptions.

Even if the water does come from the brewery's own spring or well, natural salts may have to be added or removed for the production of different types of beer.

"It's the water!" boast some breweries. "It's the beer!" would be a more convincing claim.

THE LANGUAGE OF THE LABEL

Ale The English-language term for a brew made with top-fermenting yeast, which should impart to it a distinctiv fruitiness. Ales are produced to a wide variety of colour palates and strengths (see also Bitter, Brown Ale, India Pa Ale, Light Ale, Mild, Old Ale, Scotch Ale, etc). Only in som American states is the term determined by law (wrongly) t indicate a brew of more than 4 percent weight (5 by volume)

Altbier A German term for a top-fermenting brew. Th classic examples, copper in colour, mashed only from barle malt, fermented from a single-cell yeast and cold-con ditioned, with an alcohol content of 4.5–4.7 by volume, a made in Düsseldorf.

Barley Wine An English term for an extra-strong al (implied to be as potent as wine). Usually more than percent by volume and classically closer to 11. Most ofte bottled. Copper-coloured, tawny or dark brown.

"Beer" Often misunderstood by Americans to apply onl to products that are, in fact, exclusively of the lager typ The British, on the other hand, are inclined to think that th only true beer is ale. Both lager and ale – as well as porte stout, and all the Belgian and German specialities – a embraced by the general term "beer". It is all beer.

Berliner Weisse Berlin's classic "white" (cloudy sedimented, top-fermenting wheat beer, with the quenchi sourness of a lactic fermentation, the sparkle of a hig carbonation, and a low alcohol content of around 3 percen by volume.

Bière de Garde French term originally applied to stron copper-coloured, top-fermenting brews, bottle-conditione for laying down. Today's examples have an alcohol conten in the range of 5.5–6 by volume, and may be bottom fermented and filtered.

Bitter English term for a well-hopped ale, most often o draught. Although examples vary widely, the name impli a depth of hop bitterness. There is usually some acidity i the finish, and colour varies from bronze to deep coppe Basic bitters usually have an alcohol content of aroun 3.75–4 percent by volume, "Best" or "Special" bitters com in at 4–4.75; the odd "Extra Special" at about 5.5.

Bo(c)k The German term for a strong beer. If unqualifie it indicates a bottom-fermenting brew from barley malt. I Germany, a bock beer has more than 6.25 percent alcohol b volume, and may be golden, tawny or dark brown. Outsi Germany, strengths vary, and a bock is usually dark. Boc beers are served in autumn, late winter or spring, dependin upon the country. (See also Maibock, Doppelbock, Weize bier.)

Brown Ale In the south of England, a dark-brown al sweet in palate, low in alcohol (3–3.5 by volume). In th northeast, a reddish-brown ale, drier, of 4.4–5. The slightl sour, brown brews of Flanders are also ales, though they d not generally use the designation.

Cream Ale An American designation, implying a ver pale, mild, light-bodied ale that may actually have bee blended with a lager. Around 4.75 by volume.

"Dark beer" There are many, quite unrelated, styles dark brew. If this vague term is used without qualificatio usually means a dark lager of the Munich type.

ät Pils Nothing to do with slimming, but originally tended for diabetics. A German style so popular in Britain at many drinkers think there is no other kind of "Pils". rbohydrates are diminished by a very thorough fermenta- on, creating a relatively high content of alcohol (about 6 rcent by volume) and therefore lots of calories. In German w, the alcohol now has to be reduced back to a normal lsener level (5 percent).

oppelbock "Double" bock. German extra-strong bot- m-fermenting beer, tawny or dark brown. Around 7.5 by lume or stronger. Southern speciality, seasonal to March d April. Names usually end in *-ator*.

ort Abbreviation used in Belgium and The Netherlands indicate a beer in the Dortmunder Export style.

ortmunder This indicates merely a beer brewed in ortmund, but the city's classic style is Export (see separate try).

unkel German word for "dark".

sbock An extra-strong (*Doppel*) bock beer in which tency has been heightened by a process of freezing. cause water freezes before alcohol, the removal of ice (*eis*) ncentrates the beer.

xport In Germany, a pale, Dortmund-style bottom-fer- enting beer that is bigger in body than a Pilsener, and less y, but not as sweet as a Munich pale beer. It is stronger an either, at 5.25−5.5 by volume. Elsewhere, Export ually indicates a premium beer.

ro Brussels' local style, a sweetened version of a *lambic*. 5−5.5 by volume.

stbier In Germany, any beer made for a festival. Styles ry, but such beers are usually above average strength, ten around 5.5−6 by volume.

amboise A raspberry-macerated *lambic*. 5.5−6.

ieuze A blend of old and young *lambic* beers. Around 5.

efe- The German word for yeast, indicating that a beer is ttle-conditioned and sedimented.

ell German word for "pale", indicating an everyday er that is golden in colour. Ordered as a *Helles (hell-es)*.

perial Stout See Stout.

dia Pale Ale A reminder of the days when the Indian npire was supplied with ales (high in gravity, and well pped, to stand the voyage) by the British. Today, the rm implies a super-premium pale ale.

ellerbier German term indicating an unfiltered lager, in nich there is usually a high hop content and a low rbonation. Strengths vary according to the original style.

ölsch Cologne's distinctive style of golden, top-ferment- g brew. 4.3−5 by volume.

äusen In German custom, a traditional technique of rbonation is to add a small dosage of unfermented malt gars (in English, wort) to the conditioning tank. In a rmally *kräusened* beer, the wort ferments out and the beer conventionally filtered. An unfiltered beer based on this hnique is known as a *kräusenbier*.

iek A cherry-macerated *lambic*. 5.5−6.

ger Any beer made by bottom-fermentation. In itain, lagers are usually golden in colour, but in continen- l Europe they can also be dark. In Germany and The

Netherlands, the term may be used to indicate the m(
basic beer of the house, the *bière ordinaire*.

Lambic Spontaneously fermenting style of wheat b(
unique to Belgium, notably the Senne Valley. About 4.(

Light Ale English term describing the bottled counterpa(
of a basic bitter. In Scotland, "Light" indicates the lowe(
gravity draught beer (usually dark in colour), neither ter(
implies a low-calorie beer.

Light Beer American term, indicating a watery Pilsen(
style beer. 2.75−4 by volume. Calories might better be sav(
by drinking fewer beers, eating fewer chips, or sticking (
honest water.

Maibock A bock beer of super-premium quality. Usua(
pale. Made for the first of May to celebrate spring.

Malt Liquor Not especially malty, though they are usua(
low in hop character. Certainly not liquors, though they (
usually the strongest beers in an American brewer's ran(
Malt liquor is the American term for a strong, pale lager,
anything from 5−7.5 by volume, often cheaply ma(
Regrettably, laws in some states encourage the term to (
used on imported strong lagers of far greater character.

Märzen From "March" in German. Originally a b(
brewed in March and laid down in caves before the summ(
weather rendered brewing impossible. Stocks would (
drawn upon during the summer, and finally exhausted (
October. In Germany, this tradition has come to (
associated with one specific style. *Märzenbier* has a ma(
aroma, and is a medium-strong version (classically, m(
than 5.5 percent alcohol by volume) of the amber-(
Vienna style. It is seasonal to the *Oktoberfest*, where it (
offered as a traditional speciality alongside paler beers o(
similar strength. Confusingly, in Austria the term refers (
to style but to gravity.

Mild English term indicating an ale that is only ligh(
hopped. Some milds are copper in colour, but most are da(
brown. These beers were devised to be drunk in la(
quantities by manual workers, and have in recent ye(
suffered from their blue-collar image. Around 3 by volur(
but often relatively full in body.

Munchener/Münchner Means "Munich-style". In int(
national brewing terminology, this indicates a dark-bro(
lager, a style that was developed in Munich (althou(
another Bavarian town, Kulmbach, also has a long traditi(
of − very − dark lagers). In Munich, such a brew is clea(
identified by the word *Dunkel* ("dark"), and classic exa(
ples have an alcohol content of around, or just over (
percent by volume. The brewers of Munich, and Bavaria (
general, also impart their own distinctively malty accen(
their everyday, lower-gravity (alcohol content around 3(
pale beers. These are sometimes identified as *Münchner H(
to distinguish them from the same brewers' Pilsener-st(
product.

Oktoberfest beers See **Märzen**.

Old (Ale) In Australia, "Old" simply means a dark ale.(
Britain, it is most commonly used to indicate a mediu(
strong dark ale like Old Peculier, which has just under (
percent by volume. However, by no means all a(
describing themselves as "old" are in this style.

Pale Ale Pale in this instance means copper-coloured, (
opposed to dark brown. Pale ale is a term used by so(

nglish brewers to identify their premium bitters, especially
a bottled form.

ilsener/Pilsner/Pils Loosely, any golden-coloured, dry,
ottom-fermenting beer of conventional strength might be
escribed as being of this style (in its various spellings and
bbreviations), though this most famous designation
roperly belongs only to a product of "super-premium"
uality. Too many brewers take it lightly, in more senses
han one. In their all-round interpretation, it is the German
rewers who take the style most seriously, inspired by the
Irquell (original) brew from the town of Pilsen, in the
rovince of Bohemia, Czechoslovakia. A classic Pilsner has a
ravity of around 12 Plato (4 percent alcohol by weight; 5 by
olume) and is characterized by the hoppiness of its flowery
roma and dry finish.

orter A London style that became extinct, though it has
ecently been revived. It was a lighter-bodied companion to
out, and the most accurate revivals are probably the
orters made by American micro-brewers like Sierra
evada. Around 5 percent by volume. In some countries,
he porter tradition remains in roasty-tasting dark brews
hat are bottom-fermented, and often of a greater strength.

auchbier Smoked malts are used in the production of this
ark, bottom-fermented speciality, principally made in and
round Bamberg, Franconia. Produced at around 5 percent
y volume and in *Märzen* and *Bock* versions. Serve with
avarian smoked ham, or bagels and lox.

aison Seasonal summer style in the French-speaking part
f Belgium. A sharply refreshing, faintly sour, top-ferment-
g brew, often bottle-conditioned, 5.5−8 by volume.

cotch Ale The ales of Scotland generally have a malt
ccent. In their home country, a single brewery's products
ay be identified in ascending order of gravity and strength
s Light, Heavy, Export and Strong. Or by a system based
n the old currency of shillings, probably once a reference to
ax ratings: 60/-, 70/-, 80/-, 90/-. Alcohol content by volume
ight rise through 3, 4, 4.5 and 7−10. The term "Scotch ale"
sometimes used specifically to identify a very strong, often
xtremely dark, malt-accented speciality from that country.

team Beer A name trademarked by the Anchor Steam
eer brewery of San Francisco. This brewery's principal
roduct is made by a distinctive method of bottom-fermen-
ation at high temperatures and in unusually wide, shallow
essels. This technique, producing a beer with elements of
oth lager and ale in its character (though also distinctive in
s own right), is said to have been common in California
hen, in the absence of supplies of ice, early brewers tried to
ake bottom-fermenting beers. Although there are more
omantic explanations, the term "Steam" probably derives
om the brewery's original source of power. In the days
hen it represented advanced technology, many breweries
roclaimed "Steam" (in Germany, *Dampf-*) in their names,
nd some still do. In Germany, one brewery has trade-
arked a product called *Dampfbier*, but this is not in the
alifornian style.

tout An extra-dark, almost black, top-fermenting brew,
ade with highly roasted malts. *Sweet stout*, an English
yle, is typified by Mackeson, which has only about 3.75
ercent alcohol by volume in its domestic market but more
an 5 in the Americas. Sweet stout usually contains milk

sugars (lactose), and is a soothing restorative. *Dry stout*, t
Irish style, is typified by Guinness, which comes in at arou
4 percent in the British Isles, a little more in North Ameri
and as much as 8 in tropical countries. Dry stouts sometim
contain roasted unmalted barley. *Imperial Stout*, original
brewed as a winter warmer for sale in the Tsarist Russi
Empire, is medium dry and distinguished by its gre
strength: anything from 7 to more than 10.

Trappist This order of monks has five breweries in B
gium and one in The Netherlands. By law, only they a
entitled to use the term Trappist in describing the
products. Each of them produces strong (6–9 percent
volume), top-fermenting brews, all characteristica
employing candy sugar in the kettle, and always bott
conditioned. Colour varies from bronze to deep brown.
their daily life, the monks will drink their least-stro
product, and may refer to their more potent variations (i
religious holidays and commercial sale) as Double a
Triple.

Ur-/Urquell "Original"/"-source of", in German. J
tifiable when applied to, for example, Einbecker Ur-Bock
Pilsner Urquell, but often more loosely used.

Vienna Amber-red, or only medium-dark, lager. This w
the style originally produced in Vienna. Brewers still talk
a "Vienna malt" to indicate a kilning to this amber-r
colour, but the beer-style itself is no longer especia
associated with the city. Examples include the aptly nam
Vienna All-Malt Lager, from Milwaukee; the amber E
Equis, from Mexico; and the classic *Märzen* beers of Muni
among others. Strengths vary.

Weisse/Weissbier, Weizenbier German for "white" be
implying a pale brew made from wheat. In the north
special renown is enjoyed by *Berliner Weisse*, a style in
own right (see separate entry). A different style of *Weissb*
is made in the south, with a more conventional alcoh
content (usually a little over 5 percent by volume), a hig
proportion of wheat (at least 50 percent) and a yeast (ag
top-fermenting) that produces a tart, fruity, spicy pala
sometimes with notes of cooking apples and cloves. Oft
instead of *Weissbier*, the southerners prefer the te
Weizen (a similar-sounding word but it means, quite sim
ly "wheat"). If the beer is sedimented with yeast, it m
be prefixed *Hefe-*. Southern wheat beers are also produc
in dark versions (these *Dunkel Weizen* brews have a de
cious complex of fruitiness and maltiness), and in Exp
and Bock strengths. *Weizenbock* is sometimes served a
Christmas beer.

White A term once used in several parts of Europe
describe wheat beers. Apart from those of German-speaki
countries, Belgium's Hoegaarden and Leuven white be
are of considerable interest.

Wiesen/Wies'n Among several words that are confusin
similar to the non-German speaker, this one mea
"meadow". It implies a beer brewed for a carnival
festival (an *Oktoberfest* beer may be described as a Wie
Märzen) or a rustic speciality (such as Kuppers' unfilter
Wiess).

Zwickelbier German term for an unfiltered beer with
the distinguishing features of either a *Kellerbier* or
Kräusenbier.

TIME FOR A BEER

BEFORE A MEAL

1

3

2

4

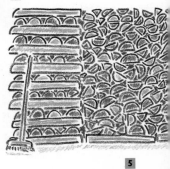

5

To sharpen the appetite . . . a dry beer. The dryness of the hop should be evident in any beer worthy of the designation Pilsener, not least the original, **1**, from Czechoslovakia. A hint of bitterness in the finish, too, to stimulate the gastric juices. A good Pilsener should be easy to find but more unusual brews add a touch of style. Drinkers who savour a Scotch before dinner might enjoy a German smoked beer, **3**, all the more teasing if it is based on wheat malt, kilned over beech logs **5**. Devotees of a pre-dinner *Kir Royale* should perhaps try a Belgian *kriek* beer, in which cherries are macerated during a third fermentation. There are *kriek* beers within the *lambic* ranges of Mort Subite, **2**, and Lindemans, **4**. Despite its threatening name, Mort Subite has a most enlivening effect.

WITH A MEAL

The London of Dickens and Disraeli knew the enigmatic pleasures of oysters (from the adjoining Thames-side counties of Essex and Kent) with porter or stout (in those days its predominant local brews). Today, the best English porter comes from a boutique brewery in Burton (a town better known for pale ales) **7**. The most famous stouts are the dry ones, from Dublin, **8**, or Cork, **3**, **7**, in Ireland. There is even a *château-* (to be pedantic, *Schloss-*) bottled example, Sir Henry's Stout, from Baron Henrik Bachofen von Echt, **1**, in Vienna. There are stouts, too, from Singapore, **5** (not to mention Sri Lanka and Japan), and from Australia, **2**. Africa, the Caribbean and North America all have stouts. They make a splendid accompaniment to crustaceans of all types, including crab and lobster. With gentler fish dishes, a pale, medium-dry, Export style beer from Dortmund, **10**, might be appropriate. Likewise with chicken or turkey. With pork, a sweeter pale beer, of the Munich *Helles* type. With spicy foods, a Vienna-style lager like Dos Equis (ideal with Mexican dishes). With noodle dishes, perhaps even a dark (*Dunkel*) lager. With red meats, a fruity ale from England (accompanying roast beef?) or Belgium (with a *carbonade Flamande*, or a French-speaking casserole), **4**, or from Canada, **9** (with a prairie steak or a Quebecois meat pie?).

And with dessert? There is a style of beer even for that occasion: a honeyish "white" wheat brew like the classic example, **6**, from the village of Hoegaarden, in Belgium.

AFTER A MEAL

the Anglo-French custom of its being served after the main meal, the cheese might be of the same origin as the accompanying beer. The French-speaking Belgian monastery, **1**, of Chimay is just one of several that produce cheese, **5**, as well as beer. Chimay's three principal strong Trappist brews are crown-corked in red, white and blue, **3**, in ascending order of potency. Among these "burgundies of Belgium", the natural accompaniment to cheese is

the vintage-dated *Capsule Bleue*, or "Chimay Blue", also available as Grande Reserve. Later still, the brandies of the beer world are those brews so strong that the warmth of alcohol comes through in the finish. The Belgian speciality Cuvée de l'Ermitage, **2**, is an Armagnac among beers. Rarer still, the German beer Abt's Trunk, **4**, from a secularized monastery brewery in Swabia, is reminiscent of an Alpine liqueur.

IN SPRING

Even before winter has retreated, but when its grip is being relaxed, the Germans strain at the leash, and reach daringly for the pleasures of outdoor drinking. It is still too cold, really, for such ventures, so a warming *Doppel* ("double") bock is proffered. The ritual begins in March or April – before Easter – with the ceremonial tapping of the first barrel of a new season's Paulaner Salvator Doppelbock, **3**, at the brewery's beer hall and garden in Munich. Echoing the original, *Doppelbock* beers usually affect names ending in *-ator*. A fine example is the brew known in Germany as Fortunator and in the United States as, appropriately, Celebrator, **2**. By May, spring can be greeted with more confidence, as it has been since pagan times. There are Maypoles in Bavaria, and there is the slightly less strong (though still potent) "single" *Bock* beer. Again in Munich, the Hofbräuhaus, **6**, the world's most famous beer garden and hall, taps its *Maibock*, **4**. There is also a *Maibock* from farther north, from Lower Saxony, from the town of Ein*beck*, **5**, where the style was conceived. Several continental European countries have *Bock* beers (though some are saved for autumn and winter, in an overlapping of traditions). In the United States, where *Bock* beers are enjoying something of a revival, they are usually served in late winter and early spring. The tradition is strongest in Wisconsin, but a fine newcomer, **1**, is from a boutique brewery in Montana.

3

4

5

6

IN SUMMER

4

5

6

In some countries, most beers are thought of as summer refreshers, but continental Europe has its own specialities to quench warm-weather thirsts. The principal categories are the wheat beers, with their sharp, tart palates. The south German type, **1**, are served in a vase-shaped glass, often with a slice of lemon. They are produced in (from right to left), dark, clear and sedimented versions. Another good range is made by Weihenstephan, **2**, the world's oldest brewery. The north German type of wheat beer, **3**, **7**, is served in a glass resembling a large champagne saucer. It is laced with essence of woodruff or, more commonly, raspberry syrup. Wheat beers, too, are enjoying a revival in the United States, with

examples from Hibernia, Kessler, Pyramid, Widmer and Anchor Steam. In addition to summer wheat beers, Belgium has intentionally sour, quenching, Flemish ales like Rodenbach, **4**, **6**, sometimes laced with grenadine. The seasonal theme is graphically portrayed when winter takes the beer it has been keeping in cold store, and presents it to summer, **5**. Sezoens is a proprietary brand in Flanders.

7

IN AUTUMN

Before September has passed, the October festivals are already beginning in the German-speaking world. This is the time when the idealized representation of the Bavarian barmaid is often exceeded in performance by the flesh and blood, **5**, **4**. She raises litre glasses, rather than consciousness, but such traditions endure. The beer she carries at *Oktoberfest* should, confusingly, be of the *Märzen* style. What was laid down in March is exhausted in October. The home of the style is Munich's Spaten brewery, which also defers to tradition with deliveries by horse and dray, **2**, **3**. American versions are produced in the Midwest by the revivalist brewers at Hibernia, **1**, and the old-established brewery of Hudepohl, **6**, **7**.

5

4

6

7

IN WINTER

1

2

A wintry country like Scotland should know how to produce warming brews. In the best traditions of the Auld Alliance, Traquair House, **2**, offers a château-bottled Scotch ale. Such delights taste best from a thistle-shaped glass, even if the Gordon's marque, **3**, is perversely only available in Belgium. Lovers of Lorimer's Caledonian might recognize MacAndrew's, **4**, which is available only in the United States. These Scottish ales are not as smoky as their compatriot whiskies, but they are more malty than most blends. Furthermore, a bottle of a strong Scotch ale is more potent than a large whisky. The English have several seasonal ales with "winter" in their name. The most famous is Winter Warmer, from Young's of London (the same name is used in the United States by Hale's Ales, of Colville, Washington). Young's is a draught ale, but its stronger, bottled counterpart is Old Nick, a devilish brew to set among the various strong ales (or "barley wines") named after bishops, **1**. Although these examples are all produced by secular breweries, the allusion has its origins in the days of ecclesiastical brewing in England.

AT CHRISTMAS

"Yule" might sound coy, but *Jule*, **1**, is Norwegian for Christmas. This Norwegian seasonal brew is a lovely tawny, nutty beer. Brewers in several countries produce special beers for the season, whether the allusion is to the gift-giving time, as in the Swiss Samichlaus (Santa Claus), or the eve of Christ's birth, as in Mexico's dark Nochebuena, **2**. Samichlaus is the world's strongest beer, at 14 percent alcohol by volume. It is produced in both pale (amber) and dark (deep red) versions, with a vintage date, a feature of several Christmas brews. All of these beers are bottom-fermenting, but a number of British and American brewers produce ales for Christmas. In the US this practice is spreading. Those

1

from the Anchor Steam Brewery, of San Francisco, are greatly prized. With both bottom- and top-fermenting brews, there is no definitive style for Christmas, but most examples are strong and of some character and quality. Some brewers, especially in Denmark, also have Easter and Whitsun brews.

2

VINTAGE BEERS

1

2

THE STRONGEST BEER IN BRITAIN
This beer is one of very few British beers bottled with its natural yeast, and it will mature in the bottle. Its flavour will improve if stored at 12°C (55°F) and will last for at least 25 years. If the bottle is disturbed before drinking, stand for 48 hours to allow natural sediment to settle and then pour carefully.
Eldridge Pope & Co. plc
Dorchester, Dorset

Most beer should be consumed as soon as possible: time is its enemy, and no further excuse should be needed. However, a handful of specialities are brewed to improve with age. That was the original significance of the French term *bière de garde* and it remains the meaning of the Flemish term *provisie bier*.

An even clearer imprecation is that on the back label of Thomas Hardy's Ale, **1**, from England. This lays down conditions that not every beer-lover can keep. Bottles from the 1960s have been offered by collectors for sale in the US at $1,000. Though not vintage-dated, Feuerfest, **2**, from Germany, carries a limited-edition number.

IMPERIAL EXTRA DOUBLE
A·LE COQ.
ANALYSES AND MEDICAL RE

АНАЛИЗЫ И ОТЗЫВЫ (
АНГЛІЙСКОМЬ ПОРТЕ
А·ЛЕ КОКЪ.

The classic vintage-dated beer is Courage's Imperial Russian Stout, **1**. This brew is made in Britain, and was originally produced for export to Russia during the time of the Tsarist Empire. Several brewers and shippers, one with the memorable name of A. Le Coq, **2**, exported "imperial" stouts during the 16th and 17th centuries. The Courage product is the last direct descendant of this trade, and has in recent years been harder to find in Britain than in some continental European countries. Since it no longer

has a long maturation perio at the brewery, it will benefit all the more from being laid down for a year o two, ideally at 12°C (55°F). Recently, another British brewer, Samuel Smith, has produced an imperial stout for export to the United States. This is not, however, intended for laying down. Neither is Kof Imperial Stout, **4**, from Finland. Another revivalist example, **3**, is produced by the Grant's boutique brewery, in Yakima, Washington. This is principally a draught beer.

The world's most widely known style of beer originates from the town of Pilsen, in Bohemia (the kingdom of Wenceslas in the Middle Ages d the province around which the modern state of echoslovakia was created).

The expression "Bohemian", meaning nonconformist, seems to have been inspired by gypsies from ross the Hungarian border, which lies to the east. It from the west, though, that this meeting point of rmanic and Slavic cultures has been seen as an cubator of brewing since the Dark Ages.

The international fixation with the term *Pilsener* n be dated, precisely, to 1842. Until that time, all of e world's beers had been dark, or at least reddish in lour, or murky. Dark malts can make for tasty ers but they were, in those days, also a way of vering up the haziness of yeasty instability.

In 1842, Pilsen's local brewery, which was then vned by the town, produced the world's first golden-loured, clear, stable, beer by bottom-fermentation, us "inventing" pale lager. This "invention" came a time when opaque drinking vessels of stoneware pewter were giving way to mass-produced glass.

At this time, the German-speaking Austrian npire ruled Bohemia. "Pilsener-style" beer soon came chic throughout the German-speaking world d beyond. By the time steps were taken to protect e name, the drayhorse had bolted.

When the American brewer Adolphus Busch ured Europe in the late 19th century to study the gering technique, he was particularly taken with the ers of a town called, in German, Budweis (in Czech, ské Budějovice), once the home of the Bohemian yal court brewery. He decided upon this allusion en he set about launching his "King of Beers" in e USA in 1876, but he had the sense to protect the me Budweiser. Busch's "super-premium" ademark Michelob (from a town now known as chalovce) is also protected.

The Bohemians' devotion to brewing has no doubt en encouraged by the availability of fine raw aterials. Although Bohemia first made wheat beers, has excellent malting barley – sweet and clean, own in a protected, temperate "continental" mate. The Bohemians have been famous for their ps since the earliest days, and still are. These are clusively of the variety known as Bohemian Red, or Saaz from the German-language name for Žatec, ntre of the growing area. The fresh fragrance of ese hops is said to be nurtured not only by the climate, with its gentle rainfall, but also by the soil rich in clay and iron.

Most Czechoslovakian breweries have an everyday beer at 7–10 Plato (3–4 percent alcohol by volume); premium product in the range of 11–12 Plato (4.5–5) sometimes a dark lager at 10 Plato and occasionally speciality of 13–20 Plato (5.5–7.5).

Where to drink

Almost every town in Czechoslovakia offers its own beer locally. The capital, Prague, has 20-odd beer taverns. The most famous, U Fleků (11 Křemencova) in the "New Town (the city centre), has its own brewery, though for some year that has been undergoing a re-fit. U Fleků has a burlesqu show. In the "Old Town", U Zlatého Tygra (17 Husova) is sociable tavern selling Pilsner Urquell; while U Medvidků (Na Perštýně) is a somewhat basic home for Budweiser Budvar in Prague. In the "Lesser Town", U Svatéh Tomáše (12 Letenska) serves beer from the small Brani brewery, of Prague; a lovely, firm, aromatic pale brew and rather thin dark one. Prague's two larger breweries make th malty Staropramen and yeasty Prazanka beers.

Budweiser Budvar

Although it has a definite hop nose and finish, **Budweiser Budvar★★★ → ★★★★** is sweet by Czechoslovakian standard clean and rounded, with a hint of fruitiness. (Units bitterness in the lower 30s; lagered for two or three months The Budvar brewery was not founded until 1895, so it mus have been the similar beers from the older Samson brewer that inspired Busch. Even today, with all the changes i barley, hops, technology and market fashion, there seems t survive a vestigial resemblance between their beers and his

Pilsner Urquell

The original. **Pilsner Urquell★★★★** has a slightly full colour than some of its latter-day derivatives. The loc. water imparts a softness, and a faintly salty tang; the u exclusively of Žatec hops ensures a big, fresh bouqu (diminished by excessive pasteurization in export shi ments) and a gentle bitterness (about 35 units); the hug traditional, pitch-lined wooden barrels used for lagering ad a touch of their own house character. An immensely comple beer. Pilsen also has the Gambrinus brewery, producing hop accented beers which evince the cleanness of Bohemian mal

EASTERN EUROPE

German/Prussian and Austrian/Bohemian influence le brewing traditions in bordering parts of Poland and Hun gary, which both countries proudly retain. There is Bohemian character to Poland's dry Zywiec/Krakus and th softer (but still hoppy) Okocim Pilsener-style beers, bot sometimes found in the West. The creator of Vienna-styl lager, Anton Dreher, founded the Kobánya Brewery, o Budapest, which proudly produces a full range of styles i Hungary. Budapest is also in the process of getting a ne micro-brewery, to produce a pale lager. The Soviet Unio has almost 400 breweries and is one of the world's bigge producers in volume. Quality and choice is variable.

AUSTRIA

When Austria had a European Empire it was an influential nation in many aspects of life, including beer, but its glories faded as quickly as the last waltz. The classic amber-red style of lager first brewed in Vienna is no longer even a speciality of the capital city. Even the term *Märzen*, which in other countries may suggest a Vienna-style beer, means something different in Austria. Here, by some perverted logic, it indicates simply a brewery's basic lager, albeit at a respectable Plato of 12-plus (5–5.25 alcohol by volume). *Spezial* indicates a beer of 13-plus (5.5–5.75). *Bock* suggests 16-plus (around 7).

Quite different speciality beers are, however, beginning to enjoy something of a revival. Baron Henrik Bachofen von Echt has his chocolatey-but-bitter **Sir Henry's Stout**★★★ (13.75; 6 by volume) and copper-coloured, ale-like **St Thomas Bräu**★★→★★★ (12.25; 5.6) at his resuscitated brewery and restaurant (☎372652) in the Vienna suburb of Nussdorf. The Piesting brewery, south of Vienna, has an **Altbier**★★★. The Zwettle brewery, northwest of Vienna, has a **Zwickel-bier**★★. These augment longer-established specialities like one or two *Weizenbiers* and the 23 Plato Ur-Bock of Eggenberg, between Salzburg and Linz. Salzburg has a brewery owned by Augustine monks but operated by a secular company. Schlägl, north of Linz, has a brewery run by Praemonstraten brothers.

Brau A.G.

This anonymous-sounding group owns the famous Schwechat brewery where Anton Dreher created the Vienna style of lager. That brewery has a premium **Hopfenperle**★→★★, relatively light in body and dry in finish, and a super-premium **Steffl**★, with a light-to-medium body and a hoppy finish. The group, which has it headquarters in Linz, also has a number of breweries producing the fruity **Kaiser**★ beers, which are a national brand. Near Salzburg, Brau A.G. has a regional brewery known for its very pale **Zipfer Urtyp**★→★★, with a hoppy aroma and sherberty dryness.

Steirische (Styrian Breweries)

Second-biggest grouping, based in Graz, embracing the local Reininghaus-Puntigam brewery and a larger company that takes its name from its Styrian home-town of Leoben-Göss. The **Reininghaus-Puntigam**★→★★ beers are generally malty and fruity. Gösser has a hearty **Spezial**★★, with a full, bronze colour, a smooth, malty palate and some hop bitterness in the finish. Its **Export**★★ is slightly fuller-bodied, with a cleaner palate. Its new **Gösser Gold**★ is lighter and relatively bland. **Gösser Stiftsbräu**★→★★ is a dark, malty, sweet beer of 12.2 Plato but only 3.6 percent alcohol by volume. It is named after the brewery's founding monastery.

SWITZERLAND

The world's strongest beer, called **Samichlaus** **** ("Santa Claus"), is produced in Swit zerland. This relatively new label has led lover of individualistic brews to take a fresh look a Switzerland, which has more speciality beers than i suggested by a reputation for products that are well made but not distinctive. Swiss beer-making tradi tion, at least in the German-speaking part of th country, is evidenced by monastic brewery ruins in S Gallen that date from the 9th century.

Samichlaus is brewed only once a year, on Decem ber 6, the day when the Swiss celebrate St Nicola (Santa Claus). It is matured throughout the followin year and released next December 6. Its startin gravity is 27.6 Plato (around 1110) and it emerge with 11.1–2 percent alcohol by weight; 13.7–14 b volume. Although it has a predictably malty nose an full body, its long maturation and high alcohol mak for a surprising firmness and a brandyish finish. *Hell* ("pale", but actually reddish) version is avail able in some markets, but Switzerland has only th dark original.

These beers are produced by Hürlimann, of Zürich Hürlimann's more conventional beers tend to b clean, light and dry, with a spritzy finish. Th company also has an interest in the city's Löwenbräu brewery (unconnected with the Munich namesake) Swiss Löwenbräu's beers are characteristically mil and dry. Among the other majors' products, those o Cardinal are perhaps more flowery, those of Halden gut slightly smoky, and those of Feldschlösschen hav a fruity bitterness; these are, however, only sligh shades of difference.

A Swiss brewery's range might embrace a basi lager (at more than 11.5; 1046; around 3.8; 4.75); a de luxe beer (12; 1048; 4.1; 5.12); a "special" (12.5–6 1050; 4.3; 5.37); a dark special (13.5; 1054; 4; 5); a "festival" brew of similar strength; a "strong" beer o 16; 1064; 5.4; 6.75; and perhaps a dark strong beer o 19; 1076; 5.9; 7.3.

Cardinal and Warteck both have *Altbiers* in thei ranges. *Weizenbiers* are produced by Calanda Frauenfeld and the Ueli brewery at the Fischerstub "brewpub" (Rheingasse 45, Basel. ☎061-329495).

The strangest speciality from Switzerland's 30-odc breweries is a beer that is intended to taste of corr (maize) – and does. It is called **Maisgold**, contains 3(percent corn (which would hardly be unusual in the United States) and is produced by the Rosengarter brewery, of Einsiedeln.

GERMANY

As northern Europe is the home of brewing in the modern world, so Germany remains its hearth. Among Germany's many claims to this central position, the strongest is that it has far more breweries than any other country. Their number is astonishing, despite many closures in recent years. Almost 40 percent of the world's breweries are in Germany; 1,200-odd in the West and more than 200 in the East, a much smaller country. Although closures outnumber openings, about ten new boutique breweries have established themselves in recent years, not only in northern cities like Essen and Dortmund but also in the more conservative south, in Munich and Nürnberg. Even a nation as lavishly served as Germany, and as rich in small breweries, has fallen for the charms of the boutique.

Germany was never for long a single state, and its relatively recent, post-war, division encouraged local loyalties. With Berlin sliced through, the other great cities of Germany vie with each other, not least in their brewing traditions. In general, the north has the driest beers; the southwest, especially the state of Baden-Württemberg, has softer brews, allegedly to suit palates weaned on wine; and the southeast (Bavaria) has sweeter, fuller-bodied products.

What is yet more interesting for the beer-lover is that each region has its own specialities. Germany has a considerable range of beers. Berlin is known for its light, slightly sour, style of *Weisse* wheat beer, a summer quencher; Hamburg and the north in general are noted for extra-dry *Pilsener*-style beers; the Old Town restaurants of Bremen and Münster have several esoteric local specialities; Dortmund, which makes more beer than any other city in Germany, has its confusingly-named *Export* style, medium in both body and dryness; Düsseldorf drinks as its everyday brew a copper-coloured, top-fermenting *Altbier*. Cologne protects through *appellation contrôlée* its pale, top-fermenting *Kölschbier*. Einbeck and Munich share the strong *Bock* beer, especially in spring, though the latter city lays claim to winter's *Doppelbock*. Munich is the greatest of cities for stylistic variety. It also shares a tradition of dark or *dunkel* beers with Kulmbach and other Bavarian towns (though Bamberg specializes in smoked-malt *Rauchbier*). Munich has a special interest in amber *Märzenbier* and various types of *Weizen* wheat beers.

Few of these varieties are wholly restricted to their own area or season, though they are always freshest at the appropriate time and taste best in their native place. Some brewers specialize in just one variety of beer, but more produce a range. Some brewers with regional roots have cross-bred with others to form semi-national groupings. The biggest are formed by Dortmunder Union, with Schultheiss of Berlin; Dortmunder Actien, with Binding of Frankfurt and Kindl of Berlin; and Bavaria St Pauli of Hamburg, with Hannen of Rhineland-Westphalia, Henninger of Frankfurt, and Tücher of Nürnberg.

Links between breweries in the north and south are less evident, though some of the bigger companies, while still quite separate, have investment from the same major banks. The biggest output of any brewery in Germany is that of Binding, which sells about 2.5 million hectolitres a year. A medium-sized brewery might produce half a million hectolitres; some small local firms have an output of less than 10,000hl; in Bavaria, there are inns producing a few hundred. The north has the greater number of very large breweries, often extremely modern. This may stem from its being mainly Protestant and therefore having a long tradition of secular, commercial brewing. A northern city but a Catholic one, Cologne, has the greatest number of breweries: a baker's dozen within its boundaries and the same number again in its hinterland. The Catholic south, with a surviving tradition of monastic brewing (albeit interrupted by Napoleon), has more village beers. Two-thirds of all the breweries in the Federal Republic are in the single state of Bavaria. Many of these are around Munich, but several smaller towns have a greater number of breweries, especially in the region of Franconia.

Within any varietal style, German breweries – especially the larger ones – are apt to make similar products. This is in part because clear standards are laid down by law. There is also the separate question of the *Reinheitsgebot*, the German Pure Beer Law of 1516. In 1985 one or two brewers were found to be in breach of this law and there was a scandal. They were also felt to have embarrassed Germany, since the Purity Law was at the time being challenged in the European Community as a restriction on free trade. The Purity Law has its origins in Bavaria, where it is observed even in the case of products made for export. Equally, Germany has always been willing to accept imports that conform to its laws. (The *Reinheitsgebot* is not applied in East Germany.) Irrespective of the law, the national standard of housekeeping in breweries in Germany is impeccable, whether they be stainless steel factories or copper classics.

The nation as a whole always features among the top two or three countries in the world's annual league table of beer consumption per head. The north, though, drinks less than the south, and does so in smaller glasses, of 20 or 30cl. In the relationship between average consumption and customary size of serving, it is not clear which is cause and which effect. Apart from the differences in size, there are also customary shapes of glass for each style of beer, in both north and south. Most German beers are served cool – at around 9°C (48°F), though there are slight variations of local habit. If the beer is to remain cool on a warm day, it had better not linger, in which case a small glass makes more sense. Nonetheless, it is in the south, where the summers can be warm, that 50cl and litre glasses are normally used. At festivals, the litre glass is often the only serving available. It is known as a *Mass* ("measure") and, whether of glass or stoneware, it qualifies as a stein only if it has a lid.

Weather, again, plays its part in the regional styles of drinking place. The northerner may well take his pleasures indoors, and there is an element of Protestant opprobium to some of the names he gives to drinking places: *Pinte*, *Kneipe* and *Wirtshaus*. *Gastwirthschaft*, *Gasthaus* or *Gasthof* sound more innocent. The southerner may drink at a similar place, or at a beer hall, but his greatest joy is when the weather permits him to go outside to the beer garden. At village festivals, there will also be a tent big enough to accommodate the entire population. The celebrations and seasons of village life in Bavaria are accompanied by religious blessings in the morning and beer in the afternoon, from the saint's day at the local church through Easter, Ascension Day, Whitsun, the harvest festival and Christmas.

HAMBURG

Around the world, imported beer from Germany often means Holsten, Beck's or St Pauli Girl. The first comes from Hamburg, the latter two from Bremen. These two cities remain the principal ports in Germany, a largely landlocked country, and they have been exporters of beer for more than 600 years. Their great importance in the brewing industry dates back to one of the early attempts at organized trade in Europe, the 15th century Hanseatic League.

The extra-dry speciality Pilseners produced in this part of Germany owe their character to the same circumstance. In the days when transport by water was easier than travel across land, Hamburg was twice blessed. Not only did it, as a seaport, have Europe's greatest sales of beer, its requirement for hops was met by trade down the river Elbe from Bohemia, the classic area of cultivation. The dryness of these Pilseners echoes Hamburg's role as a great hop market. The hops were used not only for flavour but also as a natural preservative in beer that was destined for long sea journeys.

Holsten is the best-known of Hamburg's three breweries. Next comes the confusingly named Bavaria St Pauli (nothing to do with St Pauli Girl of Bremen), then Elbschloss. All three produce generally dry beers, though with differences of emphasis. The Holsten products have an assertive dryness. Those from Bavaria St Pauli are perhaps a little fruitier. The Elbschloss beers are very clean-tasting, reserving their dryness for a long, lingering finish.

Many visitors to Hamburg, in their meanderings along the Reeperbahn, perhaps with a stop in the picaresque bars of David Street, notice the Bavaria St Pauli brewery. It stands at the top of David Street, where the St Pauli district falls away to dockland. In the next neighbourhood out of the city, the once-separate township of Altona, is the Holsten brewery. On the far edge of Altona, in the unlikely location of a stockbroker suburb, is Elbschloss, the most attractive and traditional of Hamburg's breweries, with its own maltings in its cellars.

Where to drink

Despite its brewing history, Hamburg has no traditional beer taverns. Local beers are, though, a ready accompaniment to the dubious pleasures of a seaport *Labskaus* (beef hash) or countless more appetizing eel dishes, at The Old

ommercial Room, opposite St Michael's Church, or in the
aterside restaurants of Deich Strasse. There is a good
election of northern brews at the beer bar of the Intercon-
nental Hotel. A number of new, mock-rustic places serve
eers from other parts of Germany. The biggest range
at the youthful, disco-like Posemuckel, on Bleichen
rücke.

Bavaria St Pauli

ames like "Bavaria" were adopted in the late 19th century
y brewers who were following the south's lead in lager-
rewing. The Bavaria brewery of Hamburg and the more
cally named St Pauli merged in 1922. As if its name were
ot confusing enough, the brewery markets its products
nder the Astra label. The company's basic lager, **Astra
Urtyp**★, has a pleasant, light hop aroma and palate. The
remium **Astra Pilsener**★ has a very aromatic bouquet and
alate. Astra also has a beer called **Exclusiv**★, in the style the
ermans call Export (like the Dortmund variety) and a dark
Urbock★ (again a confusing name, since this is a doppel-
ock). In addition to that fairly standard range, there is a
ght-bodied but very dry Pilsener called **Grenzquell**★ which
as for some time heavily promoted in the USA. The
ompany is best known for one outstanding product from its
ubsidiary Jever brewery, in the northern town of the same
ame in German Friesland.
   Jever Pilsener★★★★, which is regarded as something of a
riesian speciality, is the most bitter beer in Germany,
espite a slight mellowing in recent years. Jever has a big
ouquet (the aroma hops are of the Tettnang variety), a
easty palate (the brewery has had its own strain since 1936)
nd an intense aperitif bitterness in the finish. A smooth
ever **Export**★★ and a firm-bodied **Maibock**★★ are hard to
nd outside Friesland.
   A Friesian nation once straddled what are now the
orders of The Netherlands, Germany and Denmark, and its
raditional drinks suggest a liking for intense and bitter
avours. In its handsome resort town, Jever is a proud and
rosperous brewery, with a very modern plant.

Elbschloss

his brewery takes its name from the river Elbe which flows
arallel to the road on which the brewery stands. Masked by
owan trees, hawthorns and sycamores, the brewery is in its
riginal, 1881 brick building. The *Schloss* is in the woods
ehind. Elbschloss is partly owned by DUB-Schultheiss. It
as a full range of products, including the very pleasant and
plendidly dry **Ratsherrn Pils**★★★. There is also a good,
nalty Doppelbock called simply **Ratsherrn Bock**★★. None of
he Elbschloss beers are pasteurized.

Holsten

n the days when the nobility controlled such matters as
cences to brew beer, the Duchy of Schleswig-Holstein held
way over Hamburg. The Duke of Holstein who granted the
ity the right to brew is remembered in the name of this
ompany, and on its labels. The company's basic local beer is
he firm-bodied **Holsten-Edel**★. It also has a German-style
xport★, with a satisfying, wholesome texture, and a soft,
ry **Pilsener**★. Holsten is the biggest German exporter to

Britain, where one of its products has to the uninformed drinker become synonymous with the term "Pils". Ironically, the beer thus dubbed is not a regular Pilsener. It is the product that the company would prefer to be known by its full name of **Holsten Diät Pils**★★ ➔ ★★★. This very dry low carbohydrate beer was originally produced for diabetics Since it has a relatively high alcohol content, at 5.8 percent by volume, its calorie count does not suit weight-watchers Its real virtue is that it is a genuine import, with plenty of hop character. Holsten has also recently begun to export in **Maibock**★★, labelled in Britain as Urbock. This strong beer has a malty dryness, with a hint of apricot. Holsten's beer are kräusened.

Like its principal local rival, Holsten also has a super premium product from a subsidiary brewery. In this case the brewery is in Lüneburg, a spa town of stepped-gable houses, their styles evolving from the 14th–18th centuries. A group of them form the old brewery and guest-house, now converted into a beautifully-arranged beer museum and a restaurant serving local dishes. The new brewery is very modern, and its dry, hoppy beer is called **Moravia Pils**★★ The name Moravia must have come down the Elbe at some time. The beer is notable for its big bouquet, and has a rather light body. In addition to Moravia, which enjoys some prestige, there are a number of minor products, some under the Bergedorf name, and associated breweries in Kiel Neumünster and Brunswick.

BREMEN

Churches and monasteries dedicated to St Paul have given their name to a good few breweries in Germany, including one in Bremen, long destroyed. This does not altogether explain how one of the city's famous export beers came to be known as St Pauli *Girl*, and the people who might know claim they can't remember. Another noted export is Beck's while the local brewing company is called Haake-Beck Recently there has also been a tentative export called Roland Light. Roland is the legendary knight (celebrated in *chanson*) whose statue stands in the main square of Bremen (and other north German cities) as a symbol of civic, secular independence.

Bremen had the first Brewer's Guild in Germany, in 1489 and such is its beery history that it still has a large number of brewery names. Most of these names are of brewing companies that were once independent and which are still separate but linked in a complicated corporate structure Other labels to be taken into consideration are Hemelinger (nothing to do with a British brand of a similar name) and Remmer. Hemelinger produces a *Spezial*, a rather perfumy but sweetish beer. Remmer produces an interestingly malty *Altbier*. All of the linked breweries in Bremen share a single complex of modern buildings, with two brewhouses, in the town centre, close to the river Weser. Outside of this group is Dressler, which no longer has a brewery but survives as a beer brand owned by Holsten.

Where to drink

The Old Town area of Bremen, known as the Snoor, is a delight, and has some lovely taverns. Especially recom-

ended for its local speciality beers is the narrow, wedge-
shaped Kleiner Ratskeller, in an alley called Hinter dem
Schütting. This is not to be confused with the Ratskeller
itself, which is famous for the hearty consumption of wines
from the Rhine and Mosel.

Beck's

The single product brewed by Beck's carries no description
beyond a straightforward **Beck's Bier**★→★★. It is broadly
thin the Pilsener style, with a fresh aroma, a faintly fruity,
...m, crisp palate and a clean, dry finish. It is light by
German but heavy by international standards, and difficult
...place in context. A very pale malt is used, and the hopping
...ans heavily toward the Hallertau aroma variety. Within
...e Beck's brand is a dark version, available in some
...arkets. Beck's Bier is fermented with its own house yeast,
...fairly low temperatures, and kräusened.

Haake-Beck

...traditional copper brewhouse is used to produce a full
...nge of beers for Bremen and its hinterland, and also local
...ecialities. Both its regular **Edel-Hell**★ and its **Pils**★→★★
...ve a floral bouquet and a light, clean palate. While its
...smopolitan cousins do not make specific claims to the
...yle, this Pils does, and properly has a little more bitterness
...an either in the finish. It is kräusened, and – unusually – is
...ailable locally (in the Old Town, for example) in unfiltered
...rm. This version is identified as **Kräusen Pils**★★★, and has
...ing yeast in suspension. As if to emphasize the resultant
...oudiness, it is served in cracked-pattern glasses. Even by
...e standards of a German Pilsener, it has a mountainous
...ead, followed by a soft palate, with just a suggestion of
...ewy, yeast bitterness.

...Haake-Beck also produces, as a summer speciality, a
...remen interpretation of a northern wheat beer. **Bremer
Weisse**★★★ is served in a bowl-shaped glass similar to those
...ed in Berlin, and is a wonderful summer refresher. In its
...tural state, it has a palate reminiscent of under-ripe
...ums, though it is usually served sweetened with a dash of
...spberry juice. It has a gravity of 7.5 Plato, producing 2.2
...rcent alcohol by weight (2.75 by volume). In addition to a
...p yeast, there is a controlled, pure-culture lactic fermen-
...tion.

...Yet a third speciality, **Seefahrt Malz**, cannot strictly be
...ted as a beer, since it is not fermented. It is a heavily
...opped malt extract, of a daunting 55 Plato, with a syrupy
...scosity but a surprisingly pleasant taste. Seefahrt Malz
...as for a time on sale, but is now available only to eminent
...tizens who are invited to the House of Seafarers' annual
...nner in Bremen. It is ceremonially served in silver or
...wter chalices. Despite its size, the company itself has a
...ste for traditions. From among its towering buildings each
...orning emerges a line of drays drawn by Oldenburg horses
...● deliver beer to the people of the inner city area.

St Pauli Girl

...his is produced in the older of Bremen's two brewhouses.
...ike Beck's, it has a lot of aroma hopping, though it emerges
...ith a slightly lesser bouquet. **St Pauli Girl**★→★★ has floral
...nes in its bouquet and palate, and is very clean. It has

marginally less bitterness than Beck's, and is not kräusene
Although each of the two beers is made to its ov
specification, each with a different yeast background, tl
distinctions between them are less striking than tl
similarities. St Pauli Girl, too, is available in a dark versio

HANOVER AND LOWER SAXON

Famous extra-dry Pilseners like Jever and Moravia (bo)
becoming better known outside Germany) are brewed in tl
state of Lower Saxony. Neither name, though, is readi
associated with the state, which sprawls for many mil
across the north of Germany. Jever has its own, mo
localized regionality, and both beers have to a great exter
been appropriated by the city-state of Hamburg.

The most important city in Lower Saxony is Hanove
noted not only for its huge spring industrial fair but al
since the 16th century as a brewing centre. Its loc
speciality is Broyhan *Altbier*, from Lindener Gilde, one
three brewing companies in the city. Hanover's oth
breweries are the smaller Wülfel and the medium-size
Herrenhauser. Of the three, Herrenhauser is the best knov
outside Germany. This part of Germany is also well knov
for grain schnapps, including the gins of Steinhägen. A loc
trick is to hold a glass of beer and a schnapps in the san
hand and drink from them simultaneously.

To the southeast, the town of Brunswick (known
German as Braunschweig) is appreciated for its ric
architectural heritage and for the Nettelback brewer
which makes an esoteric speciality called *Braunschweig
Mumme*. This is a malt extract beer similar to that
Bremen. It is served in the Ratskeller and several oth
restaurants, either neat as a tonic or in a shandy with one
the more conventional local beers, of which there are
number. Mumme, which is named after its first brewer, w
originally produced for seafarers, and was launched in tl
year that Columbus discovered America (1492). Between tl
16th and 18th centuries "Brunswick Mumm" seems to hav
been well-known in England. The poet Alexander Po
referred to "mugs of mum" and the diarist Samuel Pepys
a "mum-house". A treatize of the time suggests tha
Brunswick Mumm should be produced in Stratford-upor
Avon, in what would presumably have been the brewir
world's first licensing arrangement. Even today, a simila
product, Mather's *Black Beer*, is produced in Leeds, Yorl
shire (associated with the county's great seafarer Capta
Cook). At this point, the story blends with those concernir
beers made from molasses and flavoured with spruce or bir
twigs. A similar *Schwarzbier* is produced across the Ea
German border in Bad Köstritz.

A much more important speciality is brewed to the sout
in the small town of Einbeck. The last syllable of Einbeck
believed to have been corrupted into *Bock*, and a goo
example of this style is produced in the town. The boc
tradition seems to date from the local nobility having at
very early stage given the citizens licence to brew. As
result, Einbeck became one of Germany's most productiv
brewing towns during the 14th century, making beers of
high gravity so that they could be transported far and wi
while fermenting-out on their journey. A high-gravity bre

us came to be known in the German-speaking world as a
ock" beer. Martin Luther is said to have been fortified
th Einbecker bock beer during the Diet of Worms in the
th century. In the 17th century, a northern Duke took
veral casks with him when he went to Munich to marry a
uthern noblewoman. Ever since, Munich has claimed bock
one of its own styles. The first bocks were probably strong,
rk wheat beers, produced by top fermentation. Today, the
rm indicates a strong beer made with barley malt and a
ttom-fermenting yeast.

here to drink

orthy of special attention, because such establishments
few in the north, is the Felsenkeller Brewery Gasthof in
uenau southwest of Hanover. The tiny brewery, owned
the Rupp family, is noted for its dark bock beers. The
joining inn has five rooms (☎05043-2275). This brewery
s no connection with the several other Felsenkellers. The
me means simply "rock cellar".

inbecker Brauhaus

e only remaining brewery in Einbeck, controlled through
bschloss of Hamburg by DUB-Schultheiss. Einbecker
auhaus produces three types of Bock. These include the
le **Ur-Bock Hell**★→★★, the dark **Ur-Bock Dunkel**★★★
★★★★ and, between the two in colour, a **Mai-Bock**. All
ree have a gravity of 16.7 Plato; a profound, smooth
altiness and a gentle Hallertau hop character. The Mai-
ck is available from the beginning of March to the end of
ay.

errenhäusen

errenhauser Pilsener★★ is the speciality of this com-
ny. It is a smooth beer with a sweetish palate and a
y dry, but not bitter, finish. Because it has just
er 4 percent alcohol by weight, it is labelled in some
nerican states as a "malt liquor". While Herrenhauser has
ery right to feel insulted about that, it compounds the
ony by labelling its beer Horsy in some markets. A sillier
me is hard to imagine, even if the company's trade-
ark is a rearing horse.

indener Gilde

e company takes its name from its origins as a civic
ewery, operated by a guild. Today it produces a range of
ry well-made beers. Its speciality **Broyhan Alt**★★★ is
med after a great Hanover brewer of the 16th century.
is is a top-fermenting *Altbier* in a similar style to those of
üsseldorf but a little stronger (12.4 Plato; 4.2 percent
cohol by weight; 5.25 by volume), slightly darker, relative-
light-bodied, malt-accented, with a delicate hop character
d a low bitterness. The brewery also has a regular **Gilde
lsener**★→★★ and a premium **Ratskeller Edel-Pils**★★, both
th a complex hop character and some Saaz delicacy, as
ll as a German-style **Edel-Export**★.

MUNSTER

e university city of Münster, rich in history as the capital
Westphalia, is regarded with affection by knowledgeable

beer-lovers all over Germany for the specialities produced a its Pinkus Müller brewery and restaurant. Pinkus Müller an institution, despite it being nothing larger than *Hausbrauerei* (small private brewery), producing fewer tha 10,000hl a year. It makes some extraordinary beers and ha the impudence to export to the USA.

It also has the impudence to survive. When Pinkus Mülle was founded in 1816, as a shop and restaurant embracing it own brewery, bakery and chocolate factory, it was not alon there were 40 breweries in town. The last of its rivals, 500,000hl brewery, closed in 1984.

Pinkus Müller's premises in the Old Town (what people i Münster call the "cow quarter", *Kuhviertel*) were original nine houses. Over the years they have been integrated, wit considerable rebuilding in the 1920s and some more recently There are four dining rooms; in the main one the centrepie is a Westphalian oven, set among Dutch tiles illustratin Bible stories. The fireplace hangs with Westphalian hams, good indication of the style of food.

Behind the restaurant is a simple, two-vessel brewhous surprisingly modern in design. The brewery uses both barle and wheat malt, and exclusively the aromatic variety Hallertau hops, in blossom form. It has its own well, use open fermenters, and has a warren of lagering cellars. It operated by Hans Müller, who is in his fifties and the head the founding family. Half a dozen members of the famil work in the brewery and restaurant. In the mid 1980s, teenage daughter departed for the famous brewing institu at Weihenstephan, so that the succession would be ensure

Where to drink

Pinkus Müller, where else? It's hard to escape, but there a other small breweries in Westphalia, and there is a brewer *Gasthof*, (nine bedrooms, ☎02522–2209), at Oelde, south east of Münster. This is called the Oelder Brauhaus, and tw beers are produced and splendidly served by the Pot Feldmann family.

Pinkus Müller

The brewery produces no fewer than four beers and is be known for what it describes as **Pinkus Münster Alt★★★ – ★★★★**. In this instance, the term *alt* indicates simply an ol style, without suggesting anything on the lines of th Düsseldorf classics. Pinkus Münster Alt is a very pale, top fermenting beer made from an unusual specification of 4 percent wheat and 60 percent barley malt, to a gravity 11.3 Plato. It has a long (six months) maturation, includin a kräusening. The maturation takes place at natural cella temperature, but in conventional lagering tanks in whic there is a resident lactic culture. The result is a very cris beer indeed, dry, with a faint, quenching acidity in th finish. In several respects, not least its higher gravit relative clarity and restrained acidity, this is a differe product from the Bremer or Berliner Weisse. It is wheati than any Kölsch, yet it does not qualify as a weizen; it is unique speciality. In fact, the brewery does produce **Pinkus Weizen★★ → ★★★**, which is worthy of special atte tion if only for its unusual lightness, though it is characteri tically low on hop bitterness, and has a fruity finish. It is rather northern-tasting *Weizen*, though it has a thoroug outhern ratio of 60–40 (wheat has the majority).

There are also two bottom-fermenting beers: **Pinkus Ils★→★★**, with a light but firm body and a hoppy dryness; nd **Pinkus Spezial★★★**, a pale beer of 12.66 Plato, brewed ith organically grown barley malt and hops. This clean, alty, dry beer, with a medium body, is sold in wholefood ops. Despite Pinkus Müller having all of these unusual ews, the house speciality is not a beer alone. The Müllers eep diced fresh fruit in sweetened water so that it forms its vn syrup. They then add a tablespoon of the fruit and rup to a glass of Pinkus Alt, so that its fresh flavours ffuse the beer and marry with the acidity of the wheat. ne availability and contents of this confection depend upon hich fruit is in season. Fruits with stones are not used, since ey impart an incongruous, almondy bitterness. In sum- er, strawberries or peaches are favoured; in winter, oranges ay be used. The fruit is steeped for a day in a pickling jar, ith a kilo of sugar. When it is added to the beer, using a lindrical glass, the result is known as an Altbier Bowl. It is Pinkus Müller speciality and a Westphalian favourite.

DORTMUND

he word "Dortmunder" features in the names of seven rewing companies, thus providing great confusion for beer- vers who are not familiar with Germany. Some of these mpanies share facilities, but there are no fewer than five zeable breweries in the city of Dortmund, plus a new *ausbrauerei*. Since each of the seven brewing companies as its own range of products in various styles, there are out 30 beers with Dortmunder names. In this respect, Dortmunder" is an *appellation contrôlée*, since no beer rewed outside the city may, in Germany, bear the designa- on. In other countries, however, brewers have over the ars produced beers that they have identified as being in ie Dortmunder style. There was a vogue in The Nether- nds and Belgium for a beer style described as "Dort".

There is, indeed, a Dortmunder style. In the days when ie great brewing cities of Europe vied for ascendency by romoting their own styles, that of Dortmund was a pale, edium-dry beer, very slightly bigger in body and higher in cohol than its rivals from Munich or Pilsen. It was drier an a Munich pale beer, but less dry than a Pilsener.

As Dortmund's efforts were repaid with sales in other arts of Germany, and in adjoining countries, the local rewers began to refer to their characteristic beer as *Export*. hat is how *Export* became a classic German style. Today a od Dortmunder Export beer has a gravity of 13 Plato, roducing 4.4 percent alcohol by weight and 5.5 by volume, nd with about 25 units of bitterness.

Unfortunately, the Dortmunder brewers' exposition of eir classic style can be hard to find outside their city and nterland. Although it made for a bigger local market, the dustrial growth of Dortmund and the Ruhr was a mixed essing for the city's image as a centre of fine brewing. In cent years especially, Dortmund brewers went through a hase of self-doubt: did a Dortmunder beer sound like a roduct for cloth-capped miners and steelworkers? In ritain, such a testimonial would be valued, but more galitarian countries like Germany and the USA have an infantile snobbism. Such a self-defeating insecurity afflicte the Dortmund brewers.

Although they have continued to make Dortmunde Export, the local brewers have in recent years neglected t promote it, preferring to concentrate on other produc within their ranges, especially the Pilseners. This policy ha not been a conspicuous success, nor does it deserve to b Dortmund is Germany's largest brewing city, and should b proud of its name. Dortmund-inspired Export beers ar after all, included in the portfolios of brewers all ov Germany. There are now, finally, signs that Dortmund beginning to remember its traditions, with the opening the Hövels Hausbrauerei and the Dortmunder Krone Brewery Museum.

Where to drink

For years, Dortmund was content to offer its beers visitors at uninspiring bars (each representing a differer brewery) set around the market square and church. Havin been damaged in the war and quickly rebuilt during th recovery years of the 1950s, this area is a little lacking romance. Now, one of the city's brewers, Dortmunder Thie (output 700,000hl) has decided to soften its own forbiddin facade by adding a separate boutique brewery (5,000hl restaurant, bar and beer garden. This new establishmen Hövels Hausbrauerei (Hoher Walls 5–7; ☎0231-141044) named after Freiherr von Hövel, one of the founders, 1854, of the parent company.

The tiny new brewhouse can be seen by drinkers an diners as they go about their pleasures. An excellent kitche provides snacks, full meals or desserts.

DAB (Dortmunder Actien Brauerei)

The middle name merely indicates a joint-stock company Perhaps that is where the phrase "a piece of the action originated. This very large brewing company is now part of national grouping, with Binding, Berliner Kindl and other In its modern brewery on the edge of Dortmund it produce beers that generally have a light, malty, dryness. I Export★ →★★ has a slight malt accent, while remaining dry and is on the light side for the style. The brewery's Meiste Pils★ (marketed in the USA under the dismissive, lower-cas name of dab beer), has a hint of malt in the nose but goes o to be dry, with some hop character in the palate and a fairl low bitterness. There is more hop aroma, with a very clea and light palate, in the brewery's Original Premium★ marketed in the USA as Special Reserve. DAB also has a Altbier★, again with a dry maltiness and a light body. Th is marketed in the USA under the unflatteringly vague nam of DAB Dark. In its local market, DAB has a pleasan Maibock★ →★★ and Tremanator Doppelbock★ →★★. DAB a very marketing-orientated company, distributing it products widely in the north of Germany.

Dortmunder Hansa

This is part of the same group as DAB, and the two share th one brewery. In Germany, Hansa has been very active in th supermarket trade. Its Export★★ has a good malt aroma, soft, full body, and a dry finish. Its Pils★ is light and crisp with some hoppy acidity.

Dortmunder Kronen

mong their home-town beers, the people of Dortmund
avour those from the Kronen brewery, one of two privately
wned breweries in the city. Its beers are, in general, big and
salty, with a clean, delicate sweetness. These characteristics
re evident especially in its **Export★★★★**, and to a lesser
egree in its super-premium **Classic★★ → ★★★**. **Pilskrone★★**
as a flowery hoppiness. The brewery also has an **Alt★** with a
elatively full body and a dense, rocky, head. And there is a
ark bock, called **Steinbock★★**, with an intense crystal-malt
ryness. It is a shame that only the Classic, and not the
hole range, is available in the bar at the brewery's museum
pen Tuesday–Sunday, closed Monday; entrance free,
rough the main gates in Märkische Strasse).

It is fitting that a great brewing city should have such a
useum, and this gesture is no doubt intended also to focus
ttention on the fact that Kronen dates back to 1430, and
as been in the same family since 1729. Something of the
rewer's devotion to his art remains in Kronen's painstaking
rocedures, with three hopping stages (using only aroma
arieties), very cold fermentation, and kräusening, for
xample – all of this taking place, however, in a plant and
uilding that are uncomprisingly modern.

Dortmunder Ritter

artly owned by DUB-Schultheiss but having its own
rewery, this company produces firm-bodied, fruity-dry
eers that generally have a long finish. These robust, matter-
f-fact Dortmunder brews are popular in the industrial Ruhr
alley. The fruitiness is perhaps most evident in the
xport★ → ★★. The **Pils★** has a malty start and a dry finish.

Dortmunder Stifts

he Stifts brewery no longer operates, but its beers are
roduced, to its own specification, under contract by Thier.
ts beers have a very local following on the south side of the
ity, and are not very evident even in the centre of
ortmund. Stifts promotes only its **Stiftsherren Pils★**,
hich has a good, "herbal" hoppy aroma, a dry start and
ot much finish. Stifts is owned by the Stern brewery, of
ssen, which is in turn part of Watney's in Britain.

Dortmunder Thier

his is a privately owned brewery and its **Export★★★
→★★★★** is malty, smooth and full-bodied. It also has a
ell-made, dry, hoppy **Pils★★**. Although its beers sell well,
hey could benefit from a wider exposure. In its marketing,
he Dortmunder Thier company kept something of a low
rofile until its opening of the adjoining Hövels Haus-
rauerei in 1984 (see Where to Drink; facing page).

DUB (Dortmunder Union Brauerei)

he "Union" refers to the merger of ten or a dozen breweries
ore than 100 years ago. That union sufficed until 1973,
hen DUB linked with Schultheiss, of Berlin. The massive
U" of the "Union" logo, illuminated at night, is a
ortmund landmark atop the imposing brewery building
hich, looking rather like a 1920s power station, broods over
he centre of the city. The DUB beers (all kräusened) have
ome malty sweetness and are generally mild in palate –

perhaps on the bland side – and smooth. The **Export★★★** i
malt-accented, and medium-bodied. The **Siegel Pils★** has a
agreeably hoppy palate but not much finish. The super
premium **Brinckhoff's No 1★**, named after a founder-brewer
has a character somewhere between the two.

Hövels Hausbrauerei

The first beer made by this new brewery was a big, malty
German export called **Hövels Urtyp★★★**, produced at the
end of 1984. It has gone on to make as its regular product a
"house" beer of bronze colour, notably full body and
smooth, malty palate. This product is misleadingly called
Bitterbier★★★, a name used in the late 19th century. It has a
gravity of 13.5 Plato but an alcohol content of only 3.5
percent by weight, 4.37 by volume. A very big **Maibock★**
→★★★ has been produced in spring, and there are plans for
other seasonal beers. Three malts are used in Bitterbier, with
blossom hops. The brewery, gleaming in copper, with brass
trim, has an open fermenter and its own lagering cellars. As
is the custom of some house-breweries, spent grain is used in
the making of bread. Bitterbier is available only at the
house-brewery bar, restaurant and beer garden, though
small barrels can be bought there. Hövels has plans to
market other beers in the free trade.

DÜSSELDORF

Where a city is lucky, or sensible, enough to have retained a
distinctive style of brewing, it often reserves a special beer
for particular occasions or moods. Düsseldorf takes a
different view and is one of those cities (like its neighbour
and rival Cologne – or Dublin) that likes to serve its
speciality as its daily beer.

Düsseldorf's prized beer is more instantly distinctive than
that of its neighbour. It has a dark copper colour, is top
fermenting and is superficially similar to a British ale. The
Düsseldorf beer has, though, a much cleaner palate, with a
complex blend of malty body and hop bitterness and has
little of the yeasty fruitiness and acidity of the classic British
ales. Since the Düsseldorf beer is a significant style in its own
right, a German might resent its being compared to British
ale. Internationally, however, the Düsseldorf style is little
known, although it has been taken up by a couple of brewers
on the West Coast of the USA. In this context, its character
can perhaps best be summed up by comparing it with ale.

The differences in the Düsseldorf product derive not only
from the typically German barley malts and hops used, but
also from the use of single cell, pure culture yeasts and –
perhaps most significant – a period of cold conditioning in
tanks, usually for several weeks. A German would no doubt
argue that the Düsseldorf beer is cleaner and smoother than
a British ale. The British would argue that their ales have
more individuality. As always, this is to compare apples
with oranges, neither is better; they are different.

A typical Düsseldorf beer has a gravity of 12 Plato, or a
fraction more. It may be made with two or three malts.
Some Düsseldorf brewers favour an infusion mash, but the
decoction system is also widely used. Two or three hop
varieties may be employed; Düsseldorf brewers have
traditionally favoured Spalt. Open fermenters are

metimes used, especially in the smaller breweries. The
armer fermentation temperatures are reflected in slightly
ss intense cold conditioning, at between 0°C (32°F) and 8°C
7°C), for anything from three to eight weeks. Alcohol
ntent is typically 3.6–3.8 by weight; 4–4.7 by volume.
nits of bitterness vary from the lower 30s to the 50s; colour
ound 35 EBC.

After its period of cold-conditioning, Düsseldorf beer is
ten dispensed in local taverns from a barrel, by gravity,
th no carbon dioxide pressure, blanket or otherwise.
lthough this method is practiced in several taverns and
staurants, notably in the Old Town, it is especially
sociated with the city's home-brew houses. Such is the joy
this city for the beer-lover: not only does it have its own
yle, of some character and complexity, it has no fewer than
ur home-brew taverns. In these establishments, the
ubby, cylindrical glasses favoured in Düsseldorf are
arged as quickly as they are exhausted.

The home-brew taverns are the shrines of the Düsseldorf
ewing style, and as such their beers must be regarded as
erman classics. The beer-loving visitor to Düsseldorf will
ant to visit all of them – and also to sample the beers made
the local style by the city's four other breweries, and
veral others in neighbouring smaller towns.

Düsseldorf's brewers may well wish that a less imitable
ame had emerged for their style; they call their brews
thing more memorable than *Düsseldorfer Altbier*. No other
ty has such devotion either to the production or serving of
er in this style, but brewers in several other towns have in
eir portfolio something which they call *Altbier*. In most
stances, though not all, it bears a great similarity to the
üsseldorf style. "*Alt*" simply means "old", and indicates a
yle that was produced before the widespread introduction
bottom-fermentation.

"*Altbier*" is the style of Düsseldorf and its brewers
roduce little else, except stronger brews variously called
Latzenbier" ("beer from the wood") or "*Sticke*" ("secret"
er) that appear very briefly in some places in winter and
utumn. Of the Düsseldorf home-brew houses, three are in
e Old Town (Altstadt seems especially appropriate in this
stance). The fourth, Schumacher, is in the more modern
art of the city centre. Among the bigger brewers' *Altbiers*,
e popular Diebels is firm-bodied; Hannen is soft, rounded
d well-balanced; Frankenheim is hoppy and light-bodied;
chlosser malty, but dry; Düssel the fruitiest; and Rhenania
n be slightly thick-tasting.

here to drink

one of the home-brew houses should be missed, and Zum
erige is mandatory. Its beer can also be sampled on
raught in the chic food hall of the Carsch Haus department
ore. South of Düsseldorf at Langenfeld, half way to
ologne, the café-restaurant Brennpunkt International has
ore than 20 beers on draught and even more in bottle. This
unusual in Germany – especially in that the beers are, as
e name suggest, international.

lm Füchschen

The Fox" is noted not only for its beer but also its food.
his home-brew house, in Ratinger Strasse, produces a very

good *Altbier*, simply called **Im Fuchschen★★★ →★★★★**. It is complex and beautifully-balanced beer, its firm, fairly fu body at first evincing malty notes, then yielding to lots hop flavour from Spalt and Saaz varieties. In the end, i hoppiness is its predominant characteristic.

The tavern's big main dining room serves hearty *Eisbei* and *Schweinhaxe*, at scrubbed tables. It can be very bus but it is a friendly place and diners are usually happy share tables.

Zum Schlüssel

"The Key" is not to be confused with the larger Schlösse ("Locksmith") brewery, however easy that may be. Zu Schlüssel, in Bolker Strasse, is a home-brew house. Th brewery is visible from its main room. **Zum Schlüsse Altbier★★ →★★★** begins with an aromatic hoppiness palate, but its predominant characteristic is a light malt ness, with a touch of "British" acidity in the finish. It has fairly light body and a bright clarity. The restaurant is qui light and airy, too, with something of a "coffee shop atmosphere. It was founded in 1936 (a little late for Heinri Heine (1797–1856), who was born in this street: the site his home is now a roast-chicken restaurant). In 1963, th company opened a second, free-standing brewery, whos **Gatzweiler Altbier★★** is widely available in Düsseldorf.

Ferdinand Schumacher

Despite being in a modern part of the city, this home-bre house in Ost Strasse, has the polite atmosphere of times pas and is a quiet place at which to relax after shopping or a da at the office. Its **Schumacher Altbier★★★** is the lightest i palate and body, and the maltiest, very clean, with a lovel delicacy of aromatic hop character. The beer is also availabl at the Goldene Kessel, in Bolker Strasse.

Zum Uerige

This rambling tavern in Berger Strasse is named after cranky proprietor. Cranky he may well have been, but it is friendly enough place today – and produces the classi **Düsseldorfer Altbier**, an aromatic, tawny brew, deep i colour and flavour, with a slowly unrolling hop bitterness i its big and sustained finish. **Zum Uerige★★★★** beer is th most assertive, complex and characterful of the Alts. It also the most bitter. Like all of the Düsseldorfer "house beer, it is produced in traditional copper kettles, but this the most beautiful brewery of them all. It also has traditional copper cool-ship, and a Baudelot cooler, bot still in use, and it is impeccably maintained and polished The brewhouse can be seen from the most picaresque of th many bars. Every few minutes, barrels are rolled throug Zum Uerige on their way to the various dispense points while drinkers jink out of the way. Meals are not served, bu Zum Uerige has its own sausage kitchen on the premises Here, sausages of pork and liver, *Blutwurst* and brawn, ar produced, with spiced dripping left over to serve wit malodorous Mainzer cheese that has been marinated in bee If those flavours are not sufficiently intense, robust gastro nomes are encouraged to look for the "secret" *Sticke* bee that mysteriously appears for one brew only in January February, and again in September-October. This is a

Altbier of 14 Plato, with an extra dash of roasted malt – and it is dry-hopped in the maturation tanks.

COLOGNE

German beer-lovers greatly admire the speciality brewing style of Cologne, even if the rest of the world has not so far noticed it. It would be widely imitated, too, if it were not protected by its appellation *Kölschbier* (the beer of Cologne). Except in cases of lengthy precedent, a beer may not label itself *Kölsch* unless it is made in the Cologne metropolitan area. Imitations are thus pointless: they cannot identify their aspirations.

Happily, there are a baker's dozen breweries in Cologne and as many again in its hinterland. All of them produce *Kölschbier*, and some do nothing else. At least one has dropped other, more conventional, styles from its portfolio. *Kölschbier* dominates Cologne: it is possible to go into an ordinary bar in the city and be unable to find a Pilsener – even though it may be advertized outside. In the city's "home-brew" houses, of course, *Kölsch* is the only beer available.

Cologne has more breweries than any other city in Germany (indeed, in the world). Being so blessed, it naturally has a great many bars and taverns, including its home-brew houses. For most of the year, it is an engrossing place in which to sample beers, except during its pre-Lenten carnival, when the drinking becomes less considered. Whether its wealth of drinking places results from, or serves to attract, the tourists is a matter for conjecture. Some people apparently go to Cologne to study its history, see its huge Cathedral, or take trips down the Rhine. They should not be distracted from the city's distinctive beer by such diversions, though it is comfortably possible to enjoy both.

For all the envy it attracts, *Kölschbier* is not at first sight especially distinctive. It is a pale beer, much the same colour as a Pilsener, but – as its lightly fruity aroma and palate should reveal – it is made by top-fermentation.

A classic *Kölsch* has that fruitiness in the beginning, a notably soft palate (influenced by the local water) and a very delicate finish. Although *Kölschbier* brewers pay a lot of attention to hop character (two or three varieties are used, often with a Hallertau accent), their aim is to achieve a light dryness in the finish and nothing too assertive.

The very subtle character of this style is no doubt influenced also by the background palate imparted by the typical Cologne yeasts. These generally create a very vigorous fermentation, which is followed by two, three or four weeks of cold conditioning at 0°–5°C (32°–41°F). The gravity range of *Kölsch* beers is from just over 11 to just under 12 Plato. A typical example has 11.5 Plato and merges at between 3.5 and 4 percent alcohol by weight. Most often, it is 4 (5 by volume). Bittering units are typically at the top end of the 20s.

To the outsider, the two dozen *Kölsch* beers are very similar, but locals have their own firm favourites. Those produced in the home-brew houses are especially enjoyed. Drinkers in the *Schwemme* (standing area) of P.J. Früh's Kölner Hofbräu see beer being served at a world-record ace. A dumb-waiter elevates barrels every ten minutes or so, they are tapped, served by gravity, and exhausted. The tall, cylindrical glasses favoured in Cologne are loaded into a specially designed tray so that they look like cartridges in a gun, and dispensed by waiters nicknamed *Köbe* (believed to be derived from *Jakob*), uniformed in blue pullovers and leather aprons. As the drinker finishes one glass, another is put in its place.

Kölschbier is a lovely aperitif (not a bad digestif, either) and it is often consumed as an accompaniment to snacks. On its home ground, this may mean "half a hen" (Rhineland whimsy for a wedge of cheese with a roll) or "Cologne caviare" (blood sausage). Or *Mettwurst* of the tartare type. "With music" means garnished with onions.

Among the home-brew beers, P.J. Früh's is especially clean-tasting, that of Päffgen the hoppiest and Malzmühle, appropriately, the maltiest. Each has its own support as a local classic, though none of the three has a clear claim to be the definitive *Kölsch*. Nor among the rest of the *Kölschbiers* does one stand out, though a good claim is staked by Garde. This is a pronouncedly fruity *Kölschbier*, produced by an old-established private company at Dormagen-bei-Köln. Garde is one of the several companies in Germany with a woman brewer.

Differences between the more widely available *Kölschbiers* are so subtle as to be very open to the influence of freshness (of the beer or the taster). Gaffel is perhaps the driest; Sion flowery and hoppy; Gereons fruitier, with a dry finish; Sester fruity and dry; Gilden fruity, with a rather heavy texture; Zunft creamy; Reissdorf light, soft and delicious; Küppers soft and sweetish; Kurfürsten and Dom sweet at the front, with a drier finish. Küppers is part of the same company as Wicküler Pils; Gereons is associated with the same group; Dom belongs to Stern, of the Watney group; and Gilden to DUB-Schultheiss.

Where to drink

Visitors who go to Cologne to see the Roman museum or the Cathedral will find P.J. Früh's Kölner Hofbräu conveniently opposite, in Am Hof. Behind Früh is the Old Town, lined with bars and restaurants, especially on the *Heumarkt* (Haymarket). At the near end of the Heumarkt, the Päffgen Kölsch brewery family has a restaurant, a couple of doors from which is the Zlata Praha bar, serving draught Urquell Pilsner and Budvar Budweiser. At the far end of the Heumarkt is the Malzmühle home-brew cafe. Beside the Rhine, a pleasant ride on tram number 15 or 16 to the stop at Schönhauser Strasse leads to the Küppers Kölsch brewery, where there is a restaurant serving local dishes and *Wiess* beer, and a very worthwhile museum of brewing.

P.J. Früh's Kölner Hofbräu

An institution: a home-brew tavern and restaurant dating from the turn of the century, in the heart of Cologne. It is a favourite meeting place for lunch or an early evening drink, and it sells between one and two thousand litres of its home brewed draught *Kölschbier* every day. Like some home-brew taverns elsewhere, Früh also sells beer by the barrel to private individuals and does a lively local trade in this way. The brewery's small, 20-litre, barrels are also on draught in some other taverns, and the beer can be found in the bottle

Früh Echt Kölsch★★★ is a soft beer, delicate in both its fruitiness of entrance and its hoppy dryness of finish. It is made with only barley malt – no wheat – and hopped with the Hallertau and Tettnang varieties.

Küppers

By far the biggest producer and exporter of Kölschbier despite being a newcomer. Küppers was established 20-odd years ago in Cologne to meet the rules of appellation, so that a *Kölschbier* could be added to the portfolio of the large Wicküler Pils company of Wuppertal. This move followed a court case over the appellation. Sales since, supported by hefty marketing efforts, have justified the determination behind Küppers establishment, but tradition is harder to build. No doubt this was in mind when Küppers established their excellent restaurant and museum. The soft and sweetish **Küppers Kölsch**★ → ★★ is unexceptional, but the brewery wins bonus points for another gesture to tradition, its confusingly-named *Wiess* beer. Although *Wiess* is the Rhineland dialect pronunciation of *Weiss* ("white"), the designation perhaps has less to do with the cloudy tone of this beer than its rustic style; Bavarians talk in the same vein about a *Wies'n* beer when they mean something that is to be served at a country fair. **Küppers Wiess**★★★ is an unfiltered version of the normal Kölsch. It still has yeast in suspension, imparting the cloudiness and an astringent, refreshing, bitter-fruit quality. The name is not intended to suggest a wheat beer. Although some wheat is used, it is present only in the small proportion typical of Kölschbier.

Malzmühle

This is a home-brew cafe and restaurant with a pleasantly insouciant, relaxing atmosphere. Being at the far end of the Heumarkt, it is easily missed, but shouldn't be. Its **Mühlen Kölsch**★★★ → ★★★★ is mild and rounded, with a warm, spicy aroma and palate, reminiscent almost of marshmallow. It is a distinctive and delicious beer, lightly hopped with Hallertau blossoms and fermented in open vessels.

Päffgen

A beautifully-kept home-brew restaurant in Friesen Strasse which has a small beer garden. Its **Päffgen Kolsch**★★★ → ★★★★ has a soft palate with a big, hoppy bouquet. By the standards of Kölschbier, it has a very hoppy finish, too.

Sion

Originally a home-brew, too. Its tavern, in Unter Taschenmacher, in the Old Town, offers brisk service and a very fresh glass of its pleasantly flowery beer. Since **Sion Kölsch**★★ → ★★★ is now produced under contract by the brewers of Gereons Kölsch, knowing drinkers whisper that the two beers are one and the same. This is not true; each is produced to its own specification. The flowery bouquet and dry finish of Sion Kölsch derives in part from Hersbrucker hops. **Gereons**★★ is hopped exclusively with Hallertau.

RHINELAND'S PILSENERS

Apart from those cities that are islands of their own style, the whole of the Rhine and its hinterland is dotted with well regarded breweries. The towns without a speciality style of their own have in several cases put their best efforts behind a Pilsener beer, developing, as Madison Avenue might term it, a super-premium product and in several instances producing nothing else.

Several of these products were among a selection dubbed "The Premium Beers" in an article some years ago in the influential newspaper *Die Welt*. The writer, Hans Baumann, is a journalist who frequently comments on both the business and social aspects of the brewing industry. His intention was not to say that these "premium" beers were the best, but that they were labels that seemed capable of commanding a high price. His "premium" tag was gratefully seized by the breweries and he now has mixed feelings about its continued use. There are, he points out, many other good beers, not all of them as intensively marketed.

The German consumer has, however, come to believe in recent years that a brewery concentrating on one style is likely to do a better job than those with a whole portfolio of products. This is a questionable proposition. If a chef prepares the same dish every lunchtime, he is unlikely to undercook or burn it, but are his the skills necessarily those of an Escoffier?

While the Pilseners of the far north are generally the driest, the same leaning is evident in Rhineland, perhaps with a softness and lightness emerging as the brewers enter wine country. Even in the far north, the extra-dry Pilseners represent a local accent rather than a varietal style, and it is again a broad regionality — even looser, but still noticed by the drinker — that groups these examples along and around the Rhine: products from as far north as Duisburg (König-Pilsener) and Essen (Stauder Pils), east into the Sauerland (Warsteiner; Veltins; Krombacher) and as far south as the Rheinpfalz (Bitburger). The north and south represent extremes of the style, too. In the north, König-Pilsener is unusually full-bodied and in the south, Bitburger is almost as light as a German Pilsener can be.

Among the products that were not included in the "premium" listing, but might have been, Herforder Pils (taking its name from its home town) and Königsbacher (from Koblenz) are conspicuous examples. No doubt Wicküler (from Wuppertal) would like to be included, too. Among smaller, local brewers, Irle (of Siegen) is a Pilsener specialist in the Sauerland. Although its emergence as a Pilsener-brewing area owes less to history than coincidence, the Sauerland has come to be especially associated with this style. With its broad, green valleys, lakes and woods, Sauerland is a pleasant place for a leisurely beer tour.

The foreign visitor who is unfamiliar with Germany had better sort out the geography before starting to drink. It is not only some of the beers but also the places that have similar names. Sauerland is far from the river with which it shares a name, for example. Oddly enough, the river Sauer is closer to Saarland, which is a different place altogether. What they all share is a selection of interesting beers, in Pilsener and other styles.

Where to drink

In Stauder's home town of Essen, one of the company's shareholders established a "house brewery" in 1984. The

rbecker Dampfbier brewery, bar and restaurant is in
inrich Brauns Strasse. The term *dampf* refers to the fact
at the premises were a steam-powered brewery in the
30s and not to the style of beer. An Export-gravity,
dium-dark Salonbier is available, with or without filtra-
n (in the latter case, it is called a *Zwickelbier*). It's a long
y from the Pilseners of the region – and a delightful
atrast.

At the opposite end of Premium Pilsner country, across
e border and into Saarland, another *Zwickelbier* can be
und, also in a "house brewery". This is the brewery
esthouse Zum 'Stiefel, run by the Bruch family, in the
wn of Saarbrücken. Another Saarland speciality, though
t from a house brewery, is Bier Eiche (Oak Beer). This was
ginally produced for a festival concerning oak trees, but is
w available all year round. It is a pale, top-fermenting
er of everyday gravity, with a delicate hop aroma and
rness. It is produced in Merzig, by Saarfurst, a local
sidiary of the region's Karlsberg brewery.

Karlsberg, in the Saarland town of Homburg, has – of
urse – nothing to do with the Danish brewery of a similar
me but different spelling.

itburger

king its name from its home town of Bitburg, this is a
ecialist "Premium" Pilsener brewery. It is a very modern
ce indeed, producing a Pilsener with a low original
avity by German standards: 11.3 Plato. This is thoroughly
enuated, to produce an alcohol content of 3.9 by weight;
/9 by volume. **Bitburger Pils★ → ★★** is very pale, extreme-
light, and dry. It has a pronounced hop flavour but not
ch bitterness.

Beer-lovers who enjoy this very light interpretation of a
sener might also appreciate **Bernkasteler Pils★ → ★★**,
ich has an even lower gravity (11.2, producing 3.8; 4.7)
t fractionally more bitterness. This is produced not far
ay by the Bürger brewery, of Bernkastel.

erforder

incipally a Pilsener brewery though it does also produce
ers in other styles. **Herforder Pils★★ → ★★★** is full-bodied,
th a clean, mild palate. Its gravity is 12.1 and its alcohol
ntent 3.9; 4.8/9. Herforder also produces a malty but dry
port★ → ★★; a pale **Mai-Bock★ → ★★** and a dark **Doppel-
ck★ → ★★**, both very malty. Herford is on the northern
rders of Rhineland-Westphalia.

le

other specialist Pilsener brewery its **Irle Edel-
s★ → ★★** having the classic combination of a 12 Plato
avity and an alcohol content of 4; 5. It has a clean palate
d is very mild.

önig

own as a "Premium" Pilsener brewery but also produces
her styles. Its Pilsener is very full-bodied but also clean
d notably dry. **König Pilsener★★★** has a rich aroma, is
stained, very smooth, bitterness and a perfumy finish. It
s an original gravity of 12.1 but this is fermented down to
alcohol content of only 3.8; 4.6. The company also has a

König-Alt★ that is fractionally less full-bodied, and muc̣ milder in hop character.

König-Alt has a rival in its home town of Duisburg. A be̦ called **Rheingold-Alt★ → ★★** is the speciality of a small̦ brewery in the town.

Königsbacher

A Coblenz brewery which produces several styles. It also ḥ a number of subsidiaries, whose products include Richmoḍ Kölsch and Düssel Alt. The enjoyable **Königsbacher Ṗ ★★ → ★★★** is complex and satisfying medium-bodied with ạ fresh, hoppy bouquet and a well-sustained bitterness in tḥ finish.

Krombacher

Taking its name from its location in Kreutzal-Krombacḥ this house is a specialist "Premium" Pilsener brewery, prọ to announce that its water comes from a rocky sprin̦ **Krombacher Pils★★** is medium-bodied, with a slight mạ accent in the nose, a clean palate, and a pleasing ḥ bitterness in its late finish. In the American market, the bẹ has been promoted as having a crispness, a "hop taste", ạ "a noticeable lack of bitterness". It is hard to say wheth̦ the copywriter was being intentionally dishonest. or cloţ tongued.

Stauder

This is known as a "Premium" Pilsener brewery althou̦ Stauder does have other products. **Stauder Pils★★** is ma̧ keted especially to expensive hotels and restaurants. advertizing in Germany emphasizes cold maturation, ma̧ ing a play on the verb to rest. Brewers sometimes descriḅ their beer as "resting" in maturation, and Stauder promoted as a product to enjoy in tranquillity. Since a lo̦ maturation also "cleans" beer, there is an implication tḥ Stauder-drinkers are strangers to the hangover. Stauder Ṗ does not, however, have an unusually clean nose or palaṭ and there is a hint of fruitiness in its character.

Veltins

This brewery led the movement to speciality Pilsen̦ brewing in Germany and is owed a debt of fashionability ḅ its fellow "Premium" producers, especially its neighbours Sauerland. It is a relatively small brewery, and its **Velti̦ Pilsener★★★** still has something of a cult following. It is ̦ clean beer, with an elegant hop bitterness in the finish.

Warsteiner

Although it does have other styles this concern is known aș "Premium" Pilsener producer. It is a very up-to-daţ brewery, aggressively marketing and exporting its pṛ mium-priced product. **Warsteiner Pilsener★ → ★★** has a li̦ hop bouquet, a dry palate, and a moderately bitter finisḥ

Wicküler

Wicküler Pilsener★★ has a delicate hop bouquet and a li̦ but firm body, with quite a bitter finish. A well-maḍ Pilsener by the standards of mass-market products (whicḥ in the Rhineland, it is). The brewery has a full range ̦ styles, and owns Küppers in Cologne.

FRANKFURT AND HESSE

the Old Town of Frankfurt, the *Sachsenhausen*, the bars
nd restaurants serve *Apfelwein*, a cloudy, medium-dry
coholic cider. If Frankfurt has a speciality for the drinker,
en this is it. There is a theory that Europe once had a cider
elt, separating the wine-growing and beer-brewing areas. It
 a tenuous theory, but in this instance the argument could,
deed, be put that Frankfurt has wine to its south and west;
er to its north and east.

In this pivotal position, Frankfurt has no beery leaning of
 own, no varietal style. Nor has the surrounding state of
esse. In so far as a country the shape of West Germany can
ave a middle, Frankfurt is the city that stands there. If its
eers are middle-of-the-road, that is only to be expected.

What Frankfurt lacks in style, it makes up in scale. With
 output in the region of 2.5 million hectolitres, the
rankfurt brewery company of Binding is the biggest in
ermany. Binding belongs to the group that also includes
ortmund's DAB and Berlin's Kindl breweries.

Frankfurt's other brewing company, Henninger, is better
nown internationally. It has an output in the region of 1.75
illion hectolitres, and is in the same group as Hannen and
avaria St Pauli.

Just as it is an important state in the matter of large
reweries, so Hesse has some significance for small – or, at
ast, independent – ones. A nationwide organization of
rivately-owned breweries, the Bräu Ring, has its headquar-
rs in Hesse, at Wetzlar, which is also the home of one of its
embers, the Euler company. Several other member-
reweries are in Hesse, including Alsfeld, the Andreas
loster brewery, Busch, Marburger and the Unionbrauerei
 Fulda.

Visitors are known to escape the post-war modernity of
rankfurt by heading for the 19th-century charm of the
rrounding spa towns, but drinkers do not have to take the
aters. The small breweries of Hesse, especially to the north,
fer an interesting alternative. Then, if the breweries of
esse prove insufficient, there is always the Bavarian
teigerwald not far east. Or, south in Mannheim across the
state line", Eichbaum brewery offers a smoked wheat beer
 2.5 Plato) called **Rauch-Weizen★★★**.

here to drink

ess than 32km (20 miles) south of Frankfurt, in the artists'
d philosphers' town of Darmstadt, is a shop stocking more
an 1,000 beers, from 250 countries. The shop is named
. Maruhn, "Der Groesste Biermarkt Der Welt", and is at
fumgstaete Strasse 174, in the district of Eberstadt, in
armstadt (☎06151-54876). Owner Bruno Maruhn is a
lly, enthusiastic chap, and his claim to have the world's
ggest beer shop is probably safe, despite earnest compe-
tion from the USA.

Binding

ermany's biggest brewing company producing a full range
f beers and perhaps most noteworthy for its premium
ersion of a German-style Export called **Export Privat★★**. It
as a fresh, light hoppiness in the nose; a clean, malt-
cented palate; and a faintly fruity dryness in the finish. A

very similar beer, but fractionally less dry, marginally fulle
bodied, and slightly paler, is brewed for the America
market under the name **Steinhauser Bier★★**. This has a littl
extra maturation, and is micro-filtered, to retain its fresh
ness. It is an enjoyable beer, and did not deserve to b
polluted by half-truth when it was launched in the USA
where a spokesman for Binding was quoted as sayin
"Steinhauser tastes the same here as it does in Germany"
Binding also produce a hearty double bock **Carolus★★**.

Busch

A famous name in brewing. Southwest of Frankfurt
Mainz, from which Adolphus Busch emigrated to the USA
start the world's biggest brewing company. Northwest
Frankfurt is Limburg, where a family called Busch run
rather smaller brewery. American Busch make 50 millio
hectolitres of beer in the time it takes their Germa
counterparts to brew 15,000hl. The two families are n
related and neither, of course, has anything to do wit
product called Bush Beer (no "c"), made in Belgium. The
are, on the other hand, historical connections, thoug
distant, between the German town of Limburg and the Be
gian and Dutch provinces of the same name. As to Limbu
ger cheese, it originated in Belgium and is still made the
and in The Netherlands, but its principal centre of produ
tion is Germany. The three Limburgs also share an intere
in beer. The German one produces a pleasant, very m
Golden Busch Pils★ → ★★ and a **Limburger Export★★**.

Euler

The cathedral in Wetzlar gives its name to Euler's **Do**
Pilsener★★, which is medium-dry. The brewery is al
known for its slightly fuller-bodied **Euler Landpils★**
Other products include a deep amber, malty **Alt Wetzlar★**
(*alt* in this instance refers to tradition, not style. This is n
an *Altbier* but a bottom-fermenting "dark" beer). Its bas
Euler Hell★ → ★★, a pale, malty beer, has an expo
counterpart called **Kloster Bier**. The Landpils is served u
filtered at the Wetzlarer Braustuben, adjoining the brewery

Henninger

This may be the smaller of the two principal breweries
Frankfurt, but it is still a sizeable concern and the bett
known internationally. Its principal products, within
considerable range, include **Kaiser Pilsner★** and the dri
Christian Henninger Pilsener★ → ★★. The latter has n
only more hops but also a second "e". Henninger expor
widely and for a time promoted its beer in the USA b
emphasizing the colour of its bottles. The argument was th
the beer is kept fresh because the bottles are made fro
brown glass. Beer bottled in green glass is more vulnerable
being harmed by supermarket lighting (and therefore mo
likely to contain additives to maintain "shelf-life"). Th
claim was intended to steal a march on those well-establ
shed imports in the American market that bottled in gree
Although the argument is valid, a more impressive clai
would have been to prove that Henninger's beer itself
more interesting than its rivals. There was for some years
Henninger brewery in Canada, and the label survives the
despite the sale of the plant to Heineken.

STUTTGART AND
BADEN-WÜRTTEMBERG

This is the place for the eclectic drinker. Here, wine and fruit brandies oblige beer to share the table, even though the state of Baden-Württemberg still contrives to have more than 180 breweries.

In the Black Forest — or, at least, its greener valleys — village brewers produce tasty, sometimes slightly fruity, beers that reveal the softness of the local water. On the west side of the forest, the Jehle family brewery of Biberach is an example, with its aromatic Privat Pils and its dry *Dunkel*. In another part of the forest, the *Schloss* brewery Zöhrlaut has a soft Edel-Pils and a fruity, coffee-ish *Dunkel*. Stuttgart has three breweries, all taking their water from Lake Constance (the Bodensee) and producing typically light and soft "wine country" beers. East of Stuttgart, towards the Swabian mountains, one or two maltier beers emerge. (The term "Swabian" is widely used in Germany to indicate the culture and kitchen of an imprecise region that might be considered a stretch from Stuttgart to Augsburg.) The Olpp brewery, a Urach, has some well-made beers, including a clean, light Grafen-Pils. In that direction, more southern styles are to be found, notably wheat beers.

Where to drink

Stuttgart, the principal city of Baden-Württemberg, is more of a wine-drinkers' than a beer-drinkers' city, but beer-lovers will want to have a nostalgic glass at the former Sanwald Brewery *Gasthof* in Silberburg Strasse. There is also a small beer garden round the corner in Rotebühl Strasse. The old Sanwald brewery's wheat beers are now made by Dinkelacker, in Tübinger Strasse. In front of the Dinkel-acker brewery is a pleasant restaurant serving the company's beers and offering Swabian dishes like *Fladlesuppe* (clear soup with strips of pancake); *Maultaschen* (Swabia's salty retort to ravioli); and *Spätzle* (egg noodles). No one ever went to Germany to lose weight and the Swabians clearly subscribe to this view.

At the end of September and for the first two weeks in October this businesslike city lets its hair down for its annual fair on the Cannstatt meadows. This *Cannstatter Volksfest* is Stuttgart's counterpart to Munich's *Oktoberfest*. Beer is supplied by all three of the local breweries (three more than some cities have, though it is only half the number mustered by Munich). Special *Volksfest* beers are produced, in the *Märzen* style, and there are very similar *Weihnachts* brews at Christmas.

About half way between Heidelberg and Stuttgart, at the salt-water spa of Bad Rappenau, the Haffner brewery has its own resort hotel (33 rooms, ☎07264-1061). Its house beer is called *Kur* ("Cure") Pils.

South of Stuttgart, on the way to Lake Constance, is a brewery called Löwen (there are about 30 such, unrelated, "Lion" breweries in Germany). This Löwen brewery, at Tuttlingen, serves a *Kellerpils* in its restaurant. Drinkers who enjoy this excessively should be warned that there are no bedrooms. Between Tuttlingen and Ulm, at Bingen, the Lamm brewery serves a *dunkles Hefeweizenbier* and, yet more exotic, *Bierhefebrannt*, a clear spirit distilled from beer.

Closer to Ulm, at Trochtelfingen, the Albquell brewery (fiv
rooms, ☎07124-733) serves a *Kellerbier*.

Where to drink in Swabian Bavaria

South of Ulm, there are four breweries with restaurant
three with bedrooms. At Roggenburg-Biberach the Schmi
brewery restaurant specializes in *Dunkel* and *Märzen* beers
but has no bedrooms. Hotel Löwenbrau (20 rooms, ☎0824
5056), at Bad Wörishofen, has a *Kurpils*, and is proud of it
Doppelbock. The Hirsch brewery, at Ottobeuren, has severa
interesting specialities including a house liqueur made b
Benedictine brothers in the local monastery. The brewery
kettles are visible to guests who soak away their hangover i
the indoor pool at the adjoining hotel (80 rooms, ☎0833
552/3). Nearby at Irsee, a secularized monastery brewer
produces some beers of outstanding interest, as well a
having a very good kitchen. The Irseer Klosterbrauerei (2
rooms, ☎08341-8331) specializes in unfiltered beers, som
matured for more than six months. A speciality called Abt'
Trunk, conditioned and sold in hand-made clay flasks, ha
been reported to have reached a record-shattering 15 percen
alcohol by weight. This sounds unlikely and the owne
reckons that 12 percent by volume is more realistic. Th
brewery also has a *Bierbrannt*. There is also a colourful rang
of home-produced *Bierbrannt* and schnapps at the Post Brewer
Hotel (22 rooms, ☎08361-238/9) in the mountain resort
Nesselwang. The hotel has a small museum of beer and hold
seminars on the subject.

Fürstenberg

The "Premium" ratings were perhaps something of
northern notion and Fürstenberg is the only souther
brewery to have been dubbed in this way. It is also a house
some nobility, controlled by the aristocratic Fürstenberg
who have been brewing for more than 500 years. The fami
are patrons of the arts and there is an impressive collection
German masters in the Fürstenberg museum, at the palac
of Donaueschingen, in the Black Forest. In the palac
grounds, the Danube emerges from its underground sourc
Donaueschingen is also the home of what is now a ver
modern brewery. A full range of styles is produced, but th
brewery is especially well known for its **Fürstenber
Pilsener**★★ → ★★★. This has quite a full body, a sustaine
lasting bead, and a nicely hoppy taste in its dry finish.

Dinkelacker

The biggest brewery in the southwest; it might just achiev
this ascendancy on the basis of local sales, but exports ar
the decider. The brewery is best known for its **CD-Pils**★
Although this is marketed as a prestige beer, the nam
stands not for *corps diplomatique* but for Carl Dinkelacke
who founded the brewery in Stuttgart in 1888. The Dink
lacker family, brewers since the mid 1700s, still control th
company. The brewery, not far from the city centre, is
blend of the traditional and the modern. Copper kettles a
used, and the CD-Pils is hopped four times with half a doze
varieties (the final addition being Brewers' Gold, in th
lauter tun). The CD-Pils is also fermented in the classi
square type of vessel and kräusened during lagering; oth
products go into an ugly forest of unitanks.

Dinkelacker produces a range of bottom-fermenting beers at adopt a middle stance between those of its local rivals ttgarter Hofbräu and Schwaben Bräu. In general, fbräu's are the sweetest, Dinkel's medium, Schwaben's driest, but these are ·fine distinctions since all three weries produce typically soft southwestern beers. In dition to its pale beers, Dinkelacker has a dark single ck, **Cluss Bock Dunkel★★**, from its affiliate Cluss brewery nearby Heilbronn – very malty in aroma and palate, but her weak in finish. At its Stuttgart headquarters Dinkeker also produces a number of specialities inherited when local Sanwald brewery was absorbed. These include a her thin **Stamm Alt★** and two wheat beers, each made to same specification: the sparkling **Weizen Krone★★** and **Sanwald Hefe Weiss★★**.

chwaben Bräu

e smallest of Stuttgart's three breweries, in the pleasant urban township of Vaihingen. It has a large, traditional oper brewhouse and splendidly cavernous lagering cellars. relative dryness of its beers is best exemplified by its **ister Pils★★ →★★★**. The parent company, Rob Leicht, o owns the Kloster brewery at Pfullingen-Reutlingen. Its **oster Pilsner★ →★★** is available not only in the local rket but travels as far as the USA. It has a lightly hoppy ma and finish, a quite full, soft, texture, and a hint of rpness in the finish. Another subsidiary, Bräuchle, in tzingen, produces a pale **Bock★★** for the whole group. The npany plans a small museum of brewing, perhaps as a ture to beer as a parent product – in the local market, it is most as well known for its soft drinks.

uttgarter Hofbräu

e Hofbräu rivals, and may surpass, Dinkelacker in local es. Its brewery is not far beyond that of Dinkelacker, on edge of Stuttgart. It's a curiously rural fold of the city, d Hofbräu's turn-of-the-century buildings have flourishes t could be Scottish baronial. Inside, however, the wery is uncompromisingly modern. The name Hofbräu ives from a former royal brewery, but the present npany is publicly held, with most of the stock in the nds of one person. The notion that drinkers of German nes have a soft, sweetish palate is emphatically accepted Hofbräu, and the brewery also takes pride in its beers' being pasteurized. Its premium product is called **Herren s★ →★★**.

BAVARIA:
MUNICH AND THE SOUTH

er-lovers in other countries may be jealous of Germany in neral but the focus of envy must be the state of Bavaria. entire nation, nor even Germany's other states put gether, can rival Bavaria's tally of breweries, which still ceeds 800. Between them, they produce about 5,000 beers. ly nine or ten of Bavaria's breweries are, by any standard, ge (each producing more than half a million hectolitres a ur). More than 500 are very small – 10,000hl or less and of se, about half are tiny, producing less than 2,000hl. Almost every village has a brewery and some have two or

three. The very small breweries almost always have the
own inn, and often their beer is available nowhere else. The
are breweries in monasteries – and convents – and in castle
The castles and baroque-rococo churches are a reminder th
Bavaria was a nation of extrovert pride in the 17th and 18
centuries and when in 1919 it joined the German Republi
one of the conditions was that its Pure Beer Law be retaine

Bavaria is the home of more beer styles than any oth
part of Germany. Its everyday beers are not especia
potent, but its specialities include the strongest beer
Germany. It grows good malting barley and virtually all
Germany's hops (and exports them all over the world), it h
water in the Alps and the icy caves where the usefulness
cold maturation – lagering – first came to be understoo

The mountain and forest isolation of village Bavaria h
helped its culture to survive, not only in costume, everyd
dress, worship, music and dance, but also in its sense of bei
a beer land. Isolation was favoured by the founders
monasteries, too, in the days when they were the sanctuari
of all knowledge, including the art of brewing. If there w
communication in these matters, it was across the mou
tains and within the forests. From the Dark Ages, the crad
of modern brewing has been slung from St Gallen
Switzerland to Munich, to Vienna, to Pilsen in Bohemi
That cradle is filled to bursting point with hearty, thirst
Bavaria, crying *ein prosit!* at every opportunity.

While the Federal Republic as a whole drinks 140-o
litres of beer per head each year, this figure is grea
exceeded in Bavaria where the figure is closer to 240.

No other state has such a defined calendar of drinki
dates and styles. It may not matter much which beer y
drink in the madness of the pre-Lenten *Fasching* (an answ
in southern cities like Munich and northern ones like Colog
to the *Mardi Gras* of Nice and New Orleans, or the *Carni*
of Rio). However, in March and April, the appropriate be
is *Doppelbock*; in May, single *Bock*; in June, July and Augu
Export-type beers at village festivals and *Weissbier*
Weizenbier in the beer gardens; at the end of September, a
for the weeks that follow, *Märzenbier* for the *Oktoberfest*;
November, it is time to think of *Weihnachts* (Christm
beer, which may be a variation on the festival speciality,
could be a *Weizenbock*.

Even the beer's accompaniments have a timetable. Wi
the mid-morning beer, the appropriate snack is *Weisswur*
a pair of succulent veal sausages coddled in a tureen of war
water. The veal is tempered with small proportions of be
and coarse bacon, and there is a seasoning of parsl
(occasionally chives) and sometimes onion or lemon. *Wei*
wurst is so important that purists argue over its prop
contents. For lunch, the beer might be accompanied
Leberkäse, which is neither liver nor cheese but a beef a
pork loaf, served hot. For an early evening snack, t
ubiquitous large radish of the region, which has a black sk
and white flesh. The flesh is sculpted into a spiral a
assaulted with salt. If the salt on the radish doesn't ma
you thirsty, the granules on the big, fresh, soft pretzels w
do the trick.

To the foreigner, not least the beer-lover, the state
Bavaria may be synonymous with its capital city, Muni
Within Bavaria, while its claims are universally recognize

Munich and its hinterland have competition from other cities and regions where yet more breweries are to be found.

Munich's claims are that it has some of the biggest and most famous breweries, and that it has nurtured more styles of beer than any other city. Within its hinterland, stretching through the regions known as Upper and Lower Bavaria, into the Alps and to the Austrian frontier, are hundreds of breweries. The city itself is ringed by small breweries making excellent beers. The Maisach and Schloss Mariabrunn breweries are just two examples. To the southwest, it is only 32km (20 miles) to the lakes and the beginning of the mountains, with more local breweries to serve the terraces and beer gardens.

South of Herrsching, on the lake called Ammersee, is the monastic brewery of Andechs, whose immensely malty *Dunkel* and *Bock* beers were the extremely distant inspiration for the American Andeker brand. The brothers also have their own bitter liqueurs and fruit brandies, and there is a *Stube* and terrace. Farther into the Alps, near the ski resort of Garmisch-Partenkirchen, is another famous monastery brewery, Ettal, producing well-made and typically Bavarian beers but better known for its fruit brandy. Northeast of Munich near Landshut is the Klosterbrauerei Furth and also the celebrated convent brewery of Mallersdorf, just off the road to Regensburg. Another convent brewery, St Josef's, is at Ursberg, west of Augsburg, near Krumbach, on the road to Ulm.

A monastery brewery founded in 1040 at Weihenstephan, near Freising, less than 32km (20 miles) northeast of Munich, was to have great historical significance. Although the evidence for continuous production is hazy, the brewery survived long enough to be secularized by Napoleon and continues today under the ownership of the State of Bavaria. The Bayerische Staatsbrauerei Weihenstephan thus claims to be the oldest brewery in the world. It may be a cobwebbed claim, but there is none better. Although there are vestiges of the monastery from the 12th century, and today's buildings are set in a restored cloister from the 17th century, the brewery is modern. It also offers some training facilities to the adjoining brewing institute.

There are only a handful of Faculties of Brewing in the world, and Weihenstephan – part of the Technical University of Munich – is the most famous. In recent years it has had difficulties, arising originally from its efforts to deal with brewers who do not work in *Reinheitsgebot* countries, but its name remains a by-word in the industry. The Weihenstephan brewery produces a full range of beers but is perhaps best known for its Kristal Export Weizenbier (very fruity, with hints of blackcurrant, and extremely dry in the finish) and its Hefeweissbier (light for the style, and refreshing).

Wheat-beer brewing is especially associated with the area to the east of Munich. About 32km (20 miles) out of the city is the Erding wheat-beer brewery, perhaps the best-known of the specialists and certainly the fastest-growing. Farther east, in Mühldorf, the Jägerhof house brewery of Wolfgang Unerti produces a wonderfully turbid wheat beer.

To the south of Munich another tiny brewery specializes in wheat beers: Gmeineder, at Deisenhofen near Oberhaching. Much farther south, at Murnau, off the road to

Garmisch, another notable example of the turbid style of
wheat beer is made by the Karg brewery.

Where to drink

Each of the principal Munich breweries has several of its own
special outlets in the form of gardens, beer halls and
restaurants. The best or most famous are detailed with their
entries below. To the west of Munich and closer to Augsburg,
the *Schloss* brewery at Odelzhausen specializes in a double
bock called Operator (nothing sinister about the name – it is
dedicated to the Munich opera). As is often the case, the
Schloss (nine bedrooms, ☎08134-6606) is more like a
country house, but it has a restaurant. To the north of
Munich, the brewery guest-house Goldener Hahn (☎08461-
419) is at Beilngries, about half way to Nürnberg. Farther
north, at Lengenfeld-Velburg, the Winkler brewery guest-
house (☎09182-326) is widely known for its Kupfer Spezial
beer. This much-loved brew is a dark copper colour, with
gravity of 14 Plato, bottom-fermented in open vessels and
matured for between ten and 16 weeks. A remarkable
feature of this family concern is that it grows and malts its
own barley. Its beer is hopped with both Bavarian and
Bohemian varieties. There are also brewery guest-houses to
the northeast of Munich at Adlersberg (Prösslbräu; ☎09404-
1822); Böbrach (Brauereigasthof Eck; ☎09923-685);
Zwiesel (Deutscher Rhein; ☎09922-1651); and Zenting
(Kamm; ☎09907-315).

Altenmünster

The name Altenmünster has become well-known among
beer-buffs in the USA thanks to the export of one of its beers
in large, 2-litre flagons. These flagons, with a sprung,
porcelain "swing top" and pewter handle, are much in
demand. In the American market, the brew is identified
simply as **Altenmünster★★**, sometimes with the after-
thought "Brauer Bier", but no indication of style. In fact, in
its full golden colour and big palate, it is a good example of
the German style known as Export. It has a firm body, with
a leaning toward maltiness that is typically Bavarian.

Altenmünster is a village near Augsburg, but exports of
this beer have been so successful that some are now handled
from a sister brewery in Weissenbrunn, northern Bavaria.
Both breweries belong to a group embracing several other
companies. These include Sailer (it rhymes with "miler")
producing a range of soft, easily drinkable but unexceptional beers in Marktoberdorf, south of Augsburg. There are
also companies at Kulmbach and at Neustadt, near Coburg.

Augustiner

The favourite brews among serious beer-drinkers in Munich
are those from Augustiner. The beers are generally the
maltiest among those produced by the city's major brewers
and in that sense are closest to the palate traditionally
associated with Munich. This is especially true of Augustiner's pale beers. The everyday **Augustiner Hell★★★★**
qualifies as the classic pale beer of Munich, with its malty
aroma and palate, soft entrance and firm, smooth finish.
The brewery's interpretation of the German Export type
has the brand name **Edelstoff★★★** in Germany and, confusingly, is described as "Augustiner Munich Light" in the

nerican market. "Light" refers, of course, to its colour
d not to its body. This is hardly the lightest of German
ers and even the slenderest of those is big by American
undards. In recent years Augustiner has been emphasizing
pale beers, perhaps to the detriment of its dark styles.
e basic dark beer is called **Dunkel Vollbier★★★**. There is
o a **Dunkel Export★★ → ★★★**, which has occasionally
peared in Germanic areas of the USA. The company has a
mber of other styles; its **Maximator Doppelbock★★★**
marketed in the USA under the unexciting description
unich Dark".

The maltiness of Augustiner's beers has sources close to
me. No fewer than three of Munich's brewers have their
n maltings and Augustiner is one. Its malt is produced in
lars that stretch like the tunnels of a mine underneath the
ewery, which itself belongs to industrial archaeology.
nstructed in 1885 and a magnificent example of the proud
ewery edifices of the time, it is now a protected building.
the brewhouse only one in three vessels is made from
pper; the other two are of stainless steel. The dark beers
ve the benefit of a triple decoction; the pale a double. Only
oma hops are used, in five varieties, from both Bavaria
d Bohemia. Fermentation is in unusual vessels, open but
th a lid that can be brought down, without pressure, to
llect carbon dioxide. Fermentation is at very cold tem-
ratures and lagering is in traditional vessels, with kräusen-
g. The brewery uses wooden casks to supply beer gardens
d some inns in the Munich area. The casks are pitched at
e brewery, adding another traditional aroma to that of the
lty air.

Augustiner has as its near neighbours Hacker-Pschorr,
aten and Löwenbräu; all four are in the traditional
rewery quarter" behind Munich's central railway station.
ross the river are Paulaner and the Hofbräuhaus brewery.
the heart of the brewery quarter, on Arnulf Strasse, is the
ugustiner Keller, relatively small and much loved by the
ople of Munich. In the centre of the city on Neuhauser
rasse, Augustiner has its elegant, somewhat eccentric,
90s restaurant and brewery tap, with a small, Italianate
rden. This building was originally constructed in 1829 to
use the brewery after secularization. As its name suggests,
ugustiner was originally a monastic brewery, and its first
e was close to Munich's landmark cathedral, the Frauen-
rche. The brewery dates at least from the 15th century,
ough there is some uncertainty about the claimed found-
ion date of 1328. It is without doubt an institution in
nich, favoured by yet a third famous outlet, the beer
rden at the Hirschgarten, a public park near Nymphen-
rg Castle. This popular picnic spot is said to accommodate
many as 8,000 drinkers, while Löwenbräu's beer garden in
nich's huge central park holds a mere 6,000. How
refully this has been counted is open to dispute.

yinger

Munich, the best-known country brewery is Ayinger. The
sition it enjoys in the city is evident: its beers are served in
e restaurant and cabaret called the Platzl, on the square of
e same name, directly opposite the Hofbräuhaus. The
staurant is owned by Ayinger and a special Platzl brew is
oduced – a miniature barrel of the beer is customarily set

in the centre of the table, to accompany the evening burlesque. After dinner, there might also be a clear fr brandy, made from apples and pears and served in p vessels shaped like tobacco pipes.

The Platzl beer is pleasant enough but a half-hour journe out of Munich to the village of Aying will provide just th freshness to make it taste delicious. In Aying (and in t USA) this brew is known as Jahrhundert. The name dat from the brewery's centenary in 1978. **Jahrhundert★★** is German Export-type beer. It has some herbal hoppiness the nose and a big, malty palate that dries in a crisp finis

Ayinger has a full range of styles, among which several a noteworthy. **Altbairisch Dunkel★★ →★★★** is a splend example of the Bavarian dark style, with a warm, sweet fruity aroma and coffee-ish finish. **Fest-Märzen★ →★★** is little pale for the style but has a lovely malt bouque carrying through in the soft palate. **Maibock★ →★★**, too, is classically malty Bavarian beer, with spicy, apricot note Most characterful of all is the double bock, labelled Germany as Fortunator and in the USA as Celebrator. whichever name, **Fortunator/Celebrator★★★** is an ou standing example of double bock style and a beautiful balanced beer, its richness mellowing out in a long, dryi finish. When strong brews are served at the end of winte Germans talk about taking the "springtime beer cure" Ayinger goes further: it dubs its home village a "beer spa"

Where the Munich basin, with its crops of malting barle gives way to the foothills of the Alps the village of Ayi provides for gentle exploration. Ayinger, with its ow elderly maltings and modern brewhouse, stands on one si of the road, facing its guest-house on the other. A small be garden, little more than a terrace, and an early baroqu church complete the village square. In the square, t typical Bavarian maypole is set into a wooden tun that w once a maturation vessel in the brewery. The brewmaster Ayinger also looks after the local museum.

Ayinger also owns Höll wheat-beer brewery in Traun stein, further up the road. This imposing brewery was bui in the late 19th century and has not changed markedly sinc It leans sleepily into a hillside in the valley of the riv Traun. Four wheat beers are produced at Traunstei **Export Weissbier★ →★★** is filtered and has a full, relative sweet, fruitiness (ripe plums, perhaps?). The unfiltere **Hefe-Weissbier★ →★★** is much more tart. The **Ur-Weize ★★ →★★★** has a fuller, amber-red colour and bursts wit fruitiness. It is also unfiltered and has the classic apples-an cloves spiciness of a traditional wheat beer. A **Weize bock★★**, 17 Plato, pale and filtered, is available in the loc market at Christmas.

Forschungs

A secret well kept by the beer-lovers of Munich is th existence of a house-brewery in the city, in the marke gardening suburb of Perlach. The place does have th qualities of a mirage. For one thing, it operates only i summer (and even then closes on Mondays). For another, looks like a cross between a seaside ice-cream parlour and th control tower at a small and dubious airport. It also happen to make the highest-gravity brew in Munich. Its speciality a 19 Plato beer called **St Jacobus Blonder Bock★★★**. Th tent product is soft and sweet but very clean with a big, alty finish. The supporting potion is curiously called **Isissimus**★★ → ★★★. It has both hops and malt in its big oma and contrives to be both dry and soft in palate. The rschungs brewery and its small, pebbled beer garden are Unterhachinger Strasse 76, Perlach (☎089-6701169).

Hacker-Pschorr

ere is a resonance about the names of Munich's principal eweries. Not so long ago, Hacker and Pschorr were two of em. They merged, and much more recently have been ken over by Paulaner. Despite that, the brewery con- ues to operate, with its own range of beers. They are the dry side and perhaps not as smooth as some Munich ews. However, by the standards of some other regions and untries, they still have a fair degree of character. Hacker- chorr has never been identified with any single speciality, ough it has recently been concentrating on its **Pils**★. Its *toberfest* **Märzen**★ → ★★ and **Animator**★★ double bock are th pleasant. The company's beers can be tasted at Zum chorr-Bräu, in Neuhauser Strasse, and in summer on a rrace in the Marienplatz.

Hofbräuhaus

rhaps the label "HB" is felt in Germany to speak for itself, t elsewhere in the world the allusion is not instantly clear. stands for "Hofbräu" ("court brew"), and is the label of ews produced for the world's most famous beer hall. The ofbräuhaus in Munich was originally the beer hall and rden of the Bavarian Royal Court Brewery. Lesser ofbräus remain elsewhere in Germany, having passed from inor royalty into commercial hands, but the most impor- nt one still belongs to Bavaria, albeit to the state vernment. The garden is pleasant, though the rambling er hall smells of stale cigarettes and the detritus of urism. The beers are excellent, the conventional brews ing malt-accented with a spritzy finish. Although the eryday beer is a fresh-tasting, malty **Export**★★ → ★★★, the ofbräuhaus (founded in 1589) is credited with having, in s early days, introduced *Bock* beer to Munich. Its smooth, alty **Maibock**★★★★ is the classic example of the style. hen the first cask is tapped at the Hofbräuhaus on May ay, the Prime Minister of Bavaria usually takes part in the remony. Maibock tastes especially good accompanied by a uple of *Weisswurst*. Since its earliest days the Hofbräu- us has also had a tradition of wheat beers. Its **Edel eizen**★★ → ★★★ has long been enjoyed, but **Dunkel- eizen**★★ → ★★★ is not to be ignored: a complex beer with nse head, lavish lacework, a sweet start, toasty maltiness, d a lemony tartness in the finish.

Kaltenberg

lthough by no means the only brewery owned by an istocrat, Kaltenberg is perhaps the best known, not least cause it is in a classic Bavarian castle. The castle dates om the 13th century, but the present structure was built in e 17th century based on designs by the architect who eated Neuschwanstein for "Mad" King Ludwig II of avaria. The third King Ludwig was the last and his great- andson, Prince Luitpold, runs the Kaltenberg brewery. In export markets Kaltenberg is known for a well-made **Diä Pils★★**, but in its local market it is noted for a rich, malt dark beer, with a coffee-ish finish, **König Ludwig Dunk ★★→★★★**, which has a gravity of 13.3 Plato.

Kaltenberg Castle is near Geltendorf, less than 50km (: miles) west of Munich. It has a beer garden and restauran and in June holds a beer festival and costumed joustin between "medieval" knights (for information, ☎0819 209). At these festivals, a **Dunkel Ritter Bock★★★** of 23 Pla is made available ("Ritter" means "rider" or "knight" Because it is outside Munich, the Kaltenberg brewery is n permitted to offer its beer at the city's *Oktoberfest* so Prin Luitpold decided in 1985 to open a *Hausbräuerei* in Munic producing a *Dunkelweizen*.

Löwenbräu

Internationally, the best-known name among the Munic breweries is Löwenbräu. About a quarter of its output exported and it licenses its name to be used on products other countries, including the USA and Japan. Despi international sales it is not the biggest brewer in Munic though it comes a good second to Paulaner, which expor far less. In local preference, Löwenbräu's beers are som where in the middle of the league table. In general, the bee are malt-accented but well-balanced, with a late hint hoppiness in the finish. Löwenbräu is not especiall associated with any one style, but promotes its **Pils★★**, whic is unusually hoppy by Munich standards. The brewery own the biggest beer hall, the 5,000-seat Mathäser, in Bayer Strasse, near the central railway station. The Mathäser h the look of a railway station itself, with its cafeteri entrance, but 15 or so inner halls are worth exploring. Th cellar restaurant features wheat beer. Löwenbräu also ha one of the biggest beer gardens in the huge central par called the English Garden. Löwenbräu's encircles the park famous pagoda, the "Chinese Tower".

Paulaner

The biggest brewery in Munich is especially associated wit its classic **Salvator★★★★** double bock. This extra-stron very dark beer, with deep amber highlights, has a gravity 18.5 Plato and is made with three malts. Only Hallerta hops are used, though of both bittering and aroma varietie The beer has a very rich start, drying out in a long finish. I alcohol content is around 6 percent by weight, 7.5 b volume. The brewery has its origins in the early 17th centur with a community of monks of St Paul, who became we known throughout the city for the strong beer they brewe called Salvator (Saviour) to sustain themselves during Len Being a very strong beer, it came to be known as a "double bock and gave rise to that style. Most other double boc beers echo the Saviour's brew by bearing names ending i *-ator*. Double bock beers are drunk to warm the soul a winter gives way to spring and the beer gardens think abou reopening. This happens a week before Easter, and the firs new barrel of Salvator is ceremonially tapped by the Mayo of Munich or Prime Minister of Bavaria at the brewery 3,500-seat beer hall and garden on the hill called Nockhe berg. There are also Salvator celebrations on March 19, th saint's day of Paulaner.

The brewery was secularized in the early 19th century and has since had several owners, but it still stands on the same site, though it has grown to straddle the hill. From the modern office block, a tunnel through the hillside leads to the maltings and the brewhouse, which is still in traditional copper. The brewery uses classic fermenters and traditional lagering cellars, maturing its everyday beers (which are *kräusened*) for five or six weeks and its stronger specialities for three to eight months. Paulaner has one of Germany's first refrigeration machines, made for the brewery by Carl von Linde, and an early water turbine powered by a stream that runs down the hill. Paulaner's beers are firm-bodied and dry for Munich, often with an assertive finish. The dark **Alt-Münchner Dunkel★★ → ★★★** has a fine colour, a smooth, full body and a maltiness in that dry finish. The export-style **Urtyp 1634★★** has, again, a full, smooth body but a slightly tannic finish. The pale **Original Münchner Hell★★★** is similar but milder. The brewery produces a full range of styles – with about ten principal beers – including a dry, rounded **Altbayerische Weissbier★★** that has helped popularize wheat beers in the USA.

Schneider

The specialist wheat-beer brewery of George Schneider and Son has been a feature of the Munich scene for more than a century, and has a restaurant on Tal Strasse. However, after World War II the company moved production out of the city, northeast to Kelheim, near Regensburg. Since Munich and the area to the east have such a long and thriving tradition of wheat beers, **Schneider-Weisse★★★ → ★★★★** might be regarded as the classic example of the style. For flavour, though, it is exceeded by the brewery's *Weizenbock*, **Aventinus★★★★** which, with its huge head and insistent sparkle, adds its own flourish to beer drinking in Munich.

Spaten

This is one of the world's most important brewing companies because of its influence on the beers most nations drink today. All lager beers, whether dark, amber or pale, owe much to the work of the Spaten brewery in the 19th century. The influence of this company should be far more widely recognized internationally, but perhaps its reputation has been subsumed, with those of its neighbours, into that of Munich itself. Although it still takes great pride in earlier styles such as wheat beers (notably the dry, spicy, full-bodied and fluffy **Franziskaner Hefe-Weissbier★★ → ★★★** and its cleaner, sparkling **Club-Weisse★★**), Spaten's contributions were in the development of bottom-fermenting beers: in the perfecting of the Bavarian dark style, as typified by its own **Dunkel Export★★★ → ★★★★**; in the popularization of the amber style, as represented by its world classic **Ur-Märzen★★★★**; and in the perfecting of the Munich pale variety, as exemplified by its **Münchner Hell★★★**. From an historical viewpoint, all these beers are classics, and they are still produced in a manner that blends tradition with modern technology. Spaten has its own maltings, uses traditional kettles and lauter tuns (copper in the old brewhouse, stainless steel in a new one), closed classic fermenters and horizontal lagering tanks.

An especially interesting feature of Spaten's methods is

that three different yeasts are used in the production o
bottom-fermenting beers. The pale beers of conventiona
gravities (including a very dry **Spaten Pils★★ → ★★★** have on
yeast; the **Franziskus Heller Bock★★** another; the darke
brews a third. Most breweries would use only one strain fo
all those types, but Spaten feels that yeasts should be chose
according to their suitability to ferment the different wort
and their contribution to background palate.

The company traces its origins to a brewery of 1397, an
its name (meaning "spade") is a jocular corruption o
Spaeth, an early owner. The royal court brewmaster Gabrie
Sedlmayr took over the company in 1807 and his son
Gabriel the Younger, became the father of modern lager
brewing. Studies carried out by Gabriel in the 1830
introduced Bavaria to more scientific methods, notably th
use of the saccharometer in the control of fermentation
Sedlmayr gathered disciples who spread the reputation o
Bavarian bottom-fermenting techniques, and Sedlmayr'
friend and rival Anton Dreher went on to introduce th
amber style of lager in Vienna in 1840/41. A year later, th
Pilsen brewery produced the first pale lager. In 1873
Sedlmayr worked with von Linde on his first refrigerator, a
the instigation of Dreher (Paulaner's Linde machine cam
later) and in 1876 he introduced the world's first steam
heated brewhouse (companies that followed liked to ca
themselves "steam breweries"). The present company wa
constituted originally from Gabriel's business and hi
brother Joseph's Franziskaner brewery.

Spaten is still predominantly owned by the Sedlmayr
family. It is proud of its family ownership and of it
traditions, and still delivers beer in Munich by horse and
dray. Regrettably, the building from which they emerg
looks less like a brewery than a fair-sized airport.

NORTHERN BAVARIA:
FRANCONIA

For the beer-drinker, Munich and southern Bavaria migh
seem like the pearly gates, but heaven is further north. U
there Bavaria has a region that is almost a state within a
state: Franconia (Franken), with Nürnberg as its largest city
and Bamberg (with no fewer than ten) and Amberg (a mer
nine) as its most heavily-breweried towns.

There are more small breweries in Franconia than any
where in the world. It remains a centre of production for dar
Bavarian lagers. It has more unfiltered beers than anywher
else and a greater number of eccentric specialities.

From south to north, the region stretches from Regens
burg to Bayreuth, Kulmbach and Coburg, on the frontie
with East Germany. Due east the Bohemian Forest form
the frontier with Czechoslovakia, with České Budějovice
(Budweis) and Pilsen nearby. To the west the small-brewery
country of the Steigerwald reaches to Würzburg and win
territory.

Bamberg is the centre for a highly unusual speciality, th
smoky *Rauchbier*. Kulmbach is the traditional centre for
dark beers and produces some especially strong *Doppelbock*
brews. Coburg has its unique, revivalist *Steinbier*, brewed
with hot rocks. Bayreuth has a proprietary speciality, the
Maisel brewery's *Dampfbier*.

Even in towns not specifically associated with a single style, many breweries have their own minor specialities. Sometimes these are dark beers. Often they are unfiltered. While an unfiltered *Kräusenbier* is cause for comment elsewhere in the country, such brews are not uncommon in Franconia. As its name suggests, this type of beer is kräusened. Then, before the kräusen has worked out, the maturation vessel is tapped, revealing intentionally cloudy beer. Another type of unfiltered beer is not kräusened. This *Kellerbier*, which is allowed to settle in the maturation tanks before being tapped. As might be expected it has a notably low carbonation. Traditionally, this type of beer has been heavily hopped to guard against infection. A well-known example is made by St Georgenbräu, of Buttenheim, just south of Bamberg. Another excellent *Kellerbier* comes from Maisel of Bamberg (there are four Maisel breweries in Bavaria, each quite separate but linked by family).

Bamberg is a town of only 70,000 people but it is a remarkable centre of brewing. High on the hill that overlooks the town is the 17th-century Romanesque church of St Michael, part of a former monastery which had a brewery (the monks' brewhouse has now been converted into a Franconian Beer Museum). The town itself is a living museum, not only for its German Renaissance buildings but also for its selection of breweries. There is plenty of half-timbering and gilding about the breweries and their guest-houses, too, but their principal contribution is in terms not of architecture but of social and economic history. Two even have their own maltings so that they can do the kilning necessary to produce *Rauchbier* (made by kilning the malt over beech logs). There are also two free-standing maltings.

By no means do all of Bamberg's ten breweries regularly feature *Rauchbier* and, though the town is the centre for its production, companies elsewhere have been known to produce a beer in this style. In Bamberg, the Heller brewery has Aecht Schlenkerla Rauchbier as its principal product; the family Merz's Hausbrauerei Spezial produces nothing else; Greifenklau's beer has only a faint hint of smokiness; and Kaiserdom Rauchbier is produced in Eltmann for Burgerbrau-Bamberg; Maisel's Rauchbier is made by another Eltmann brewery.

Among other Bamberg breweries, Fässchen offers as its specialities a *Kellerbier* and a *Märzen*; Keesman emphasizes its malty but dry Herren Pils; the secular Klosterbräu has a dark beer; Löwenbräu has a range of products; Mahrs has a relatively well carbonated *Kellerbier* and a delicious, rich dark brew called Wunderburger Liesl. The pale beers of Bamberg all have a dry maltiness.

To the west is the Steigerwald, with woodland walks and scores of small breweries, many with their own taverns. About 24km (15 miles) north of Bamberg, at Pferdsfeld, the Kunigunda Leicht brewery lists its production at 250 hectolitres a year, which probably makes it the smallest in Germany. To the east, in the countryside known as the Frankische Schweiz, are more small breweries.

Some towns and villages have communal breweries where members of the public can brew their own beer. Falkenburg, Neuhaus-on-Pegnitz and Sesslach are examples. This facility is generally exercised by barley farmers or tavern keepers. In the days before commercial production, a

communal brewer who had a new batch ready would displa
a garland or a six-pointed star outside his house. The latter
a symbol of the brewer, deriving from alchemy rather tha
from any religious significance. In some places this practi
is still followed, although it is also used by small commerci
brewers. Ecclesiastical brewing was significant in the past
Franconia, but only one monastery brewery remains, th
Klosterbrauerei Kreuzberg at Bischofsheim, north of Wür
burg, near the frontier with East Germany.

Where to drink

In Bamberg, the obvious places to stay are the guest-house
of Brauerei Spezial (Obere König Strasse 10, ☎0951-24304
which is in the shopping area; or Brauerei Greifenkla
(Laurenziplatz 20, ☎0951-53219) which has a spectacul
valley view. The mandatory stop for a drink is th
Schlenkerla tavern, in Dominikaner Strasse, but oth
brewery taps are also worth a visit; the low-ceilinged taver
of the Mahrs brewery, in Wunderburg, is a delightf
"local". The Steigerwald can be explored from the Kloste
bräu Hotel in Ebelsbach (☎09522-235), which specializes
a dark *Märzen* beer. To the north, between Bamberg an
Coburg, the Goldener Stern at Ebersdorf (24 bedroom
☎ 09562-106163) has a splendid *Zwickelbier*. Northwest
Coburg, at Gauerstadt, near Rodach, the Wacker brewer
(20 bedrooms, ☎09564-225) has a pale draught bee
Northeast of Coburg, the Grosch brewery (17 bedroom
☎09563-547) in Rodental, on the way to Neustadt, has a
excellent dark beer. In the old brewing town of Lichtenfe
the Wichert *Gasthof* has a *Kellerbier* but no bedrooms. Th
Frankische Schweiz can be explored from the Drei Krone
brewery inn at Memmelsdorf (☎0951-43001), where a
unfiltered lager and a dark *Märzen* is served. Another Dr
Kronen ("Three Crowns") in nearby Strassgeich produces
lovely, firm-bodied Kronenbräu Lager with a gravity of 12.
Plato and a "1308" Pilsener of 12.4 (unusual, in tha
everyday lagers usually have lower gravities than the
companion Pilseners). The "1308" is named for the fou
dation date of this tiny (3,000hl) brewery, which so captur
the imagination of an executive from a large internation
company that its name was bought for use on somewha
lesser beers in Canada and South Africa. This Drei Krone
has no rooms. Neither does the Schinner brewery restaura
in Richard Wagner Strasse, Bayreuth, but it does serve a
excellent Braunbier. In Nürnberg, the Altstadt brewery
an essential visit, with beer on sale by the bottle and avai
able on tap nearby. Regensburg has a number of bee
restaurants. In Arnulfsplatz, the Kneitinger brewer
produces beer mainly for its own restaurant. The Spita
garten, in Katharinenplatz, dates from the 14th century an
serves local beer.

Altstadthof

The name indicates "Old Town Courtyard", which is th
corner of Nürnberg where this delightful *Hausbrauerei* is t
be found. The brewery, a bakery and one or two wholefoo
shops share a restored courtyard off Berg Strasse. In the Ol
Town, in a building dating from the 16th century and wit
brewing rights from that time, the *Hausbrauerei* firs
charged its traditional copper kettle in 1984, taking care t

se organically grown barley malt and hop blossoms.
Fermentation is open, wooden tuns like those in drawings
of medieval breweries and lagering is in wooden hogsheads of
the type often kept as museum pieces in large breweries. The
year-round product is an unfiltered dark beer with a gravity
of 12–12.5 Plato. **Hausbrauerei Altstadthof**★★★ beer has a
deep, tawny colour, almost opaque; yeasty fruitiness and
malty sweetness in the aroma; a yeasty dryness overlaying
the rich, smooth, malty palate; dark malt tones in the finish,
with some local, Hersbrucker hop coming through. Seasonal
Bock and *Märzen* versions have also been produced. A tiny
antique bottling machine fills the beer into swing-top litres,
which are then sold at the brewery in crude wooden six-
packs. The beer is also available on draught at two
Altstadthof cafes (one, opening at lunchtime, is called the
Dampfnudel and specializes in sweet steamed puddings; the
other, opening in the evening, is the Schmelztiegl). The
brewery has only two full-time employees.

The *Hausbrauerei* was established, initially out of enthusiasm for beery history, by the owners of the Lamms
brewery in Neumarkt, south of Nürnberg. Lammsbrau
provides not only the yeast but also the water for Altstadt.
The *Hausbrauerei* does not have an adequate supply of its
own water, nor space for treatment facilities.

EKU

The EKU brewery in Kulmbach boasts the highest gravity of
any beer in the world, with its **Kulminator 28**★★★ → ★★★★.
As its name suggests, this beer has a guaranteed gravity of
28 degrees – though analysis has revealed levels as high as
30.54. The brewery claims to mature the beer for nine
months with a short period of freezing to settle protein. Since
this is not done specifically for the purpose of raising alcohol
content, Kulminator 28 is not labelled as an *Eisbock*. As the
name Kulmin*ator* implies, it is a *Doppelbock* by style, though
it is labelled merely as *Urtyp* ("original") and *Hell* ("pale").
In fact it is not especially pale – the great density of malt
provides an amber cast – but it is not a dark beer. It has an
intensely malty nose and palate, with a strongly alcoholic
character. Its alcohol content has been analysed at 10.92 by
weight, 13.5 by volume.

The world heavyweight title is contested between Kulminator 28 and the Swiss Hürlimann brewery's Samichlaus
a Christmas beer. Samichlaus has a lower gravity (27.6), a
longer period of maturation (a year) and a higher alcohol
content (11.1 by weight; 13.71 by volume). While this
contest is too hard to resist, such muscle has limited
application. These are beers of excellent quality but they
would best be dispensed from small barrels suspended from
the necks of mountain-rescue dogs. Whether they revive or
stun the recipient depends upon the constitution of the
drinker. Certainly, in their fermentation, the yeast is
stunned by the alcohol it produces. That explains why these
beers take so long, and are so difficult to make. Nor do they
contain any of the sugars (or, sometimes, enzymes) that are
used in the relatively lightweight strong beers (or "malt
liquors") of the USA.

EKU also has a dark double bock, simply called **Kulminator**★★ → ★★★ (with a gravity of 18.5); a pale, single
Edelbock★★; a conventional dark export-style beer called

Rubin; a rather full-bodied **Pils★→★★**; and a pleasan
Weizen★.

The first two initials of EKU stand for Erste ("First"
Kulmbach. The "U" derives from the union of two earlie
breweries that created the company in 1872.

Hofmark

The traditionalist Hofmark brewery is interesting for a
number of reasons: its location, east of Regensburg at Cham
on the Bavarian side of the Bohemian Forest, means that it
soft water emerges from the same quartz-granite bed as tha
of Pilsen; it was founded in 1590 and has been in one family
for more than 200 years; and it still uses some traditiona
techniques, not least the method of fining with beechwoo
chips. It is also unusual in that its premium beer Das fein
Hofmark is prepared in two variations: mild and bitte
(designations that sound more English than German). Bot
are firm, smooth, beautifully balanced beers of som
complexity. Das feine Hofmark **Würzig Mild★★** has a mal
accent; **Würzig Herb★★ →★★★** (meaning "dry" or "bitter")
has a lovely hop character in both nose and finish. Thi
brewery was a pioneer in the use of swing-top bottles.

Kaiserdom

A full range of beers is marketed under the Kaiserdom labe
by the Bürgerbräu brewery of Bamberg. Most tend toward
the dry maltiness of the region but are unexceptional
However **Kaiserdom Rauchbier★★★** has the distinction o
being the only smoked beer exported to the USA.

Kulmbacher Mönchshof

The dark-beer tradition of Kulmbach is best maintained by
the "Monks'" brewery. Its **Kloster Schwarz-Bier★★★★** rate
as a classic, with a gravity of 12.5, a full, smooth body and a
dark-malt palate unrivalled among major labels. The con
noisseur of Bavarian dark beers might, of course, prefer the
earthier character to be found in some of the many
Hausbrauerei examples. Mönchshof goes back to the begin
nings of monastic brewing in Kulmbach in 1349. It wa
secularized in 1791, becoming a family brewery, and i
now part-owned by Kulmbacher Reichelbräu. Even at the
peak of Kulmbach's international repute as a brewing
centre, at the turn of the century, Mönchshof was one of the
smaller houses. Today, it remains an active exporter
especially to the USA. Its range includes a very full-bodie
dark double bock called **Urstoff★★ →★★★**; a very flavourfu
single **Klosterbock Dunkel★★★**; a malty **Märzen★★**; a malty
export called **Maingold★★**; and what is for Bavaria ar
unusually dry **Mönchshof-Pilsener★★**.

Kulmbacher Reichelbräu

If Germany can have Eiswein, then it can have icy beer, too
The tradition of Eisbock is especially kept alive by Kulm
bacher Reichelbräu. Eisbock is a strong beer in which alcoho
content is enhanced by freezing and then removing the ice
Because alcohol has a lower freezing point than water thi
concentrates the brew. The resultant **Eisbock Bayrisch
G'frorns★★ →★★★★** ("Bavarian Frozen") has a gravity o
24 and an alcohol content of around 8 percent by weight, 1(
by volume. It is a most interesting beer, dense and potent

eichelbräu, which is named after its founder, has the iggest local sales and offers a full range of styles.

Kulmbacher Schweizerhof

Kulmbacher Schweizerhof was founded in 1834, but since 980 has been part of the same group as Rauchenfels, Altenmünster and Sailer. It has a range of styles but its principal beer, identified simply as **Kulmbacher Schweizer-of-Bräu★→★★** ("feinherb aus Kulmbach") is a rather malty Pilsener with a firm, dry palate.

Maisel

Among the four Bavarian brewing companies called Maisel, this one in Bayreuth is by far the biggest. It has also become well known for its speciality brews, notably its highly individualistic **Maisel's Dampfbier★★★**. This is a top-fermenting beer, very fruity, with vanilla-like tones. It has a gravity of 12.2 Plato, is made with a triple decoction mash from four barley malts, hopped with Hallertaus and fermented with its own yeast in open vessels. It emerges slightly redder and paler than a Düsseldorfer Altbier, and about 4 percent alcohol by weight, 5 by volume. It is not pasteurized, even for export to the USA. "Dampfbier" is a registered name, not intended to indicate a recognized style and Maisel earnestly disavows any intention to sound like Anchor Steam (which is different both in production process and palate). In the late 1970s, the brewery decided that, "all beers were beginning to taste the same. We wanted something distinctive. We experimented, and this was the brew we liked." The decision may also have had something to do with the move out of a magnificently castellated and steam-powered brewery of 1887 into a remorselessly modern plant next door. There is an element of nostalgia to a "steam beer" (which is how Dampfbier would, inescapably, translate). For the two Maisel brothers who own the brewery, nostalgia is not a cheap emotion. The entire old brewery has been mothballed, in working order, and is now open for tours, at 10 o'clock each morning, or by appointment.

Meanwhile, Maisel continues in its spotless new brewery to produce an interesting range of products, including three wheat beers. **Weizen Kristall-Klar★★** is, as its name suggests, a crystal-clear beer, very pale, with a champagne-like sparkle and a tannic, apple fruitiness. **Hefe-Weiss★★** is fermented out with a mixture of yeasts, kräusened and given a dosage at bottling. It has a deep bronze colour, an apple-like palate and a big, fluffy body. **Weizenbock★★→★★★**, at 17.5 Plato, has a deep tawny colour, a big body, and a sharpness that recedes into smooth vanilla and licorice tones at the finish.

Rauchenfels Steinbiere

One of the world's oddest speciality beers, **Rauchenfels Steinbiere**, is also among the most drinkable. This is a 1980s revival of a brewing method used before the development of metal kettles. When brewing vessels were made from wood they could not be heated directly, and one method of boiling the brew was to mull it with hot stones. This is said to have been done in Alpine areas where stones could be found that would accept great heat, and sudden cooling, without shattering. The inventive and entrepreneurial German

brewer Gerd Borges, on the lookout for new specialities
acquired a quarry with suitable graywacke stones, de
veloped a way of handling the hot stones in a brewery and
revived the technique. A clay hearth and a beechwood fire
heat the stones, which are held in a steel basket, to a
temperature of 1,200°C. The stones are then immersed in a
pre-heated brew. The kettle bubbles, hisses, and exhales
steam as though it were a volcano. Within a few seconds, the
malt sugars in the brew have caramelized on to the stones. In
this modern version, the heating function of the stones is less
significant than the caramelization of the malt sugars.
"Stone Beer" is top-fermenting, but the caramelized malt
comes back into play when the cooled stones are placed in
the maturation vessels with the brew. At this point, a violent
secondary fermentation starts, settling down over a three
week period. **Rauchenfels Steinbiere★★★ → ★★★★** has a very
smoky palate, less dry than smooth, with a long, rounded
finish. A companion "stone" Weizenbier is also produced.
The beers are made at Neustadt, near Coburg, in an old
established brewery acquired for the purpose.

Schäffbräu

After a bruising collision with the *Reinheitsgebot*, the Schäff
bräu brewery now probably produces the purest beer in
Germany. Whatever its other claims to fame, it is notable for
its "Fire Festival" double bock. **Schäff-Feuerfest★★★** has a
gravity of 25 Plato, and the brewery claims that it is
matured for 12–18 months before emerging with an alcohol
content of more than 8 percent by weight; 10 by volume. It is
a dark, fruity beer, with a low carbonation. Although the
brewery recommends Feuerfest as an aperitif, both its name
and its prune-brandy palate seem more suited to accompany
crêpes Suzette. So does its bottle, with wax seal and limited
edition number. The brewery is south of Nürnberg, in the
Altmühltal Natural Park at Treuchtlingen.

Schlenkerla Rauchbier

The most famous Bamberg *Rauchbier* is Schlenkerla,
produced for the tavern of that name by the Heller brewery.
Like Scotch whisky, *Rauchbier* gains its smoky palate at the
malting stage. Again as with Scotch, the method stems from
the available means of kilning the malt. What the Scots had
at hand was peat; the Franconians had beechwood. As more
modern methods of kilning evolved, a degree of tradition
survived in both Scotland and Franconia, especially in the
wooded countryside that surrounds the town of Bamberg.

Ricks of beechwood logs still wait to burn in the tiny
maltings (though it has both Saladin and drum systems) of
the Heller brewery, which dates from 1678. The traditional
brewhouse, in copper trimmed with brass, sparkles. In
another room, a whirlpool makes a strange contrast before
the open fermenters. Ninety-five percent of the brewery's
production is *Rauchbier*, usually at a *Märzen* gravity of just
over 13.5 percent. It is made entirely from smoked malt
mashed by double decoction, hopped only once (the magic
cone can hardly fight the smoke), bottom-fermented,
matured for six or seven weeks without kräusening and no
pasteurized. The resultant beer has a smoky aroma and a
dryness the moment it hits the tongue, and a full, smoky
flavour that lingers in a long finish. Some people have to

nk as many as five litre glasses before they begin to enjoy
uchbier. It is, not only among beers but also among all
oholic drinks, a classic. **Aecht Schlenkerla Rauchbier
rzen★★★★** is the definitive example, and in October,
vember and December there is a 19 Plato version called
-**Bock★★★**. The brewery also has a *Helles*, but even that
s a hint of smokiness.

ezial

e oldest *Rauchbier* producer is believed to be Bamberg's
auerei Spezial, which dates from 1536. It is an unassum-
; *Hausbrauerei* in a main shopping street. The Christian
rz family have their own tiny maltings and produce only
oked beers. Their everyday product, if it can be called
t, is a *Rauchbier* simply called **Lager**, at 12 Plato. It has a
tly insistent smokiness and a treacle-toffee finish. A
rzen★★★ version of around 13.5 is even smokier in
ture, bursting with flavour in the finish. There is also a
vember **Bock★★★**.

ucher

e of the two large breweries that dominate the Nürnberg
rket is Tucher, the other being Patrizier. On their home
und, both have upset beer-lovers by swallowing smaller
weries, but Tucher's exports have brought a welcome
te of Germany to parts of the New World. The brewery
s a full range, including a dryish **Pilsener★ →★★**; a tasty,
lty dark beer called **Alt Franken Export Dunkel★★**; a
ooth double bock called **Bajuvator★★**; and a couple of
eat beers, **Weizen★** and **Hefe-Weizen★**. Sad to say, the
endidly bitter **Doppelhopfen** has not been available in
ent years.

ürzburger Hofbräu

rzburg is in wine country and tried, in 1434, to banish its
wers forever. A couple of hundred years later it had
uired a Hofbräuhaus, which still produces pleasant
rs, malt-accented but well balanced. **Pils★ →★★** has a
lty nose, a firm body and a hoppy finish. **Burkardus★** (in
ne export markets **"Bavarian Dark"**) is tawny and trans-
ent with a dry, malty palate. **Oktoberfest★** is on the dark
e and quite dry. There is also a **Maibock★**, a **Sympator★**
ble bock and a **Hefe-Weissbier★★**.

BERLIN

e champagne of beers" is a soubriquet too generously
osed. It is appropriate only to wheat brews, notably
liner Weisse. Napoleon's troops during their Prussian
apaign coined the description "the champagne of the
th". Long after Napoleon was vanquished, the same
ampagne" was a fitting toast in Imperial Berlin.
 Berlin white beer" has a very pale colour, an insistent
rkle, a fragrant fruitiness in the nose, a sharp, dry palate
 a *frisson* of quenching, sour acidity in the finish. It is
ved in large bowl-shaped glasses, like beer-sized cham-
ne saucers. To soften its acidity, it is often laced with a
h (a *Schuss*) of raspberry syrup, as though it were a *kir*
ale. The green essence of the herb woodruff is also
netimes used for this purpose, though this is becoming less

common. To complete the presentation, candy-strip
straws of white and pink or green may be offered as
decoration. It is a speciality style of beer, produced as
summer refresher by the principal breweries on both sides
the Berlin Wall. Despite its limited, seasonal popularity,
distinctiveness and nobility remains a matter of civic prid

The term "white" has been used over the centuri
throughout northern Europe to describe pale, sometim
cloudy, wheat beers. In the north of Germany it became t
practice for such beers to contain a relatively low proporti
of wheat and be characterized by a lactic fermentation. N
doubt the lactic fermentation was originally accidental, b
it is now a feature of the style. There are vestiges of this ty
of brewing elsewhere in the north, notably in Bremen, but
is mainly associated with Berlin.

Although *Berliner Weisse* beers were once produced in
wide variety of gravities, the quenching quality of this sty
is best suited by a low alcohol content and this has becom
the custom. For the same reason, this type of beer is brew
to have only very slight hop bitterness. The classic examp
Berliner Kindl Weisse★★★★, is produced from a gravity
7.5 Plato and emerges with an alcohol content of just und
2.5 percent by weight; around 3 by volume. It has only fo
units of bitterness.

Hops are used in only small quantities and in an unusu
way. They are added in the mash tun, in a technique th
presumably dates back to their role as a preservative. Eith
an infusion or decoction mash may be used. Only about
quarter of the mash comprises wheat, which is malted. T
rest of the mash is barley malt. A top-fermenting yeast
used, but in a mixture with rod-shaped lactic acid bacteri
The classic method is to bottle without filtration and let t
beer undergo a secondary fermentation at 15—16
(59—62°F). There may then be three or four weeks' co
maturation in the bottle while the yeast settles. After sa
the beer should continue to improve in the bottle for mont
(but perhaps not years), gaining a greater complexity
aroma in particular. *Berliner Weisse* should be stored in
dark, cool but not refrigerated place. Because there is
sediment, handle the bottle carefully, and because the be
has such sparkle and foam, pour gently, ideally into a lar
wide vessel. *Berliner Weisse* should be served lightly chil
or at a natural cellar temperature.

Berliner Kindl Weisse has a little more sharpness than
rival from Schultheiss. These two breweries dominate W
Berlin and each produces a wide range of more conventio
beers. Schultheiss also owns West Berlin's third brewer
Engelhardt, which does not produce a *Weisse*. These th
family names are also used by breweries in the East, toget
with Bürgerbräu and Bärenquell. The East German Schu
heiss and Kindl breweries both produce *Berliner Weisse*

Where to drink

In summer, *Berliner Weisse* is widely available througho
Germany, especially the north, and readily in outlets serv
by the parent groups of Kindl and Schultheiss. In Berlin, t
cafes of the Kurfürstendamm and the city's beer halls
"palaces") serve *Weissbier* in summer. It is a popular dri
at the writers' and actors' bar and restaurant called Dien
at 47 Grolman Strasse in the Charlottenburg district.

he northernmost nations of Europe evoke
images of icy *fjords* bristling with longboats full
of Norsemen inflaming themselves with mead
some early form of beer. Nordic legend certainly
ys great stress on brewed beverages, but the modern
putation of Scandinavia in this respect derives from
egant, civilized Copenhagen.

Outside Germany, the Danes did more than anyone
popularize lager brewing, and they did so with
eat resourcefulness. In 1845, pots of bottom-fer-
enting yeast were brought from Munich to Copen-
agen by the founder of the Carlsberg brewery. In a
urney of at least 600 miles (965km), by stagecoach,
e is said to have kept the yeast cool under his
ovepipe hat and by dousing it with cold water at
very stop. In 1883, the Carlsberg laboratory crossed
other frontier by isolating for the first time a single-
ll yeast culture. Pure bottom-fermenting yeasts
ere subsequently identified as *carlsbergensis*.

Denmark continues to remember its earlier, top-
rmenting wheat beers by producing a barley malt
rivative, of low alcohol content, called *hvidtøl*. But
is, of course, best known for pale lagers, brewed in
a unusually wide variety of strengths, and typically
ith a malty mildness of palate.

Not only in tradition but also in consumption of
er per head, Denmark is an important brewing
ation. It has, though, only about 30 breweries.
mong those, Carlsberg, Tuborg, Wiibroe and Nep-
n are controlled by United Breweries of Copen-
agen, which also has a stake in Jyske breweries
eres and others).

Norway has 16 breweries, producing by law all-
alt beers, principally clean, crisp Pilseners. Prob-
ly the best-known brewery is Ringnes, producing
od examples of the style, while the beers of its
sociate Frydenlunds have more hop character. In
e same group are two provincial breweries, Aren-
als and Lundetangens. Most towns have their own
eweries, marketing only locally. One of them —
ack, in Tromsø — is the world's most northerly
ewery. In Tromsø, which is north of the Arctic
rcle, beer is served with a snack of seagulls' eggs.

A typical Norwegian brewery might produce a
lsener of 10.5–11 Plato (1042–44), with around 3.6
ercent alcohol by weight; 4.5 by volume. Other
roducts may include a summer beer of around 10.5,
tenuated to a similar alcohol content and hopped
r flowery aroma rather than bitterness; a
Bavarian-style" dark lager of 11–12 (1044–48), less

well attenuated, to achieve again a similar alcohol
content; a German-style "Export" of 13, 1052, 4.5,
5.6; a Christmas beer of 15, 1060, 4.8, 6; and a dark
Bock of 17, 1068, 4.9, 6-plus. There might also be
special product marking an anniversary or other
celebration, usually at around 11.5, 1046, 3.6, 4.5.

In Norway and Sweden, beers are heavily taxed
and their strength and availability is beset with
restrictions. Sweden's laws on beer strength mean
that supermarkets sell only low-alcohol or light beers.
The former, designated as Class I, have a maximum of
1.8 percent alcohol by weight (2.25 by volume). The
latter, Class II, have 2.8 (3.5), from a gravity of at
least 10.5 Plato (1042) and often considerably higher.
Although such a specification is not unusual elsewhere in the world, Swedes complain that restrictions
make it difficult for them to find a beer of a more
typically international "medium" strength (which
they describe as *Mellanøl*, at 3.6, 4.5). Given this
difficulty, serious beer-lovers in Sweden often find
themselves in restaurants or state liquor stores where
strong beers (Class III, 4.5, 5.6) are available. Thus
laws that are intended to favour low-strength beer
have the opposite effect, and visitors being enter-
tained in Sweden can gain the impression that the
country's beers are unusually full-bodied and strong.

Sweden has 16 breweries, four of which are owned
by Pripps and a fifth by its associate Falken (which
spells its brand Falcon). Despite the rigid alcohol
brackets, most brewers have a wide variety of
products. The same product may be brewed in two or
three strengths, each clearly labelled as to its class.

The most unusual Swedish beers are two from a
company called Till, which has three breweries in the
far north. One, with the Viking name **Röde** (Red
Orm, is described as a mead. It is primed with honey
and spiced, though it is brewed from barley malt, and
hopped. It has hints of honey in the aroma and finish.
Despite its fierce name, it is a low-alcohol beer (Class
I). The other, in Class II, is called **Spetsat**. It is a dark
beer seasoned with juniper, angelica and sweet gale
(*Myrica gale*, also known as bog myrtle). It has some
juniper in the nose and a sweetish, faintly resinous
palate. All three ingredients were widely used in
brewing in Europe before the ascendancy of the hop,
and may still be found – along with alder twigs – in
traditional home-brews in Nordic countries.

Finland has 11 breweries, owned by five companies. The Fins do not tax beer so heavily, since they see
it as a temperate alternative to hard liquor. Their
alcohol limits on beer are also generally a little higher.
Finland's Class I beers may have a maximum alcohol
content of 2.25 by weight; 2.8 by volume. Class II (at

,75) is generally ignored by brewers. Class III has
.7; 4.5. Class IV has 4.5; 5.6. The laws also encourage
ll-malt beers, though some other brewing sugars are
llowed. Beers tend to be broadly in the Pilsener style,
ery clean and firm, with some fruitiness.

Aass

mbarrassingly named (at least to English-speakers)
rewery in Drammen, near Oslo. The name means "sum-
it", so perhaps the owning family originally came from the
ountains. A small brewery by international standards and
ly middle-sized in Norway, but an exporter. Range
cludes the well-matured **Aass Export**★★, firm and smooth,
ith Saaz hops in the nose; **Aass Bayer Øl**★★, a good
xample of the Bavarian style; **Aass Jule Øl**★★★, a Christ-
as beer with a tawny colour and a lovely, nutty finish; and
ass **Bokk**★★ →★★★, splendidly creamy.

Albani

ledium-sized indpendent producing a typical range of
anish beers, with some good strong seasonal specialities as
ell as the popular **Giraf**★★ pale lager (15.4 Plato; 1063; 5.4
ercent alcohol by weight; 6.8 by volume) and an all-malt
orter★★ →★★★ (20; 1083; 6.2; 7.8).

Carlsberg

nternational name, producing or licensing its beers in at
east a dozen countries, some of which have as many as four
r five different strengths and styles of Carlsberg. The
ompany also makes at least half a dozen special export
eers, and within its own country has yet more. The basic
ager Beer (known in some markets as Hof, after the Danish
oyal Court)★ →★★ has the soft, smooth, malty dryness that
typical of Carlsberg and its home country. The same
haracter can be found in the much stronger **Elephant**★★
n some markets, Carlsberg '68), which has 16 Plato; 1064;
069; 7.1. There is, predictably, a chewier character to the yet
tronger **Carlsberg Special Strong Lager**★★★, which
epresents something of a style in itself. At Easter, Danes
ave the pleasure of **Carlsberg Påske Bryg 1847**★★★ (17.4;
069; 6.2; 7.8), which has a lovely, deep-amber colour, a
estrained sweetness in the nose and a malty dryness in the
nish. A beautifully balanced and delicious beer. A similar
rew, of slightly lower gravity, is produced for Christmas.
amle Carlsberg Special Dark Lager★★ is a true Munich-
tyle beer, of conventional gravity. **Gammel Porter** (or
mperial Stout)★★★ has a gravity of 18.8; 1075, producing
.1; 7.5. It is bottom-fermenting, but has a splendidly stouty
burnt toffee" palate. Carlsberg's premises include the
vorld's most beautiful brewhouse, like a cathedral of beer.
he founders turned the company into a foundation to
upport the arts and sciences, and it remains such, despite
eing a component of United Breweries.

Ceres

Vhile its own **Ceres Pilsner**★ →★★ has a classically clean
naltiness, this medium-sized Danish company also has
oppier beers from its associate Thor brewery. The group,
vhich also includes the Urban brewery, produces a very

wide range of tasty beers in typically Danish styles. A bee
colourfully dubbed **Red Eric★★** has a gravity of just unde
13; 1058; and an alcohol content of 4.5; 5.6. It is a firm, dr
lager, pale in colour despite its name. A pink version wa
dropped after a Community ruling on food colourings.

Faxe

Unpasteurized beers, sterile-filtered, from an aggressiv
independent. The principal local product is **Faxe Fad★→★**
(meaning "draught-style"), at 3.6; 4.5. An export versio
called **The Great Dane★→★★** has 4.5; 5.6. In some market
there is a **Fest Bock★→★★**, at 6; 7.5. Typically Danish beers
perhaps less distinctive than they were a few years ago.

Koff

A genuinely top-fermenting **Porter/Imperial Stout★★★→
★★★★**, dry, very roasty and satisfying, is an especiall
noteworthy product from this Finnish brewery. Full nam
Sinebrychoff.

Neptun

A green beer is the speciality product of this house. The bee
is called Green Rooster in the American market, Bacchus i
Japan, and **Pinsebryg★★** (Whitsun brew) in Denmark. Th
colour was devised to celebrate the beginning of spring, bu
it merely distracts attention from a pleasantly soft, dryis
palate, big body, and alcohol content of 6; 7.5. Anothe
brewery provides the wort; Neptun ferments and matures

Polar Beer

Iceland (with only 200,000 people) has just one brewery, an
severe laws mean that its local products, a "Pilsner" an
(surprisingly) a "*Märzen*-type", have only 6.2; 1025; 1.78
2.25. However, the brewery does export a well-made **Pola
Beer★→★★** of 13; 1052; 4.2; 5.3.

Pripps

Sweden's biggest brewing company. Its **Nordik Wölf★→★
is very well attenuated (9; 1036; 3.8; 4.75). In Sweden, i
rates as a Class III beer, and it has more alcohol and flavour
especially hop character, than most competing "light beers"
in the US market. In the Swedish market, the brewery i
very proud of its **Royal★★**, a Pilsener-style beer with a lot o
Hallertau hop in the nose, a soft palate and a spritzy bu
long finish. Within an extensive range, another interestin
product is a sweetish, chocolatey, Munich-style beer with th
British-sounding name **Black and Brown★★**. The mos
distinctive of all the Pripps products is Sweden's only top
fermenting brew, **Carnegie Porter★★★**, which in its reintro
duced Class III version has a big, dry, "burnt" palate.

Spendrup's

Sweden's most aggressive independent. Its all-mal
premium **Spendrup's★★** and its super-premium **Old Gold★
have a lot of hop character, in both aroma and palate.

Tuborg

International name, producing a full range of Danish styles
Tuborg's beers are perhaps a little lighter in body an
hoppier than those of its partner Carlsberg.

ecause it has become the most international of all beer brands, Heineken is not always perceived to be Dutch: to originate from Holland , as the nation is properly known, The Netherlands. g names are a feature of brewing in this small untry (Heineken, Amstel, Skol – even Oranjeboom d Three Horseshoes are to some extent international brands) and until recently they tended to scure the presence of interesting middle-sized comnies like Grolsch, not to mention the smaller houses ke Brand that dot the southern provinces of Brabant d Limburg. There is even a Trappist monastery ewery: Schaapskooi in Brabant. Now, the Dutch e beginning to pay more attention to these small eweries, in addition to which three or four utiques have been established.

Initially, it tended to be the small houses that were ntract-brewing for prospective boutiques. An Arnm company had a strong ale called Sloth; a firm in ouda had a copper ale, Kuyt: these ran into ccoughs. In the northern town of Groningen, a firm lled De Munte marketed a contract-brewed dry out while also producing its own abbey-style Triple, heavily sedimented ale with lots of hop bitterness, lled **Noorderblond**★★ → ★★★.

In the cheese town of Alkmaar, a boutique called e Noorderbierbrouwerij began with a most unusual roduct: an alcoholic ginger beer, called **8 Oktober**★★★. his is appropriately gingery and beery, if a little too easty, and it deserves points for boldness. Early roducts also included a "white" beer, **Burg-wit**, tually reddish in colour and very tannic; a rather eesy-tasting **Golden Brown** (6.5 percent alcohol by olume); and a **Winterbier** (7.5), astringent in the nose d sweet in palate.

Near the eastern town of Nijmegen, a boutique lled Raaf produces a well-balanced, honeyish ale at percent, known simply as **No 12**★★ → ★★★. The same rewery has a **Nijmeegs Dubbel**★★ (6.5), tawny, fruity d very dry. An ale is also produced for the local Café e Fuik. Also in the east, a prospective boutique in peldoorn began with a contract-brewed, claretloured, "sweet and sour" beer in Flemish style, lled **Palinckx**★★.

In 1985, Amsterdam's first boutique, 't IJ, began ith a Triple called **Zatte**★★★, well balanced, with malt d fruit in the nose and lots of hop bitterness in the nish.

Until recently, a typical Dutch brewery would roduce a low-alcohol Old Brown (around 9 Plato;

1036; 2-3 percent by weight; 2.5-3.5 by volume);
Pilsener (in The Netherlands, this term indicates th
classic gravity of 11-12; 1044-48; with an alcoh
content of around 4; 5); a "Dortmunder-style" (som
as might be expected, at around 13.5; 1054; 4.7; 5.
but others considerably stronger); and a season
Bock (15.7-16.5; 1063-66; 5-5.5; 6.25-7). Now, ne
styles are being introduced, often with a Belgia
accent. There are 20-odd breweries.

Where to drink

The Dutch pioneered speciality beer bars, and it is doubtf
whether any in the world can surpass Café Gollem,
Amsterdam. This has the best elements of Amsterdam
cosy, friendly cafes, while also serving around 200 beers: n
the biggest selection in the world, but chosen and presente
with knowledge and care. Behind the Royal Palace, turn le
into Spuistraat, right into Raamsteeg (☎020-254634. Ope
4 o'clock). There are at least 20 specialist beer bars in Th
Netherlands, and another notable example, in the tow
of Utrecht, is Jan Primus (27-31 Jan van Scorellstraa
☎030-520347).

Alfa

Small Limburg brewery making exclusively all-malt beer
smooth and well-balanced, with Hallertau and Saaz hop
ping. Noted for its sweetish **Super-Dort★★★**, the stronges
example of the style (16-16.5; 1064-66; 5.5; 7).

Arcen

Revivalist Limburg brewery making a wide range of al
malt, top-fermenting specialities, including the stronges
beer in The Netherlands, **Arcener Grand Prestige★★★** (2
1088; 8; 10); very dark, with a malty nose, fruity vanill
notes in the palate and a dry finish hinting at licorice; a goo
bottle-conditioned, winter ale. Other products includ
Arcener Stout★★★ (16.5; 1066; 5.2; 6.5), which has a smok
dryness; and The Netherlands' first *Altbier*, **Altforster★**
→★★★, which is dry and rather thin. A range of specialities
also produced under the Hertog Jan name.

Bavaria

Light, malty-tasting beers under the **Bavaria★** and **Swinkel**
names. This brewery, in Lieshout, Brabant, produces a wid
range of supermarket and other "own-brand" labels.

Brand

Oldest-established brewery in The Netherlands. This Lim
burg company has attracted attention in the United State
by marketing its pleasant **Pils★★** in a porcelain-style bottle
as Royal Brand. This beer has a malty nose, light body, an
dry finish. The super-premium, all-malt **Brand Up★★ →★★★**
dry and hoppy, is a much more interesting beer (12.5; 1050
4.25; 5.5). A pale (actually, amber) *Bock* called **Imperato**
★★ →★★★ is also all-malt, as its palate suggests (16.5; 1066; 5
6.5). A new strong, all-malt brew (19.5; 1078; 7; 9) calle
Sylvester★★★, is available regularly, despite its New Yea
name. It is highly unusual in that, while its primar
fermentation is with a "bottom" yeast, its secondary – i

both tank and bottle – is "top". Bottle-conditioning takes about 15 weeks. The beer has a dense head, a bronze colour, a malty nose, a suggestion of alcohol in the palate, and a dry hoppiness in the finish. A nice, warming, winter beer.

Breda

This Brabant town gives its name to a company making the once-famous **Three Horse(shoes)**★ beers (generally fresh-tasting, with some hoppiness), and now linked with Rotterdam's **Oranjeboom**★ (whose products tend to be firmer in body), as part of Allied Breweries (with the bland **Skol**★ labels). A confusion of similar-tasting beers, with export markets also having the low-cost **Royal Dutch Post Horn**.

Budels

Small Brabant brewery with several interesting new products: **Budels Alt**★★→★★★ is in the German style but from the relatively high gravity of 13.5 (1054; 4.4; 5.5). **Parel**★★→★★★ is a top-fermenting pale beer of 14 (1056; 4.8; 6). **Capucijn**★★→★★★ (16; 1064; 5.2; 6.5) is first bottom- and then top-fermented. It is a most unusual beer, with hints of smoked applewood. All of these beers are notably smooth, and are not pasteurized.

Dommels

Brabant brewery owned by Artois, of Belgium. **Dominator Dommelsch Speciaal**★★, a strong (4.8; 6), very pale lager, dry and lightly fruity, is a new product. A similar *speciaal* is produced by the sister brewery in Hengelo.

Grolsch

The pot-stoppered bottle was set to be phased out in the 1950s, but consumers objected. It helped **Grolsch**★★ become a cult beer, first in The Netherlands, more recently in export markets. Judged (as it now must be) among the bigger-selling Dutch Pilseners, Grolsch has a hint of new-mown hay in the nose; a soft, fluffy body; and a dryish palate. It is unpasteurized.

Gulpen

Small Limburg brewery already known for one speciality, and now gaining attention for a second. The original speciality, **X-pert**★★→★★★, is a super-premium Pilsener with a notably full colour, a gravity of 12 (1048; 4; 5), and a lot of Tettnang hop in both aroma and palate. It is kräusened, and well-matured. The newer product, **Mestreechs Aajt**★★★, is a revival of a regional speciality, with a nod in a southerly direction. It is a sour-and-sweet summer beer, claret in colour, and with some wild fermentation. It is brewed from a refreshingly low gravity of 8.5 (1034; 3.2; 4), and matured for a year. It is ironic that Gulpen should intentionally produce a sour beer. In the days before refrigeration, if beer in a brewery went sour, it would be sold off as malt vinegar. Gulpen's vinegar was so popular that the company continues to produce it (by less empirical methods), and also makes mustard.

Heineken

International trade (in beer even before tea, spices and diamonds) has always been a way of life in The Netherlands, a tiny but densely populated nation pushing into the sea. Heineken was the first brewery in the world to export to the United States at the repeal of Prohibition, and the company now controls the production of more beer in the international market than any rival. Its principal product, **Heineken Lager Beer★→★★**, is in the Pilsener style, and in its production the company stresses the use of summer barley and a total process time of not less than six weeks. The beer has a characteristically refreshing hint of fruitiness, only a light hop character, and a spritzy finish. In the Dutch market, the company produces a full range of local styles. It also has specialities like the tasty, though bottom-fermenting, **Van Vollenhoven Stout★★ →★★★** (16.2; 1065; 4.8; 6). Seasonal *Bock* beers have been marketed locally under the Heineken, Hooijberg and Sleutel names, in what seems to be ascending order of dryness. A full range of beers is marketed internationally under the Amstel brand. These are generally lighter, and sharper, in palate (see also Canada). A third international brand is Murphy (see Ireland). The company also has substantial stakes in the local brewing industries of France, Italy and several smaller countries.

De Kroon

Very small Brabant brewery. A new speciality called **Egelantier★★** is a bronze, bottom-fermenting beer of conventional gravity but full body. The Dortmunder-style **Briljant★★** (12; 1048; 5.2; 6.3) seems to have developed more of its own character in recent years. It has a malty nose, firm but surprisingly light body, and dry palate.

De Leeuw

Small Limburg brewery. It is to be hoped that the soft, all-malt **Jubileeuw★★** (originally produced for the brewery's centenary) has a permanent place in the range. This is a pale, bottom-fermenting beer of conventional gravity. **Super Leeuw★★** (13.5; 1054; 4.7; 5.9) is a well-liked Dortmunder. These beers are unpasteurized.

Lindeboom

Small Limburg brewery noted for its dry **Pilsener★★** and a pleasant **Bock★★**.

De Ridder

Small Limburg brewery noted for its creamy, fruity, Dortmunder-style **Maltezer★★**. The products of this brewery do not seem to have changed in character since it was acquired by Heineken.

Schaapskooi, Trappist Monastery

Proud monastery, near Tilburg, recently much more assertive in its brewing activities. The basic **Schaapskooi Trappisten Bier★★★** has a copper colour, a sherryish nose, and a gently malty palate, with fruity undertones (4 percent alcohol by weight; 5 by volume). There is a more pronounced fruitiness to the yeasty, dry **La Trappe★★★ →★★★★** (17 Plato; 1068; around 5.5; 7) which is also a little paler. Slightly paler again – though still full in colour – is a Trappist beer of similar gravity and strength, but maltier in character, brewed under the name **Koningshoeven★★★** and marketed by Allied Breweries in The Netherlands.

BELGIUM

The secret is out. Beer-drinkers have begun to realize that Belgium has the most diverse, individualistic brews in the world. Its cidery, winey, spontaneously fermenting *lambic* family pre-date the pitching of yeast by brewers and its cherry *kriek*, strawberry *framboise* and spiced "white" brews pre-date the acceptance of the hop as the universal seasoning in beer. Other countries have monastery breweries but it is only in Belgium that the brothers have evolved their own collective style. Whether produced in the country's five monastery breweries or a secular plant, "abbey"-style beers are always strong, top-fermenting and bottle-matured. They often have a heavy sediment and a fruity palate, sometimes evincing hints of chocolate. Within these characteristics, however, there are substantial differences between the brews, and a couple of sub-categories, but that is the way of Belgian beer. Some Belgian specialities are hard to categorize, although most are top-fermenting and many are bottle-matured. No country has a more diverse range even within the bottle-matured group – the Belgians are keen on this means of conditioning and sometimes refer to it as their *méthode champenoise*.

In a Belgian cafe, the list of beers will identify at

least one member of the *lambic* family (occasionally a sweet *faro*, often a sparkling *gueuze*); perhaps a honeyish "white" beer (*witbier* or *bière blanche*) from the village or a brown (*bruin*) from the town of Oudenaarde; a local *spécial*; and a strong, bottle-conditioned monastery (*abdij* or *abbaye*) brew. There may also be a Belgian *ale*, as well as local interpretations of English, Scottish and sometimes German styles. This is in an ordinary cafe; there will be a far greater categorization in a cafe that makes a feature of speciality beers, listing them by the hundred.

After decades of decline when they were regarded as "old-fashioned", speciality beers began to enjoy a revival in the late 1970s. They are a joy to the visiting beer-lover, although it is necessary to know what to order. A request simply for "a beer" is likely to be met by a mass-market Pilsener.

With the revival of interest in speciality beers within Belgium, more of them have also entered export markets. They present a bewildering choice. As always, the selection of beers reflects both history and geography. The influence of the brewing customs of the surrounding nations has been accepted with shrewd selectivity by the Belgians, yet they have also contrived to be conservative and inward-looking to the point that their principal regions maintain their own traditions. The country is divided not only into its Dutch-speaking north (Flanders) and French-speaking south (Wallonia) but also has a German-speaking corner in the east and a bilingual knot around the city of Brussels. Some styles of beer are perceived as belonging not to a region but to a province, river valley, town or village.

The Belgians like to talk about beer as their reply to Burgundy. They suggest that beer is to them what wine is to France. Cheese might be an even better comparison. The beers of Belgium, like the cheeses of France, are often idiosyncratic, cranky, artisanal. Some drinkers could never learn to enjoy one of the cloudy, sour specialities of the Senne Valley any more than they could acquire a taste for a smelly cheese. In both cases, the loss would be theirs. This is drink at its most sensuous.

In its native gastronomy, Belgium is a land of beer, seafood and — after dinner — the world's finest chocolate. It is a land of German portions and French culinary skills. Beer may be served, with some ceremony, at a family meal, and might well have been used in the cooking. Other countries have the odd dish prepared with beer, but Belgium has hundreds. The Belgians even eat hop shoots, as a delicacy, in the brief season of their availability, served like asparagus, with poached or scrambled eggs.

Beer is also a central theme in Belgium's history
and culture. St Arnold of Oudenaarde is remembered
or having successfully beseeched God, in the 11th
century, to provide more beer after an abbey brewery
collapsed. He is the patron saint of Belgian brewers,
some of whom display his statue by their kettles.
French-speakers can, if they prefer, remember
another beery miracle, that of St Arnold at Metz.) The
13th-century Duke Jan the First of Brabant, Louvain
and Antwerp has passed into legend as the King of
Beer: "Jan Primus" has been corrupted into "Gam-
rinus", by which name he is remembered not only in
Belgium but also in Germany, Czechoslovakia and far
beyond. Jan Primus is said to have been an honorary
member of the Brewers' Guild, although their present
gilded premises on Brussels' Grand' Place were not
built until 1701. Today, the "Brewers' House" is the
only building on the Grand' Place still to be used as
the headquarters of a trade guild. A small museum in
its cellars is open to the public.

Today's Confederation has about a hundred members, and that represents roughly the number of
breweries in Belgium. The figure has been declining
or some years, although recently a number of new
micro-breweries have opened. Many Belgian
breweries are family-owned, which can lead to
problems when there is no clear succession. But
however much the number of breweries fluctuates,
the tally of beers increases, with new specialities
constantly being launched. At any one time, there are
probably more than 500 Belgium beers on the market.

FLANDERS

Flemish painters like Bruegel and the aptly named Brouwer
depicted the people of their home state as enthusiastic beer-
drinkers. It has been like that for a thousand years. As
Emperor of Europe, Charlemagne took an interest in
brewing, and perhaps he brought the news from Aix to
Ghent. The nationalistic Flemings might, however, secretly
resent their famous artists' depiction of beery excess. They
take pride in being hard-working, and the Early and Late
Flemish schools of painting were made possible by the
prosperity of Flanders at different times as an exporter of
beer as well as textiles, and as a commercial centre. Flanders
emerged as a principal component of the new Belgium in
1830, and has in recent years reasserted itself through the
trading prosperity of the river Scheldt – with beer exports
once again on the upswing.

As a region, Flanders stretches from the Dutch side of the
Scheldt to a slice of northern France. Politically, it com-
prises the Belgian provinces of West and East Flanders,
Antwerp and Limburg.

West Flanders, with its 15th-century canalside capital
Bruges, has traditionally been known for its sour, burgundy-
coloured style of beer – the classic example is Rodenbach.

The province is well served by small breweries and has two o the strongest beers in Belgium, from the revivalist Doll Brouwers and the monastery brewery of Westvleteren.

East Flanders, with the proud city of Ghent as its capita is noted for slightly less sour brown ales, produced in or nea the town of Oudenaarde, which has a cluster of smal breweries to the east.

The province and city of Antwerp is noted for th beautifully made De Konick beer (a copper ale). Th province also has the monastery of Westmalle, whic created the Triple style of abbey beer, and in the south, it strong, golden ale called Duvel, the potent, dark Goude Carolus and the well-liked Maes Pils.

Limburg has a less gilded capital, the pretty little town o Hasselt, which is known for the production of *genever* gin It is a thinly breweried province but has the distinctiv Sezoens beer from the Martens brewery, Cristal Alken, a especially well-respected Pilsener beer.

Where to drink

The biggest selection of beers in any one cafe in the world i probably that at Het Grote Ongenoegen (9 Jeruzalemstraa in the Old Town of Antwerp. This specialist cafe has mor than 1,000 beers, although it seems to have lost some of it energy since the departure of the original owner. Th publicity attracted by the collection at Het Grote Ongen oegen helped to make specialist beer bars fashionable i Belgium. The best in Antwerp, although service varies fror the obliging to the dour, is the small cafe Kulminator (32–3 Vleminckxveld) with 350–400 beers. Patersvaetje (1 Blauw moezelstraat) has about 80 beers.

There are good selections in many other places, althoug Belgian cafes in general do not always offer much to ea Where they do, Flanders is at its best with seafood. Vagan (25 Reyndersstraat) has some interesting beers and gins, an offers herring in season (in the same street, De Groote Witt Arend marries beer with fine art and recitals of chambe music). De Arme Duivel (in the street of the same name) ha *kriek* on draught, and mussels in season; 't Waagstuk (2 Stadswag) has 60 beers and offers fish dishes; Fouquets (1 De Keyserlei) has beers, oysters in season and desserts.

After Antwerp, the largest city in Flanders is Ghent which has a popular and well-run specialist beer cafe calle De Hopduvel ("The Hop Devil", at 10 Rokerelsstraat). Th Hopduvel also features the growing number of Belgia cheeses. Bruges, too, has an excellent beer cafe, a pubb place that also specializes in pancakes. It is called 't Brug Beertje (5 Kemelstraat) and has an adjoining shop sellin unusual brews by the bottle. Farther afield, the Limbur town of Hasselt has adjoining beer and gin bars in the tow centre in an establishment called the Hasselt Cafe (3 Maastrichterstraat). The cafe also has its own juniper bee called Dikkenek ("Thick Neck", a self-mocking nicknam for the people of Limburg). Nearby, the Hemelrijk cafe (i the street of the same name) specializes in beer and whisky Not a town for the abstemious.

Cristal Alken

The hoppiest of the principal Belgian Pilseners is **Crista Alken**★★ → ★★★. This well-made Pilsener with a notably pal

olour, fresh, hoppy nose; very clean, crisp palate and a
mooth dryness in the finish. It is hopped principally with
ossoms, including Saaz for aroma, fermented at relatively
old temperatures, lagered for a respectable period and not
asteurized. Cristal is a much-loved beer and its character
as been maintained despite a change in the ownership of the
rewery. It has also been retained as the exclusive property
the brewery in the village of Alken in Limburg. There were
ars, which have been proved groundless, that production
ight ultimately be shared with a sister brewery in East
landers, whose **Zulte★★** is a good example of the sour,
urgundy-coloured style of the region. Both breweries are
wned by Kronenbourg, of France.

De Dolle Brouwers

The Mad Brewers", they call themselves. It is a typically
emish, sardonic shrug on behalf of a group of enthusiasts
ho rescued from closure a village brewery near Diksmuide,
ot far from Ostend. As a weekend project, they renovated
e brewery, which dates from the mid 19th century and is a
assic of its type. (Tours welcome; ☎051-502781.) They
ecialize in strong, top-fermenting beers, all bottle-
atured. The house speciality is **Oerbier★★★**, very dark and
nooth, with a sweetness that is offset by licorice tones
riginal gravity 1100; alcohol content 6 percent by weight;
5 by volume). There are also several seasonal products: the
assy-coloured, honey-primed **Boskeun★★★**, an Easter beer
about 8 percent by volume; the pale, dry-hopped
rabier★★★, for summer, with a similar alcohol content; and
ille Nacht★★★, a claret-coloured Christmas brew, with
nts of apple in its aroma and palate, and an alcohol
ntent of around 9 percent. With an original gravity of
ound 1120 (12 degrees Belgian), this matches West-
eteren's Abt, although that has a higher alcohol content,
ving been known to weigh in at 10.6 percent by volume.

De Koninck

classic. This perilously drinkable, copper-coloured, top-
rmenting beer fits in stylistically somewhere between an
nglish ale (a fruity "best bitter") and a smooth Düsseldorf
tbier. For all its complexity of character, it pursues an
iassuming occupation as the local beer of Antwerp, from
e city's only brewery. The company stayed with top-
rmentation when other big-city breweries were switching
Pilseners. Its sole product is **De Koninck★★★**, an all-
alt beer of 12 Plato, brewed by direct flame in a cast-iron
ttle. It is cold-conditioned and emerges with an alcohol
ntent of a little over 4 percent by weight and 5 by volume.
e Koninck has an excellent malt character, a yeasty
uitiness and a great deal of Saaz hoppiness, especially in its
g finish. Its full palate is best experienced in the draught
rm, which is unpasteurized. Opposite the brewery, at the
lgrim Cafe (8 Boomgardstraat), drinkers sometimes add a
rinkle of yeast to the beer. In the heart of Antwerp, the
er is available at the city's oldest cafe, Quinten Matsijs (17
oriaanstraat) and at Den Engel (3 Grote Markt).

Duvel

nis means "Devil" and is the name of the world's most
guiling beer. With its pale, golden sparkle, **Duvel★★★★**

looks superficially like a Pilsener. Its palate is soft and seductive. Beneath its frothy head, behind its dense lace work, this all-malt, top-fermenting beer has the power (6. percent alcohol by weight; 8.2 by volume) to lead anyon into temptation. The pale colour is achieved with the help c the brewery's own maltings; Styrian and Saaz hops are used a very distinctive yeast imparts a subtle fruitiness (remi niscent of Poire Williams; the cleanness and smoothness i enhanced by both cold and warm maturation; and, in th classic, sedimented, version, the *mousse* develops fron bottle-conditioning. Duvel is customarily chilled as though it were an *alcool blanc*. It is produced by the Moortga brewery in the village of Breendonk near Mechelen/Malines Other Moortgat products include tasty, abbey-style beer under the **Maredsous★★** label, for the monastery of tha name. Duvel is sometimes compared with the variou monastic Triple beers, but this is self-evident heresay. Duve is lighter in body, less sweet, more delicate. It is the origina and therefore classic, example of what has become a distinc style. Broadly in this style are **Deugniet★★**, **Hap kin★★ →★★★**, **Ketje★**, **Lucifer★**, **Sloeber★★** and **Teutenbier★**

Gouden Carolus

This is the classic strong, dark ale of Belgium. Its nam derives from a gold coin from the realm of the Holy Roma Emperor Charles V, who grew up in the Flemish City c Mechelen (better known to the outside world by its Frenc name, Malines) where this beer is brewed. **Gouden Carolu** has a dense, dark colour, a gentle, soothing character, a hin of fruitiness in the finish and, from a gravity of 19 Plato, a alcohol content of 6 percent by weight; 7.5 by volume. lovely after-dinner beer; or, better still, a nightcap.

Kwak Pauwel

The odd name derives from an antique Flemish speciality This revival, a strong (9 percent by volume), garnet coloured, top-fermenting brew, is notable for its licoric aroma and palate. Licorice is actually added; the characte does not derive from the malt, as it does in some dark brew **Kwak Pauwel★★★** is a hearty, warming brew. When it firs appeared in Belgium, it won attention by being served in "yard of ale" glass, of the type allegedly handed up t coachmen in times past when they stopped for a restorativ drink.

Liefmans

Liefmans is the classic brown-ale brewery in Oudenaard where such products are a speciality. The brewery's basi brown ale, known simply as **Liefmans★★ →★★★** is made fron at least four styles of malt and a similar number of ho varieties. It spends an extraordinarily long time in the brev kettle – a whole night – and is cooled in open vessels. It pitched with a pure-culture, top-fermenting yeast that ha slightly lactic character, imparting the gentle sournes typical in such beers. It has six weeks' warm-conditioning i tanks and is then blended with a smaller proportion of similar beer that has had eight to ten months' conditionin It has an original gravity of around 12 Plato (1048) and a alcohol content of 3.7 percent by weight; 4.6 by volume.

The longer-conditioned "vintage" brew is bottle

straight" as **Liefmans Goudenband★★★★** (Golden Band)
nd is surely the world's finest brown ale. After tank-
onditioning, it has 3–12 months' bottle-maturation (with-
ut dosage) in the brewery's *caves*. It is called a *provisie*,
dicating that it can be laid down. If it is kept in a cool (but
ot refrigerated) dark place, it will continue to improve,
erhaps reaching its peak after two years. For a brown ale, it
unusually spritzy and very dry, with a finish reminiscent
Montilla. It has an original gravity of about 13 Plato
052), and an alcohol content of 4.4; 5.5. The brown ales are
so used as the basis for the unusual **Liefmans Kriek★★★**,
hich has a notably smooth body, a sour-and-sweet palate
d a port-wine finish. It has an original gravity of 18.25
lato (1073), 5.76 by weight; 7.2 by volume. Liefmans craft-
rewing approach is emphasized by the use of tissue-
rapped bottles. These appear in a variety of sizes including,
r very good customers, hand-filled Nebuchadnezzars
ntaining enough beer to fill 20 normal bottles.

The town of Oudenaarde also has brown ales from its
udde and Clarysse breweries, the latter under the Felix
bel, and in a less sour style from Roman. Similar beers are
ade nearby by the wonderfully artisanal brewer of
rombe in Zottegem and Van Den Bossche in St Lievens-
sse, and there are many more distant imitators.

Maes

flowery, "Riesling" bouquet imparts distinctiveness to
aes Pils★★ →★★★. In other respects the brewery is un-
ually faithful to the Pilsener tradition, extensively using
alt produced in Bohemia specifically for Maes and Saaz
ossom hops. Maes is also painstaking in its use of open
oling vessels and a very slow, cold fermentation in the
louble", Darauflassen method. Lagering is for two to three
onths and the result is a light, soft beer, definitely dry but
t assertively so. Maes is one of the principal Belgian
lseners and is very well made for a relatively mass-
arketed beer. The brewery is in the village of Waarloos,
rth of Mechelen. The company also produces two top-
rmenting beers for the abbey of Grimbergen, a Flemish
llage near Brussels. **Grimbergen Double★★** is a dark,
uity beer, with a chocolatey palate; it has a gravity of 15.8
ato and an alcohol content of 5.2 percent by weight; 6.5 by
olume. **Grimbergen Tripel★ →★★** is paler, fruity, but with
more winey character; it has a gravity of 19.6 Plato and an
cohol content of 7.2 by weight; 9 by volume.

Rodenbach

he unimaginative are apt to consider Rodenbach's beers
drinkable, yet they are the classics of the "sour" style of
est Flanders. They gain their sourness, and their bur-
undy colour, in a number of ways. The sourness derives in
art from the top-fermenting yeast a blend of three strains
at has been in the house for 150 years, and from cultures
sident in wooden maturation tuns. The colour, too,
iginates partly from the use of reddish Vienna-style malts
t also probably from the caramels and tannins extracted
om the oak of the tuns. These vessels, made from
avonian oak, from Poland, are uncoated. They make a
markable sight, each tun standing vertically from floor to
iling. The smallest contains 15,000 litres of maturing beer;

the largest 60,000 litres. There are 300 in all, filling severa
halls, as though this were a winery or a brandy distillery
When the maturing beer has attained its typical palate, it
stabilized by flash pasteurization so does not mature in th
bottle and is not intended for laying down.

The basic **Rodenbach**★★★ →★★★★ is a blend of "young
beer (matured five to six weeks) and "vintage" brew
(matured 18 months to two years). The longer-matured bee
is also bottled "straight" as **Rodenbach Grand Cru**★★★★
The basic Rodenbach has an original gravity of 11.5−11.7
Plato, emerging with 3.7 percent alcohol by weight; 4.
volume. The Grand Cru has an original gravity of 15, but a
alcohol content of only around 4.1; 5.2. The gravity
heightened by the use of non-fermented sugars and th
alcohol content is diminished because some of the fermer
tation is lactic. There is both a sharpness and a restorativ
quality about these beers: perfect after a game of tennis. Th
Grand Cru has a slightly bigger palate and a smoothe
texture. Even then, some Belgians add a touch of grenadin
as though they were making a red *kir*. The Rodenbac
brewery is in Roeslare, the centre of an agricultural area

Several breweries in West Flanders produce similar bee
to Rodenbach's but none with such a distinctive characte
Examples include Paulus from Van Eecke; Oude Piro fror
Bevernagie; Bacchus from Van Honsenbrouck; Petrus fror
Bavik; and Vichtenaar from Verhaege. In East Flander
beers very much in this style are produced under the nam
Bios by Van Steenberge.

St Louis

The widely marketed St Louis beers of the *lambic* family
including a novel strawberry brew, come from the Va
Honsenbrouck company in Ingelmunster. In buccaneerin
fashion, this brewery tackles a wide variety of "speciality
styles and carries this off surprisingly well on occasion. S
Louis **Gueuze Lambic**★ may be a trifle on the sweet side bu
the **Kriek Lambic**★ →★★ is well balanced, if a little blanc
The **Framboise**★★ is full and fruity. The strawberry **Beze
bier**★★★ has to win points for effort. It has a rich strawberr
aroma and is sweet when young, drying to a considerabl
tartness as it ages. In addition to its **Bacchus**★ →★★ (se
previous entry), the brewery has an interesting top-fermen
ing speciality called **Brigand**★★. This is an amber, stron
brew, with a secondary fermentation in its corked bottle. I
has a gravity of 20 Plato, emerging with 7.2 percent alcoh
by weight; 9 by volume. While it superficially resembles
saison in its immense liveliness and fruitiness, it has a mo
rounded texture and its palate is less citric, more reminiscen
of soft fruit.

St Sixtus

See Westvleteren, Trappist Monastery of St Sixtus

Sezoens

While seasonal *saison* beers for summer are a recognize
style in the French-speaking part of Belgium, they are les
evident in Flemish tradition. **Sezoens**★★★ has the sam
connotation, but is the registered trademark of a distinctiv
and delightful product from the Martens brewery, in th
Limburg village of Bocholt. It has a delightful label, to

owing a well-clad personification of winter handing the
eer to a sunny "Mr Summer". Sezoens is a pale, golden top-
rmenting brew of 13.5 Plato, with 4 percent alcohol by
eight; 5 by volume. It has a fresh, hoppy aroma (Saaz is
sed), a firm, clean, notably dry palate, and plenty of hop
aaracter throughout, especially in the finish, where the
arty dryness is that of the Northern Brewer variety. At
e moment, this product is not bottle-conditioned though it
ight be in the future. In all of these respects, Sezoens is
iite different from the amber, stronger, yeastily fruit
ison brews of French-speaking Belgium. Martens also
:oduces a rather German-tasting **Kwik Pils★★**. Devotees
ho track these beers down to their far-flung home village
aould arrange in advance to visit Martens'museum
3rouwerij Martens Museum, Dorpstraat 32, Bocholt, Bel-
um B3598; ☎011-461705), which is open by appointment
lly. In Brussels, Sezoens is the speciality of the cafe De
ltieme Hallucinatie (316 Koningsstraat/Rue Royale), in
1 Art Nouveau house near the Botanical Gardens.

tropken

he aniseed finish in Stropken makes it especially interest-
g among the several idiosyncratic speciality beers launched
Belgium, and especially in Flanders, during the 1980s.
'ith its flowery bouquet, fruity start and firm, creamy
)dy, it is the beer world's answer to *pastis*. The first
tropken was assertively spicy, but this subsequently
elded to a more refined Grand Cru version. **Stropken
rand Cru★★ →★★★** is a well-made, top-fermenting beer,
ith an original gravity of 17.5 Plato and an alcohol content
' around 5.5 percent by weight; 6.75 by volume. The name
tropken is an ironic Flemish reference to the halters that
ie rebellious Lords of Ghent were obliged to wear by
mperor Charles in the 16th century. Stropken, originally
:oduced as the house brew at the Hopduvel specialist beer
afe in Ghent, is now produced under contract by the
aghmuylder brewery also in East Flanders. Slaghmuylder
:oduces well-made abbey-style brews and an unusual,
pper-coloured all-malt, bottom-fermenting speciality beer
' conventional gravity called **Cornel★★ →★★★**, beautifully
alanced, with a hoppy dryness in the finish.

Westmalle, Trappist Monastery

he classic example of the pale, Triple style of Belgian
rappist brew is produced by the monastery of Westmalle, a
llage northeast of Antwerp. The monastery, established in
321, has brewed since its early days, though it was slow in
aking its beer available commercially, and remains one of
ie most withdrawn of the Trappist monasteries. Visits are
ot encouraged, though the brewery can sometimes be seen
y appointment. The smart, traditional copper brewhouse is
a strikingly 1930s building. It produces three beers. The
Single", confusingly known as **Extra**, is available only to
ie brothers; a shame, since this pale, top-fermenting brew is
product of some delicacy. The **Double★★** is dark brown,
alty, but quite dry. It has an original gravity of around 16
lato and an alcohol content of about 5.5 by weight; just
ider 7 by volume. The **Triple★★★★** offers an unusual
)mbination of features, being a strong, top-fermenting beer
' pale, almost Pilsener, colour. Its mash is entirely of

Pilsener malts from Czechoslovakia and France but, in th
classic procedure, candy sugar is added in the kettle. Ther
are three hopping stages, using Fuggles, a number o
German varieties and Saaz. The brew is fermented with
hybrid house yeast, then has a secondary fermentation o
one to three months in tanks, and is given a priming of suga
and a further dosage of yeast before being bottled. It i
warm-conditioned in the bottle before being released from
gravity of around 20 Plato, it emerges with an alcohc
content of around 6.4 percent by weight; 8 by volume. Witl
its faintly citric fruitiness, its rounded body and its alcoholi
"kick", the Triple expresses a very full character within si:
months of leaving the monastery, though bottles from 192
are still in good condition. Westmalle is jealous of th
individuality of its product, but several secular brewerie
produce beers in a similar style, using the designation Tripl
(in Flemish, Tripel). Good examples include Vieille Viller
Triple from Van Assche; Witkap from Slaghmuylder and th
slightly fuller-coloured Affligem from De Smedt.

Westvleteren, Trappist Monastery of St Sixtus

The strongest beer in Belgium comes from by far th
smallest of the country's five monastery breweries. This i
the monastery of St Sixtus, at the hamlet of Westvleteren, i
a rustic corner of Flanders, near the French border an
between the coast and the town best known by its Frenc
name Ypres (Ieper in Flemish). Although it overlooks a ho
garden, the monastery produces beers in which malt
sweetness is the predominant characteristic, with spicy an
fruity tones also notable. As well as being tiny, th
brewhouse is antique. Its own output is limited – artisana
Trappist beers, bottled without labels and identified by th
crown cork – though further supplies are produced b
arrangement in a nearby commercial brewery. From th
monastery's own output there is no Single, and the basi
beer, with a green crown-cork, is called **Double★★**. Ther
comes the **Special★★** (red crown-cork), drier, with hints o
vanilla and licorice, a gravity of around 15 Plato and a
alcohol content of about 4.8 percent by weight; 6 b
volume. The **Extra★★** (blue) has more fruity, acidic tone
and some alcohol character (20 Plato; 6.4; 8). Finally
the strongest beer in the monastery (and the country) is th
Abbot★★★★ (yellow), very full-bodied, creamy, soft an
sweet. This is sometimes known as a 12-degree beer, it
gravity in the Belgian scale. That works out at about 3
Plato (1120) and the beer has around 8.48 percent alcohol b
weight; 10.6 by volume.

These beers can be bought by the case at the monaster
and sampled next door in the Café De Vrede, but they ar
less easy to find elsewhere. Their crown-corks identify th
beer as Westmalle, while the commercially produced versior
has a label and is designated St Sixtus. The commerciall
produced counterpart to Abbot, with a yet yeastier charac
ter (very lively, and with an acidic finish) is exported to th
USA simply as **St Sixtus★★★**. This is remarkable in that th
producing brewery, St Bernard, is itself very small. S
Bernard is in Watou, near Poperinge. Its local rival Va
Eecke produces a similar range of tasty yeasty, abbey-styl
brews, and a hoppy speciality called **Popering
Hommelbier★★ →★★★**.

BRUSSELS AND BRABANT

Within the extraordinarily colourful tapestry of Belgian brewing, the most vivid shades are to be found in the country's central province, Brabant, and especially around the capital city, Brussels. If the Germanic north of Europe and the Romantic south intertwine in Belgium, it is in the province of Brabant and the city of Brussels that the knot is tied. As the nearest thing Europe has to a federal capital, Brussels has some lofty French kitchens, but it also takes pride in the heartier *carbonades* of what it terms *"cuisine de bière"*, in which several restaurants specialize. On its Gallic avenues, it has some splendid Art Nouveau cafes, but the Grand' Place and the older neighbourhoods are Flemish in flavour and so is the beer.

To the east, the Flemish village of Hoegaarden is the home of the Belgian style of "white" beer. Louvain (in Flemish, Leuven) is the home of Stella Artois and the biggest brewing city in Belgium. The greatest splash of colour by far is, however, Brussels. Although it has one conventional brewery, Brussels is the local market for the *lambic* family, the most unusual beers in the world, with palate characteristics that range from a hint of pine kernels to a forkful of Brie cheese. *Lambic* is produced in the city itself and, in great variety, by a cluster of specialist brewers and blenders in the Senne Valley.

The Senne is a small river that runs diagonally, often underground, from northeast to southwest through Brussels. There used to be *lambic* breweries on both sides of the city and even today *lambic* is served as a local speciality on the eastern edge of the city at Jezus-Eik. South of Brussels it is served at Hoeillaart-Overijse, where Belgium's (dessert) grapes are grown. However, it is on the western edge of Brussels that production is concentrated today spreading out into the nearby scatter of farming villages collectively known as Payottenland. Traditional *lambic*-makers brew only in the winter, and the number in production at any one time varies. Some have closed in recent years, but it is not unknown in such cases for a brewery to reopen.

There are a couple of *lambic* breweries within the western boundary of Brussels itself and a further eight or nine active ones in Payottenland. There are also about half a dozen companies that contract or buy brews which they then ferment, mature or blend in their own cellars. A further two or three breweries beyond the traditional area also produce beers of this type (notably St Louis and Jacobins, both from West Flanders). With 20-odd houses producing *lambic* beers to varying degrees of authenticity, and seven or eight derivative styles, some available in more than one age, there are usually about 100 products of this type on the market, though many are obtainable only on a very limited scale and in specialist cafes.

The *lambic* family are not everybody's glass of beer, but no one with a keen interest in alcoholic drink would find them anything less than fascinating. In their "wildness" and unpredictability, these are exciting brews. At their best, they are the meeting point between beer and wine. At their worst, they offer a taste of history, as though one of those stoneware jars of beer had been lifted from the canvas of a

Bruegel or Brouwer.

The basic *lambic* is a spontaneously fermenting wheat beer, made from a turbid mash of 30–40 percent wheat and the rest barley. The barley is only lightly malted; the wheat not at all. The boil can last three to six hours and the brew is hopped very heavily but with blossoms that have been aged to reduce their bitterness. The hops are used for their traditional purpose as a preservative; their bitterness is not wanted in a fruity wheat beer. In the classic method, the brew is taken upstairs to the gable of the roof, where vents are left open so that the wild yeasts of the Senne Valley may enter. The brew lies uncovered in an open vessel, and consummation takes place. The brew is allowed to be aroused in this way for only one night, ideally an autumn evening, and only the wild yeasts of the Senne Valley are said to provide the proper impregnation.

After its night upstairs the brew is barrelled in hogsheads where primary and secondary fermentations take place, further stimulated by microflora resident in the wood. For this reason, *lambic* brewers are reluctant to disturb the dust that collects among the hogsheads, which are racked in galleries with no temperature control.

Brewers outside the traditional *lambic* area who wish to make a beer of this type have been known to acquire a barrel of a Senne Valley vintage to use as a starter. In the classic method the brewer never pitches any yeast. No doubt it was originally just a question of supply, but some barrels used in the maturation of *lambic* originally contained claret, port or sherry – the last reminiscent of whisky-making in Scotland. Like the whisky-maker, the *lambic*-brewer wants his barrels to respond to the natural changes in temperature.

The primary fermentation takes only five or six days, the secondary six months. If a brew of less than six months is made available for sale, it is customarily identified as young (*jong*) or "fox" (*vos*) *lambic*. The classic maturation period, however, is "one or two summers" and occasionally three.

Terminology is imprecise, not least because of the two languages in use (and Flemish manifests itself in several dialects). *Lambic* may appear as *lambiek* and both the beer and yeast are said to derive their name from the village of Lembeek, in Payottenland. In its basic form *lambic* is hard to find, but it is served on draught in some cafes in the producing area. The young version can be intensely dry, sour, cloudy and still, like an English "scrumpy" or rustic cider. The older version will have mellowed, settled, and perhaps be *pétillant*.

A blended version of young *lambic* sweetened with dark candy sugar is known as *faro*. If this is then diluted with water, it becomes *mars*. Sometimes cafes provide sugar and a muddler. If the sugared version is bottled, it is effectively chaptalized and develops a complex of sweetness in the start and fruity sharpness in the finish. If young and old versions of the basic beer are blended in the cask to start yet a further fermentation, the result, sparkling and medium-dry, is known as *gueuze-lambic*. This term is also sometimes used to describe a version that is blended and conditioned in the bottle, though such a product is properly known simply as *gueze* and is the most widely available member of the family. The bottle-conditioning may take three to nine months, though the beer will continue to improve for one or two years.

fter leaving the brewery and will certainly last for five.
ecause the atmosphere in the brewery is dusty and perhaps
amp, some small brewers feel it pointless to label their
ottles but do put a dab of whitewash on the bottle to show
hich way up it has been stored.

The version in which cherries have been macerated in the
ask is known as *kriek*. If raspberries are used, it is called
amboise. Strawberries (*aardbeien*) and even grapes
druiven) have also been used. The cherry version is a very
aditional summer drink in the Brussels area, and the
riginal method is to make it with whole fruit, which ferment
own to the pits. Another technique is to macerate whole
uit in juice and add the mixture to the brew.

The original beer is brewed from a conventional gravity of
2–13 Plato (1048–52), though the density and alcohol
ntent varies according to dilution, blending and macera-
on. A basic *lambic* has only about 3.6 percent alcohol by
eight; 4.4 by volume. A *gueuze* might have 4.4; 5.5. A *kriek*
an go up to 4.8; 6.

Even with all of these variations at their disposal some
fes choose to offer their own blend, perhaps to offset the
urness of a young *lambic* with the fruitiness of a mature
e. Such a blend may be offered as the *panache* of the house.
ese beers are sometimes accompanied by a hunk of brown
ead with cheese, onions and radishes. A spready *fromage
anc*, made from skimmed milk, is favoured. Or a salty
usselsekaas might be appropriate. The beers are served at
ool cellar temperature of around 10°C (50°F). In the USA
ey have proved themselves to be elegant aperitifs, over ice,
though they were vermouth.

As if such colour were not enough, there are a number of
breweries in Brabant, especially northwest of Brussels.

here to drink

Brussels: Beer-lovers who also enjoy Art Nouveau will
preciate the cafe De Ultime Hallucinatie (31b Rue
yale). Something a little later, reminiscent of the bar in a
ilway station of the period, is offered by the wonderful
20s, Mort Subite (serving the *lambic* beers of the same
me) at Rue de Montagne-aux-Herbes Potagères, not far
m Grand' Place. Another *lambic* cafe, even closer to
and' Place, is Bécasse, in an alley off Rue Tabora. Easily
inkable and sweetish *lambic* beers are brewed for the
De Neve and served with snacks in a cosy "Dutch
chen" atmosphere. On Grand' Place, La Chaloupe d'Or
s a wide selection of beers. Another cafe in the "Dutch
chen" style, also in the centre of the city, is 't Spinnek-
ke at Place du Jardin aux Fleurs, with a good range of
ll-kept beers. Not far away, Place Sainte Catherine has
veral atmospheric cafes selling *lambic* beers.

Around the edge of the city centre there are several
tstanding specialist beer cafes: La Houblonnière, a
ident spot with hearty hot food, in Place de Londres; Le
roir, with a knowledgeable owner, some unusual
eciality beers and a "coffee shop" atmosphere, at Place
ine Astrid in Jette; Moeder Lambic, which also has a
taurant, at Chausée de Waterloo; Au Père Faro, in
aussée d'Alsemberg, Uccle; and Bierodrome, with jazz, at
ace Fernand Cock in Ixelles.

In Louvain/Leuven, the town-centre cafe Domus in Tien-

sestraat has a wide selection of beers and brews its ow
Munich-style pale lager.

In Payottenland, every village has at least one caf
serving *lambic* beer. In the aptly named village of Beerse
there are two cafes that blend their own *lambic*. One, Dri
Fonteinen, has hand-pumps. The other, Oude Pruim, als
specializes in *boudin* (black pudding, or blood sausage
Beersel has a 13th-century castle that can be visited i
summer or on winter weekends.

Artois

A major European brewing company that is the biggest i
Belgium. The name derives from a family, not the region
northern France. **Stella Artois★** is a Pilsener-style beer wit
a hint of new-mown hay in the nose. Artois, based in Leuve
also produces a "Danish"-style premium lager calle
Loburg★ and the top-fermenting **Ketje★**. Products of it
subsidiaries include **Wiel's★**, a local Pilsener in Brussel
Vieux Temps★ and **Ginder★**, both Belgian-style ales, an
the **Leffe★★** and **Tongerlo★★** ranges of abbey-style ales.

Belle-Vue

In so far as the phrase "mass-market" can be applied t
lambic beers, it describes the relatively bland and swee
Belle-Vue★ products from the sizeable Vandenstoc
brewery in Brussels. The same company owns the excellen
De Neve *lambic* brewery in Payottenland at Schepdaal. I
its unfiltered form, **De Neve Lambic★★→★★★** has a
almondy, aperitif dryness.

Boon

A well-respected blender of *lambic* beers, Frank Boo
(pronounced "Bone") has contributed much to the revival o
interest in *lambic* styles since he started to blend his ow
products some years ago at the former De Vit brewery i
appropriately, Lembeek. Boon's *lambic* beers are aromati
very lively, fruity and dry. He makes a speciality of offerin
a variety of ages and even of *caves*. His speciality blends ar
labelled **Mariage Parfait★★**. Other blenders include D
Koninck (no connection with the Antwerp brewer of th
same name), Hanssens and Wets.

Cantillon

Tiny, working "museum brewery" producing *lambic* beers i
Brussels. Well worth a visit at 56 Rue Gheude, Anderlech
(☎5214928). Its beers are smooth, with a sustained head
dry and with a sharply fruity finish. A full range of *lambi*
beers is produced, and the **Framboise Cantillon★★★★** is
classic.

De Troch

Very small *lambic* brewery in Wambeek in Payottenland
Despite its small scale it exports to France where its beer i
well-regarded. **De Troch★★★** beers are generally on the dar
side, quite full in body, and rather carbonic. There is also
blender called De Troch in Schepdaal.

Eylenbosch

The extreme dryness and woodiness formerly found in th
Eylenbosch *lambic* beers seems to have retreated since th

ewery was rented to new management. The beers are still ry but balanced with hints of sweetness against a smoother ackground. Distinctiveness has been traded perhaps for a roader acceptability. An Eylenbosch speciality has been e **Festival Supergueuze★★★**, which has more than three ears' maturation before being bottled, according to the rewery which is at Schepdaal, in Payottenland.

Girardin

good, traditional *lambic* brewery in Payottenland at St lrik's Kapelle. Girardin produces big-bodied, fruity and ther bitter beers. Its **Lambic Girardin★★★** is a well-garded example of the basic style.

Haacht

eyond its everyday beers (usually on the malty side) and a leasant Belgian ale called **Aerts 1900★★** this brewery, in oortmeerbeek, has made some effort to promote a **Gilden-er★★★**. This is an unusual, Belgian style of top-fermenting ark brown beer that is notable for its rich sweetness. It may ave limited application – as a restorative, perhaps – but is a art of tradition. This example has a hint of iron in the nose d licorice tones in the finish. The style was originally local Diest, not far away on the northeast border of Brabant. evivalist examples are also made by the brewery De Kluis d by Gouden Boom of Bruges.

Hoegaarden "White"

oegaarden is a village in the far east of Brabant that is mous for cloudy "white" wheat beers. There were once 30 reweries in the area producing beers in this style. The last osed in the mid 1950s and a decade later a revivalist brewer -started production on a small scale. This unlikely venture as proved to be both a critical and commercial success. The rewery is called De Kluis and the beer **Hoegaardse itte★★★**. It has a very old-fashioned specification: in ercentages, 45 wheat, 5 oats and 50 barley. The wheat and ats are raw, and only the barley is malted. This strange rew is also old-fashioned in that it is spiced, with coriander d curaçao, both of which were more commonly used before e universal adoption of the hop as a seasoning. A top-rmenting yeast is used and there is a further dosage in the ttle, with a priming of sugar. The nature of the grist and e use of a slowly flocculating yeast in the bottle help ensure e characteristic "white" cloudiness. The beer has a nventional gravity of 12 Plato, and emerges with an cohol content of 3.84 percent by weight; 4.8 by volume. As ages, it gains a refractive quality known as "double ine", and its fruity sourness gives way to a honeyish veetness. A similar beer, aromatic and pale but stronger 8.4 Plato. 6; 7.5) and made exclusively from barley malt, is lled **Grand Cru Hoegaarden★★★**.

Also in a similar style is a slightly darker beer, **Echte real") Peeterman★★★**. The darker hue comes from rrefied barley malt and it is a beer of conventional gravity. he name derives from the church of St Peter in nearby ouvain, a city that once had its own "white" beer adition. Another Peeterman, also from eastern Brabant, is ade by Verlinden of Lubbeek, and there is a sweet, cidery rsion in broadly the Louvain tradition from De Kroon of

Neerijse. This is called **Dubbel-Wit** and is, indeed, ver
cloudy. White beers in the Hoegaarden style are also made i
Flanders by Riva (whose Wittekop is exported to the US
and Gouden Boom (which calls its entrant, with civic prid
Brugs Tarwebier).

Meanwhile, the Hoegaarden brewery's taste for ex
perimentation is unquenchable. Another of its products
called **Forbidden Fruit. Verboden Vrucht**★★→★★★ (L
Fruit Defendu) is a claret-coloured, all-malt, strong ale o
19.5 Plato (6.4; 8), which combines a spicing of coriande
with a hefty helping of Challenger and Styrian aroma hop
The spicy, sweet fruitiness is very evident in the aroma, an
the earthy hoppiness in the palate. A very sexy strong ale, a
its label implies.

Lindemans

This classic Brabant farmhouse brewery in *lambic* country a
Vlezenbeek, Payottenland, seems an unlikely location fro
which to attack world markets. Nonetheless, its craftsman
made **Faro**★★★→★★★★, **Gueuze**★★→★★★, **Kriek**★★→★★
and **Framboise**★★★ are variously well-known in The Nethe
lands, France and the USA. In their whitewashed brewer
the Lindemans family have seen *lambic* beer, once writte
off as a "farmers' drink", capture the imagination of win
lovers. In so doing, their products have lost a little of the
sharpness and become a trifle sweeter, but they remai
authentic and interesting examples of their style.

Mort Subite

The name may mean "Sudden Death", but it derives simpl
from a dice game played at the famous Mort Subite cafe i
Brussels. Despite the Bruxellois joke "from beer to bier"
the Mort Subite brews are not especially lethal. On th
contrary, they have a conventionally modest alcohol con
tent. They are brewed by the De Keersmaeckers in Payo
tenland. The family have been brewers since the 18t
century and still have some cellars dating from then, thoug
their 1950s brewhouse is modern by *lambic* standards. The
beers, including a **Faro**★★, a **Gueuze**★★ and a **Kriek**★★, hav
in the past varied from being sharp to being on the blan
side. Recently there have been some rather sweet, "beery
bottlings.

Palm

Typically Belgian ales are produced by this medium-size
family brewery in the hamlet of Steenhuffel, to the nort
west of Brussels. In Belgium, a top-fermenting beer of n
regional style is often identified simply as a "special" t
distinguish it from a Pilsener. Hence **Spéciale Palm**★★, no
exported to the USA under the more precise name **Palm Al**
It has an original gravity of around 11.25 Plato and its yea
is a combination of three strains. Palm Ale has a brigh
amber colour; a light-to-medium body; a fruity, bitte
orange aroma and a tart finish.

Timmermans

Widely available *lambic* beers made by traditional method
at Itterbeek in Payottenland. Timmermans' **Lambic**★★→
★★★, **Gueuze**★★→★★★ and **Kriek**★★→★★★ are all fruity an
acidic but easily drinkable.

Vanderlinden

xcellent *lambic* beers, produced at Halle in Payottenland.
anderlinden's **Vieux Foudre Gueuze★★ →★★★** has a full
olour, a dense, soft, rocky head and a palate that is smooth
nd dry, with a "sour apple" tartness. **View Foudre
riek★★ →★★★** is lively, with lots of aroma, starting with
ints of sweetness and finishing with a dry bitterness. The
rewery also has a fruity **Framboise★★ →★★★**. Its house
peciality **Duivel★★★** is an odd combination of a *lambic* with
 conventional top-fermenting beer.

FRENCH-SPEAKING
BELGIUM

'erhaps it is the softness of the language: summer beers
alled *saisons*, winter-warmers like Cuvée de l'Ermitage and
himay Grand Reserve, aperitifs like Abbaye d'Orval. Or
laybe the rolling, wooded countryside, occasionally hiding
 brewery in its folds. The French-speaking south seems a
estful, contemplative place in which to drink. Just as there
re fewer people in the south, so the breweries and beer styles
re thinner on the ground, but they are rich in character.

Contemplative beer drinking (an aperitif here, a digestif
here) suits the pace. No gastronome would go to Belgium
ithout wishing to taste the hams, pâtés and game of the
rdennes – the sprawling forest that occupies much of the
outh, forming and straddling the borders with France,
uxembourg and Germany. This is country for touring
ather than tourism. The Ardennes are the dominant feature
f French-speaking Belgium, especially east of the river
Ieuse, and to the outsider they identify the region more
eadily than its official name, Wallonia.

When, as sometimes happens, a beer menu in Belgium
sts "Wallonian specialities" (in whichever language), it is
eferring to *saisons* and monastery beers from four prov-
ices. Among these, the province of Hainaut (with interest-
g industrial archaeology around the cities of Mons and
harleroi) has the most breweries, including the celebrated
ne at the abbey of Chimay. The province of Namur, named
fter its pleasant and historically interesting capital city,
as the Rochefort monastery brewery. The province of
iège, also named after its principal city, has the Jupiler
rewery, producing the biggest-selling Pilsener in Belgium.
his province also has the German-speaking pocket in which
he Eupener Brauerei produces an excellent Pilsener and a
tronger, amber Kapuciener Klosterbrau. The Belgian
rovince of Luxembourg (which borders on the sovereign
tate of the same name) has the Orval monastery brewery.

Where to drink

lmost every town in Belgium has at least one specialist beer
afe, and there are many in the French-speaking provinces.
ood examples include: in Mons, Le Bureau, on Grand Rue,
nd La Podo, in Marché aux Herbes; between Brussels and
harleroi, at Nivelles, Le Pado; near Namur, at Jambes,
scapade, and – a little further away – Le Relais de la
Ieuse, at Lustin; between Namur and Liège, at Huy,
'avern Big Ben; in Liège, Le Cirque d'Hiver and Le Pot au
ait; south of Liège, in the direction of the Ardennes, Le
'audrée, at Angleur.

Bush Beer

This distinctive and extra-strong brew takes its name from that of the family Dubuisson (*buisson* means "bush") by whom it is made, in the village of Pipaix near Tournai in the province of Hainaut. Retaining the botanical theme, the family re-named the beer Scaldis, after a local flower, for the American market, to avoid conflict with the US brewer Busch. Under either name, **Bush Beer/Scaldis★★★** might be more accurately described as an ale. It has a copper colour, a gravity of 9.5 Belgian degrees (24 Plato; 1095) and an alcohol content of 7.34 percent by weight; 9.4 by volume. Produced with a top-fermenting yeast matured for three months, dry-hopped and filtered but not pasteurized, it emerges with a chewy, malty, perhaps nutty, palate and with a hoppy dryness in the finish.

Chimay Trappist Monastery

The best-known and biggest monastery brewery in Belgium. Its long-serving brewmaster, Father Théodore, is a greatly respected figure in the industry, and Chimay's products have been a model for many others. They are, in the monastic tradition, top-fermenting strong ales, conditioned in the bottle. Within this tradition, the Chimay beers have a house character that is fruity, both in the intense aroma and the palate. Beyond that, each has its own features. Each is distinguished by its own colour of crown cork (*capsule*). The basic beer, **Chimay Red★★★**, has a gravity of 6.2 Belgian degrees, 15.5 Plato, 1063, with 5.5 percent alcohol by weight; 7 by volume. It has a full, copper colour, a notably soft palate and a hint of blackcurrant. The quite different **Chimay White★★★** has a gravity of 7 Belgian; 17.35 Plato (1071) and an alcohol content of 6.3; 8. It has a firm, dry body, slender for its gravity, with plenty of hop character in the finish and a quenching hint of acidity. This noble beer is very highly regarded by the brewery, but it does not have the most typically Chimay character. A return to type is represented by the **Chimay Blue★★★★**, which has a gravity of 8; 19.62 (1081) and an alcohol content of 7.1; 9. This has, again, that characteristically Chimay depth of aromatic fruitiness – a Zinfandel, or even a port, among beers. Chimay Blue is vintage-dated on the crown cork. If it is kept in a dark, cool place (ideally 19°C (65°F), but definitely not refrigerated), it will become markedly smoother after a year and sometimes continues to improve for two or three, drying slightly as it progresses. After five years, it could lose a little character, but some samples have flourished for a quarter of a century. A version of Chimay Blue in a corked 75 cl bottle is called **Grande Reserve**. The larger bottle size and different method of sealing seem to mature the beer in a softer manner. With different surface areas and air space, a slightly larger yeast presence and the very slight porosity of cork this is not fanciful.

The full name of the abbey is Notre Dame de Scourmont, after the hill on which it stands near the hamlet of Forges, close to the small town of Chimay in the province of Hainaut. The monastery was founded in 1850, during the post-Napoleonic restoration of abbey life. The monks began to brew not long afterward, in 1861–62. They were the first monks in Belgium to sell their brew commercially, introduced the designation "Trappist Beer" and in the period after World War II perfected the style. The monastery was damaged in the war and has been extensively restored, but in traditional style. It has a classic copper brewhouse and very modern fermentation halls.

The monastery also makes a cheese, called Chimay, of the Port Salut type. A restaurant not far from the monastery sells both beer and cheese. In the area, a favourite local dish is the spiced trout escavèche derived from the tastes and cooking techniques of occupying forces during the period of the Spanish Netherlands. There are also several local recipes featuring Chimay beers.

Cuvée de l'Ermitage

Hermitages were the first homes of monks in the western world and there were many in the forests of Hainaut in the early Middle Ages, but no one is certain which of two sites gave their name to this brew. It is certainly worthy of being enjoyed in a reflective moment, though not necessarily to the ascetic taste. **Cuvee de l'Ermitage★★★** is a very dark and strong all-malt brew of 18.7 Plato, with an alcohol content of 6 percent by weight; 7.5 by volume. It is produced from three malts and heavily hopped with an interesting combination of Kent Goldings and Hallertaus (both for bitterness) and Northern Brewer and Saaz (both for aroma). It has a distinctively creamy bouquet, a smooth start, with hints of sweetness, then a surprising dryness in the finish – almost the sappiness of an Armagnac. **Cuvée** is the local speciality of the old Union brewery at Jumet, on the edge of Charleroi. The brewery produces a range of top-fermenting beers for its parents, Maes and Watney.

Jupiler

The biggest-selling Pilsener beer in Belgium takes its name from Jupille, near Liège, where it is produced by a brewery that for many years rejoiced in the odd name Piedboeuf. In recent years, the company itself has become known as Jupiler. Although it has lost some of its hoppiness, **Jupiler★** remains dry and soft and is a pleasant enough mass-market beer. The company has recently acquired Lamot and Krüger.

Orval Trappist Monastery

There is a purity of conception about both the brewery and the monastery of Orval. The brewery provides its own distinctive interpretation of the monastic style and offers just one beer: **Orval★★★★**. This brew gains its unusual orangey colour from the use of three malts produced to its own specification, plus white candy sugar in the kettle; its aromatic, aperitif bitterness derives from the use of Hallertau and (more especially) Kent Goldings, not only in the kettle but also in dry-hopping; its characterful acidity comes from its own single-cell yeast in its primary and secondary fermentations and a blend of four or five bottom cultures in a slow bottle-conditioning. As to which of these procedures is most important in imparting the gout d'Orval, there may be some debate. The triple fermentation process is certainly important, but the dry-hopping is perhaps the critical factor. The beer has an original gravity of 13.5–14 Plato (1055+) and emerges with an alcohol content of more than 4.5 percent by weight, around 6 by volume. Its secondary fermentation lasts for five to seven weeks, at a relatively warm temperature of around 15°C (60°F). Its bottle-conditioning, regarded by the brewery as a third fermentation, lasts for two months, again at warm temperatures. The beer should be kept in a dark place, ideally at a natural cellar temperature. If it was bought in a shop, give the beer a few days to recover its equilibrium and pour gently. It should improve for about a year and, although its character may then diminish, it could keep for five years.

This is a short period in the life of an abbey that was founded in 1070 by Benedictines from Calabria, rebuilt in the 12th century by early Cistercians from Champagne and sacked in several conflicts along the way, in the 17th century leaving most of the ruins that stand today. From the 18th century, there are records of brewing having taken place in the restored abbey, which was then sacked in the French Revolution. The present monastery, with its dramatic, dream-like purity of line, subsumes Romanesque-Burgundian influences in a design of the late 1920s and 1930s. The monastery makes its beer, crusty brown bread and two cheeses, of the Port Salut and (in a somewhat distance interpretation) Cheddar types, and sells them to tourists in its gift shop.

Meanwhile, in its corner of the province of Luxembourg, not far from the small town of Florenville, the "valley of gold" dreams. Legend says that Countess Mathilda of Tuscany lost a gold ring in the lake in the valley. When a fish recovered the ring for her, Mathilda was so grateful that she gave the land to God for the foundation of the monastery. The fish with the golden ring is now the emblem of Orval and its beer.

No other beer can be said to match the character of Orval, but there are secular products in a broadly similar style. An example from this part of Belgium is the beer of the new micro-brewery at Montignies sur Roc. From Flanders, there is Augustijn, produced by the Van Steenbergen brewery.

Rochefort Trappist Monastery

A low profile is perhaps appropriate to a Trappist monastery and it cannot be said that Rochefort, in the province of Namur, has any clear image. The first impression created by its beers is that they are classic examples of the Trappist style and certainly very well made. If they have a house characteristic, it is a subtle chocolate tone. **Rochefort★★★** has beers at 6, 8 and 10 Belgian degrees.

Saison Régal

This is the most widely available *saison* beer, from the Du Bocq brewery of Purnode in the province of Namur and Marbaix in Hainault. **Saison Régal★★** is neither the strongest nor the most efflorescent example of the style, but it is a useful introduction. It has a gravity of around 13 Plato (1052) and around 4.5 percent alcohol by weight; 5.6 by volume. It is produced with a mash of more than 90 percent malt, pale and crystal, has a Kent Goldings accent in the hopping (with also Hallertau and Saaz) and spends a month stabilizing in closed tanks. The beer has a full, amber colour, a surprisingly light but firm body, and a teasing balance between aromatic hoppiness and fruitiness. The brewery so produces a characterful strong ale, **Gauloise**★★ → ★★★. This has nothing to do with the well-known brand of cigarette.) The beer celebrates those most brave of Gauls, the early Belgians. Gauloise is available 6 and 8 degrees Belgian gravity, producing slightly higher figures for alcohol by volume. Du Bocq produces a great many other products, in some instances marketing the same beer under more than one name. It is a colourful old brewery, but this practice of "label-brewing" does not win friends in Belgium.

Saison Silly

"Saison" is emphasized in English-speaking markets to prevent this name from sounding too silly. In fact, Silly is the name of the village in Hainaut where the beer is made. In Belgium, **Saison Silly**★★ → ★★★ has a gravity 13.75 Plato, a firm body, a hint of intentional, quenching sourness in the palate and a sweeter, soft finish. The *saison* sold in the US is **Speciale Enghien**★★★, which has a higher gravity, at around 16 Plato, with a softer, rounder palate, quenchingly acidic but notably clean in its long finish. A companion of 15 Plato is called **Doublette Enghien**★★ → ★★★. Beers in this *saison* style usually have a big, rocky head; good lacework; a full, amber colour; a firm but sometimes quite thin body and a delicate balance between sour acidity and sweet fruitiness; with a soft, clean finish. They are usually bottle-conditioned and often dry-hopped. Other examples include *saisons* Dupont, Pipaix, Roland and Voisin. These artisanal *saisons* come in corked wine bottles and are something of a speciality of the western part of Hainaut.

There are beers that are not described as *saisons* but are similar in style. These include the Allard and Groetembril range from Hainaut and La Chouffe from a new micro-brewery in the province of Liège.

THE GRAND DUCHY OF LUXEMBOURG

Although it shares its name with a province of Belgium, and has economic ties with that country, the Grand Duchy of Luxembourg is a sovereign state. In the matter of beer, the Grand Duchy leans in the opposite direction, towards Germany. It even claims that its Purity Law is similar to that of Germany, though it does, in fact, permit adjuncts. The typical product range of a Luxembourgeoise brewery includes a relatively mild Pilsener; a slightly more potent brew, perhaps in the Export style; and a bottom-fermenting strong beer, sometimes seasonal.

Luxembourg has five brewing companies, each with just one plant. The biggest, just, is Diekirch, which has a fairly full-bodied, clean-tasting, all-malt **Pils**★★, with a good hop aroma. There have also been occasional sightings of a stronger (4.9 by weight; 6.1 by volume) pale, bottom-fermenting beer called **Premium**★★ from Diekirch.

The second largest brewery (in which Artois, of Belgium, has a small stake) is Mousel and Clausen, with the Royal-münster brand. Then comes Brasserie Nationale, of Bascharage, with the Bofferding and Funck-Bricher labels. The small Simon brewery, of Wiltz, produces some excellent beers. So does the tiniest of them all, Battin, of Esch, with its Gambrinus label.

FRANCE

As well as making the world's most comple
wines, France has a beer tradition stretchin
from the beginnings of brewing. It is mos
evident in the north: the Flemish corner of Franc
specializes in top-fermented beers; Alsace an
Lorraine in bottom-fermented brews. A link has eve
been forged with Britain, with the opening of a Breto
ale brewery, Brasserie de Deux Rivières, in Morlai

Between Valenciennes and the Belgian border,
Crespin, there was once a monastery that is remem
bered in a tart, fruity, bottle-conditioned, abbey
style beer, **Réserve St Landelin★★★**, from the loc
Rimaux brewery. Just south of Valenciennes, Duyc
produces **Jenlain★★★ →★★★★**, a classic *Bière de Gard*
with a deep, amber colour, fruity nose and hints
licorice in its long finish. In the tradition of this styl
it is a top-fermenting, all-malt, 16 Plato (106
5.2; 6.5), not pasteurized, although it is filtere
(ideally, it should not be – the original idea of a *Biè
de Garde* was that it could be laid down).

The area between Valenciennes, Lille and Boulog
is the heartland of this style. Good examples inclu
the bottle-conditioned **La Choulette★★★**, counter-poi
ting a citric fruitiness with a hoppy dryness; t
beautifully balanced **Réserve du Brasseur★★ →★★★**; t
lively, soft, **La Cave des Pères★★ →★★★**; the malty **Peti
Suisse★★ →★★★**; the perfumy, strong **Septante 5★★ →★★**
and the profoundly fruity **Ch'ti★★ →★★★**, whi
appears in dark and pale versions. Outside Franc
the easiest to find are the relatively hoppy
Léonard★★ →★★★ and the malty **Lutèce★★**, from Pari

The Lille area also has the world's strongest pa
(truly golden) lager, **La Bière du Démon★★★** (21.7; 9
12). For its weight, this beer is surprisingly dry, b
with honeyish tones. It is brewed by Enfants
Gayant, who also own the Boxer brewery in Sw
zerland. George Killian's **"Irish Red"★★ →★★★** is brew
by Pelforth of Lille (16.8; 1067; 5.3; 6.6) in a mal
full-bodied interpretation that also characterizes t
brewery's darker **Brune★★**. Both are top-fermentin
Pelforth and Union de Brasseries (whose bran
include **"33"** and **Mützig**) are part-owned by Heineke

A yet more unusual speciality, **Adelscott★★★** (16
1065; 5.2; 6.5) is produced with whisky malt, which
this case imparts a very light smokiness. It is brew
by Fischer/Pêcheur, a major independent based
Alsace. This region is also the base of Kronenbou
the biggest brewer in France. Its beers are genera
fruity and slightly sticky. The premium product is t
relatively dry **1664★ →★★**.

E ngland, Wales and Scotland are the only nations in which the principal brewing tradition is
to produce ales. Ireland is the only nation in
which the principal tradition is to produce stouts.

These island nations were at the peak of imperial
arrogance when the rest of the world started to
abandon such top-fermenting brews in favour of
bottom-fermenting lagers, in the mid and late 19th
century. Imperial power may be a mixed blessing, but
here is something to be said for national pride.

Even to the British, their ales and stouts present a
taste which has first to be acquired. The writer
Graham Greene, whose own family have a renowned
brewery, recalls in his book *A Sort of Life* that he
"hated" his first pint but that when he tried a second,
he "enjoyed the taste with a pleasure that has never
failed me since". The delights afforded by the classic
draught ales of the British Isles might be compared to

the pleasures offered by the red wines of Bordeaux. Both have subtlety of colour; a fresh fruitiness; dashes of sweetness and counter-strokes of dryness; and sometimes a hint of oak. The dry stouts of Ireland have the qualities ascribed by Hugh Johnson in his *World Atlas of Wine* to true Amontillado sherries: "Dry and almost stingingly powerful of flavour, with a dark, fat, rich tang".

In Britain, the seeker after "real" ales will look out for the designation "cask-conditioned" at the point of sale, and for hand-pulled pumps, the most common (though not only) form of dispense. A British ale served as cask-conditioned draught is like a Bordeaux wine bottled at the château.

In 1986, Britain's "Big Six" brewing companies (Bass, Allied, Whitbread, Watney, Courage, Scottish and Newcastle) had 39 breweries; the old-established independents had 81; new boutiques, all established within the previous decade, had 91; and there were 7 brewpubs, most of them equally new. Among these, 278 out of 287 produced cask-conditioned ales.

Where to drink

Of Britain's 70,000 pubs, half serve the cask-conditioned product. Among those, the 5,000 chosen each year for the *Good Beer Guide* are the ale-lovers' favourites. This invaluable guide is published by the Campaign for Real Ale (34 Alma Road, St Albans, Herts AL1 3BW), and available from WH Smith and other bookstore chains. Not every visitor to Britain has time to visit all 5,000 although it is praiseworthy to try. Most visitors land in London, where there are some good "real ale" pubs, but where out-of-town brews can be expensive and badly kept (to be fair, most don't travel well).

A much more satisfying experience will be obtained if the drinker does the travelling, whether for a long weekend or for a browse of two or three weeks around the British Isles. Below, the ale territories are viewed anti-clockwise from London. Since Britain has not only a great many pubs but also a huge range of ales, only those of special interest or reputation (and not all of those) can be detailed, and scores are accordingly high. The ★ and ★ → ★★ ales generally did not make the list.

LONDON AND THE SOUTH

The capital has two classic breweries, Young's and Fuller's. In Central London, Young's is well served at the Lamb (94 Lamb's Conduit St, Bloomsbury); Fuller's at the Star Tavern (6 Belgrave Mews West, Belgravia). The breweries are both on the west side of town, in Wandsworth and Chiswick respectively, whence their pubs generally fan outward toward pretty London "villages" like Richmond. Lamb's Conduit St also has the Sun, famous for its wide range of out-of-town ales. Not far away (at 208 High Holborn) is another such specialist pub, the Princess Louise. Another, near Waterloo Station, is the Hole in the Wall.

epham St), with ales from one of the longer-established ondon boutiques, Godson-Chudley. The Beer Shop (8 tfield St, near Old St Underground station) has a wide lection of bottled products, and has its own boutique ours: ☎739 3701). London has many brewpubs. None ands out for its beers, but the Firkin chain is famous for ving popularized the idea. A good example is the Frog and rkin (41 Tavistock Crescent, Westbourne Park Underound, near Portobello Road market).

here to drink: long weekends

est to Oxford along the Thames Valley, where every ewery offers good, country ales. Go via Marlow (Wethed's ales, a Whitbread subsidiary, try the Royal Oak); enley (Brakspear's: Three Tuns); Abingdon (Morland's: e Ox Inn or the riverside Old Anchor); and Oxford Iorrell's: lots of good pubs; try the King's Arms, 40 olywell St). Return via the B474 to visit the Royal andard of England (Marston's Owd Roger) at Forty reen, near Beaconsfield.

South to Brighton. Via Horsham (King and Barnes: the out House) or Lewes (lovely, buttery-malty ales from arvey's/Beard's: the Brewer's Arms); and Brighton (the aven boutique brewery has its ales at the Coachmaker's rms, 76 Trafalgar St; Alexandra Becket's at the Queen's ead, 69 Queen's Road).

East to Canterbury, via Maidstone (Goacher's: the Pilot, 3 pper Stone St) and Faversham (Shepherd Neame at the n; Fremlin's, a Whitbread subsidiary, at the Phoenix). anterbury Brewery's ales can be found in its home town at e Millers Arms in Mill Lane.

rakspear

mong a remarkably good crop of breweries in the Thames alley, Brakspear, at Henley, is outstanding. Its "ordinary" tter★★★★ (1035), hoppy from its nose to its lingering ish, is the classic example of this English style.

uller

rsistent award-winner. Beautifully balanced ales, with ppiness being countered by fruitiness as gravities ascend. elightful "ordinary", Chiswick Bitter★★ (1035+); comex "special", London Pride★★ → ★★★ (1041+); renowned xtra Special Bitter★★★★ (1055+). The bottled Golden ide★★★ → ★★★★ (1084–92) has the colour, smoothness and arming finish of a cognac. The brewery is on the way into ndon from Heathrow

iale

ne corked and bottle-conditioned Prize Old Ale★★★ → ★★★ (1092–98) has such a dry fruitiness, and alcoholic armth, as to be reminiscent of a Calvados. This dry uitiness characterizes the range. The brewery is about 60 iles (96 km) from London, on the edge of Portsmouth.

ing and Barnes

untry brewery specializing in "real" ale. Malt, hop and uitiness beautifully balanced in ales like Festive★★ (1050). ie brewery, at Horsham, Sussex, is an interesting blend of adition and modern technology.

Shepherd Neame

The Queen Court vineyard, growing a prize-winning Mülle[r]
Thurgau, is owned by this brewery. Since the location o[f]
both, the country town of Faversham, is in the 'Grand[e]
Champagne' of the English hop, it seems a shame tha[t]
Shep's no longer grow their own East Kent Goldings. After [a]
period of flirtation with other hops, the brewery is, howeve[r,]
now re-emphasizing this wonderfully aromatic local variet[y.]
The hop bitterness comes through most strongly in th[e]
"ordinary" **Masterbrew Bitter**★★★ → ★★★★ (1036). **She[p-]
herd Neame Stock Ale**★★★ (1037) is dark and dry, with a l[ot]
of character for its gravity. **Invicta**★★ (1044) is a "best["]
bitter with a nice balance of hop and malt.

Watney

Bête rouge of the "real ale" movement, though past sin[s]
should by now be forgiven. Perhaps because of the hous[e]
yeast, its London cask ales are not as characterful a[s]
devotees would wish. Albeit a minor category, **Mann['s]
Brown Ale**★★★ (1034−5) is a classic example of the souther[n]
style. **Stingo**★★★ (1076) is a dark barley wine in a distinctive[-]
ly dry interpretation, with a touch of burnt stoutines[s.]
Watney's affiliate Truman produces more assertive ales.

Whitbread

A well-ordered portfolio of 30 or 40 products (each with it[s]
own specification) includes about 15 middling-to-goo[d]
"real" ales from local subsidiaries (the company has eigh[t]
breweries). National bottled products include the definitiv[e]
sweet or "milk" stout (both brewed and primed wit[h]
lactose), **Mackeson**★★★★ (1038−42 in Britain; higher in th[e]
Americas). Surprisingly, this brew is not filtered, just fined[.]
The brewing world's answer to Bailey's Irish Cream per[-]
haps? Whitbread also has **Gold Label**★★★ → ★★★★ (1098; [8]
percent alcohol by weight; 10 by volume), a classic pal[e]
barley wine, which spends three hours in the brew-kettle[,]
has its own yeast and in the bottled (but not canned) form i[s]
unpasteurized. Strong and warming, but mellow. Th[e]
brewing world's answer to whisky?

Young

Fiercely independent London brewery serving real ale in a[ll]
of its pubs. Its "ordinary" **Bitter**★★ → ★★★ (1036), soft an[d]
complex, is still a classic, despite being less assertively dr[y]
than it once was. Its **Special**★★★ → ★★★★ (1046) is beautifull[y]
balanced, with a malty finish. Its bottled **Ramrod**★★ (104[6]
has a smooth bitterness and an interesting balance o[f]
maltiness and strength. **Young's Export Special Londo[n]
Ale**★★★ (1062−3) has, when it is fresh, a massive bouquet o[f]
floral East Kent Goldings. **Old Nick**★★★ → ★★★★ (1084) is [a]
classic dark barley wine, warming, with some liqueuris[h]
fruitiness (a hint of banana?) in the finish.

EASTERN ENGLAND

From London, a round-trip east for two or three days wi[ll]
reveal some intensely traditional ales and interestingly rur[al]
(if often flat) countryside. The first stop would be one of th[e]
villages near Chelmsford, where Ridley's brewery sells it[s]
very hoppy, dry beers, often from wooden casks.

Further down the road, Ipswich has pleasantly hoppy ales from Tolly Cobbold. Beyond Ipswich, the road heads for the main destination, the pretty little harbour town of South-wold, the home of Adnams brewery.

Further north in Norwich, the boutique brewery Wood-forde has its very hoppy ales at the Plasterers' Arms, in Cowgate, and the Rosary Tavern, in Rosary Road. From Norwich, the road runs through The Fens to Wisbech, where Elgood's fruity **Bitter**★ → ★★ is brewed. Further west lies Oakham, home of the famous Ruddle's brewery, which has no pubs of its own. Ruddle's ale can be found in Peter-borough, at the Still, in Cumbergate. South of Peter-borough, Paine's makes very fruity, strawberry-ish ales at St Neots, on the way to Cambridge.

From Cambridge, the route presents a tough problem: to the east lies Bury St Edmunds, with the classic Greene King brewery; to the west is Bedford, home of Charles Wells. Whichever the way home, pass through Hertford, home of McMullen's, noted for its lightly dry **A.K. Mild**★★ → ★★★.

Adnams

Noted wine merchants as well as brewers. It seemed like a scotch whisky allusion, too, when British beer-writer Roger Protz observed that he found a salty, tangy, "seaweedy" character in Adnams' tawny ales. Perhaps this is merely suggested by the maritime location but there does, indeed, seem to be a salty dryness along with the firm body and derby hop character. The **Mild**★★ (1034), **Bitter**★★ (1036) and **Extra**★★★ (1044) are all distinctive and very complex.

Greene King

Graham Greene, as a celebration of his 80th birthday, mashed a special "edition" of the family brewery's **St Edmund Ale**★★★ (1056–62). This pale strong ale has a surprising crispness in its malty palate. The brewery is better known for its fruity draught ales, especially **Abbot**★★★. Greene King also owns Rayment.

Ruddles

Regards itself as an ale specialist. The characteristically fresh fruitiness of English ales is more evident in Ruddle's draught products than their bottled counterparts, though the latter are still enjoyable. The **Bitter**★★ → ★★★, with lots of Fuggles character but a gravity of only 1032, shows just how much palate can be found in a very light English ale. There is a greater Goldings character in the persistently award-winning **County**★★★ (1050).

Wells

Home of the full-bodied **Bombardier Ale**★★ (1042), a "special" bitter with a creamy texture and a dry maltiness, well-liked in Britain and a sought-after export.

YORKSHIRE
AND THE NORTHEAST

Instead of being happy to be England's biggest county, Yorkshire has always felt itself to be a nation in its own right, steadfastly preserving its customs. Even today, its brewing tradition of using double-deck fermentation vessels leaves it with a family of yeasts that are as headstrong as a Yorkshireman. Perhaps that is why the character of its ales has been better sustained than that of the brews from the counties further north, clustered around the city of Newcastle.

An ale tour might follow the Pennine hills and dales, whose villages are always within easy reach of the big industrial cities. In South Yorkshire, the city of Sheffield has a brewpub, the Frog and Parrot (Division St ☎0742-21280), which has in recent years brewed a winter (October and November) dark ale, aiming for a world-record gravity of 1125 and a commensurate alcohol content. Although the record has not yet been ratified, **Roger and Out**★★★ → ★★★★ is immensely potent yet soft and smooth. Sheffield has two breweries owned by Bass, one producing the tasty **Stone's Best Bitter**★ → ★★. It also has a Whitbread brewery, producing **Trophy Bitter**★. Yet a third sizable brewery, owned by Vaux, produces the under-rated Ward's ales. In the nose, they seem malty, but there is a dense interplay of hop and yeast in a full flavour and texture that is typically Yorkshire. Vaux also has malt-accented ales from the Darley brewery, not far away in Doncaster.

In West Yorkshire, Wakefield has a boutique called Clark's, with an adjoining pub, the Henry Boon, in Westgate, selling its flowery **Bitter**★★ (1038). Halifax has a Watney subsidiary, Webster, making dry ales with a pleasantly oily texture. Keighley, near Bradford, has a classic brewery, Timothy Taylor's. Leeds has another classic, Tetley's. In East Yorkshire, a boutique called Old Mill has a herby, hoppy **Traditional Bitter**★★ (1037).

In North Yorkshire, the village of Tadcaster became for reasons of its water an important brewing centre. It has the classic Sam Smith's; former family rival (now part of the Courage group) John Smith's, producing a pleasantly drinkable **Bitter**★ → ★★ with some Yorkshire character; and a Bass brewery with several local ales. North Yorkshire has not far from Ripon, in the village of Masham, the classic Theakston brewery, owned by Matthew Brown.

Further north, there are lovely, nutty ales from Cameron's in Hartlepool. Nearby, a Whitbread brewery produces sweetish ales at Castle Eden.

Vaux has its principal brewery at Sunderland. Its **Samson** ★ → ★★ is a hoppy, fruity "best" Bitter. Its range also includes **Double Maxim**★★★ → ★★★★, a brown ale in the higher-gravity style (around 1045) regional to the Northeast; not so much brown as amber red, with a full, crystal-malt character, its sweetness steadied with an underlying hint of dry roastiness. Its neighbour and more famous rival **Newcastle Brown Ale**★★★ (1045) is less malty. Newcastle Breweries' other products include a hoppy cask ale called **Exhibition**★ → ★★. In something of a revival of the city's tradition, Newcastle now has a boutique, called Big Lamp, and producing an intensely hoppy-tasting **Bitter**★★.

Samuel Smith

Classic exponent of the Yorkshire brewing system, fermenting in "stone" (actually, slate), double-deck vessels, which make for a circulation of the yeast. The character developed by the yeast in this system produces brews with a very full texture. "Sam's" products do have their own roundness. They are often thought to be malty, but they also have a great deal of interwoven hop character. While British drinkers seek them out as cask-conditioned draught (always from the wood), export markets have to make do with bottled products. Britain's "Strong" (1048) **Pale Ale**★★★ has become chic in the US. So, at the same gravity, have Britain's **Strong Brown**★★★, known in the US as Nut Brown (it is, indeed, nutty-tasting) and the delightfully named **Nourishing Strong Stout**★★★ (again, 1048), confusingly offered to Americans as Porter (it is arguably dry enough, but surely too full-bodied for that designation?). If the British have a serious complaint it is that they cannot buy the silky **Oatmeal Stout**★★★→★★★★ (1048) or a new **Imperial Stout**★★★→★★★★ (1072), immensely rich, with a flavour of slightly burnt currants on a cake.

Tetley

Classically creamy Yorkshire ale, **Tetley Bitter**★★★ (1035.5), comes from this independently minded outpost of Allied Breweries.

Theakston

Never mind the spelling, **Old Peculier**★★★ (1058–60) is a strong dark ale with a sweet richness that is positively embracing in the cask-conditioned draught. In bottled form, it is as satisfying as a chaste kiss. If it is chilled, so is the kiss.

Timothy Taylor

A splendidly Yorkshire-sounding brewery, in the land of the Brontës (or, if you prefer it, Rugby League). A quirky but wide, and excellent, range includes a hoppy "best", **Landlord**★★→★★★ (1042) and the beautifully balanced, dark **Ram Tam**★★ (1043).

SCOTLAND

A cold country that specializes in rich, warming ales. Scotland, and especially Edinburgh, were once known throughout the world of brewing for their strong ales. The quality and diversity of these products was pummelled by brewery takeovers in the 1960s, and the dust has yet to settle, despite the arrival of one or two boutiques.

Among the British giants, Bass has two Scottish breweries, mainly concerned with the better-than-average Tennent's lagers. They also have one or two cask ales, and a pleasant strong brew called **Fowler's Wee Heavy**★★ (1067–73). Allied brews Skol in the brewing town of Alloa, and has a cask ale called **Archibald Arrol's 70/-**★★ (1037), with a typically Scottish maltiness in the entrance but a surprising hop acidity in the finish. Wathey owns Dryborough, whose dark, malty **Eighty**★★ (1042) has a good Scots accent. The nation's own giant, Scottish and Newcastle, produces a variety of products under the McEwan and Younger labels. Vaux has the excellent Lorimer and Clark brewery. Belhaven and Maclay are the only old-established independents, both cherished.

Good ranges of Scottish ales can be found in Edinburgh at the Guildford Arms (West Register St, in the city centre) and the Starbank Inn (on the waterside at Newhaven); and in Glasgow at the Bon Accord (153 North St) and the Victoria Bar (159 Bridgegate).

Alice

Boutique in the Highland capital of Inverness. Principal product is the intensely fruity and dry **Alice Ale★** (1040).

Argyle

Boutique in Edinburgh, brewing a full-bodied, dark, Scottish-accented ale, **Argyle 80/-★★**.

Belhaven

With monastic beginnings and a site in a harbour village at Dunbar (between Edinburgh and the border), Belhaven has romance enough. It probably still has the finest ales in Scotland, too, although its performance has experienced the upheavals of takeovers and modernizations. Its **70/- Heavy★★→★★★** (1035–6) is a beautifully balanced beer; its maltier **80/- Export★★★→★★★★** (1041–2) is perhaps the classic Scottish draught ale.

A bottled version of the Export is gaining popularity in the US as Belhaven Scottish Ale.

Borve House

Brewpub/boutique on the remote Outer Hebridean island of Lewis. Britain's most northerly brewery produces the delightful **Borve Ale Extra Strong★★→★★★** (1085), with a smoky aroma, a full palate and a long, intense finish.

Devanha

Aberdeen boutique producing a sweetly fruity **80/- Pale★** (1042).

Greenmantle

An interesting balance of malt and hop in **Greenmantle Ale★★** (1038). Boutique at Broughton, near Biggar, Lanarkshire, in the south of Scotland.

Lorimer and Clark

Old-established small brewery in Edinburgh, especially noted for its strong Scottish ale (1080; 5.7; 7.1), available on draught in its home country as **Caledonian★★★→★★★★**, and also marketed in the US as MacAndrew's.

Maclay

The lesser-known of Scotland's old independents, probably because its ales can be hard to find outside its home town of Alloa. Rarity value aside, there is a school of drinkers that favours Maclay's as the best ales in Scotland. They are, though, a tad too hoppy to be regarded as classically Scottish. Perhaps the national taste is most evident in the **60/- Light★★★** (1030).

McEwan/Younger

In Scotland, the ale known as **80/- or IPA★★** (1042) is enjoyed for its fullness of flavour. In England, the richer and darker **Younger's No 3★★** (1043) has a small cult following. In Belgium and the US, another dark brew, **McEwan's Scotch Ale★★★** (1088), packs a more obvious punch.

Strathalbyn

Boutique at Dalmuir, near Glasgow. Its **Strathalbyn II★ →★★★** (1043) is a rich, malty-fruity Scottish ale.

Traquair

manor house (perhaps even a castle?) in which Bonnie
Prince Charlie once took refuge. Like any other large
residence, it had its own brewery, enterprisingly put back
into operation by the present Laird in 1965. The castle can
be visited (☎0896-830323). Its principal product, **Traquair
House Ale**★★★★ (1073–1080), is the classic example of a
dark Scottish ale, rich and full without being excessively
sweet: not unlike a good port.

THE NORTHWEST

South of the Scottish border, the Lake District and Lanca-
shire are dotted with breweries all the way to Manchester,
which has a cluster of its own. The trouble with breweries in
the Northwest is that they keep buying each other.

It is to be hoped that independence can be preserved by
the region's classic country brewery, Jennings, of Cocker-
mouth, Cumbria – a "real ale" specialist, producing a wonderfully hoppy **Bitter**★★ → ★★★ (1035), with a hint of fruity
sourness in the nose and a tingle at the back of the tongue.

Elsewhere in the county, Carlisle has a Theakston
brewery, but that company belongs to the Blackburn firm of
Matthew Brown (which has itself been the subject of
takeover attentions from Scottish and Newcastle). The old
Cumbrian Brewers, of Workington, also belongs to Matthew
Brown, whose own ales are pleasant but unexceptional. In
Ulverston, Hartley's is known for its beautifully balanced
"best" Bitter, **XB**★★ → ★★★ (1040), but the brewery is now
owned by Robinson's, of Stockport. Lancaster lost a
brewery in 1985 after a takeover by another Blackburn
company, Thwaites (itself well-known for a malty but dryish
Best Mild★★, at 1034). Lancaster's survivor, Mitchell's,
produces pleasantly smooth ales. The Manchester company Boddingtons owns the nearby Oldham Brewery and
Higson's, of Liverpool.

Despite all of this activity, there remains a remarkable
selection of ales. Greater Manchester has (apart from the
interestingly malty ales of Wilson, a subsidiary of Watney)
some very dry brews. These include those of Chester's, a
subsidiary of Whitbread, as well as several independents.
The once-revered pale **Bitter**★★ of Boddingtons has lost a
little of its character, but each of the smaller breweries has
its own partisans. **Robinson's Best Bitter**★★ → ★★★ (1042)
has lots of hop character in aroma as well as palate, and a big
body. This brewery also has a strong (1079) dark ale called
Old Tom★★★, surprisingly dry for its gravity, with a lot of
alcohol character in the finish. The small Lees brewery has a
similar product but of less personality, called **Moonraker**★★
→ ★★★ (1072). Holt's ales are extremely hoppy, and its
Bitter★★★ (1039) is a local classic. The smallest of the old-
established Manchester breweries is Hydes, easily over-
looked, it certainly should not be. Its ales are deceptively
drinkable, but with a great deal of character in the finish.

Between Manchester and Liverpool, the town of Warring-
ton has the independent Burtonwood brewery, producing
creamy-textured ales; a Tetley branch brewery; and the
acquisitive Greenall Whitley (making unexceptional ales
itself, and having taken over Wem, Davenport's and
Shipstone, among others).

BURTON AND THE MIDLANDS

The most famous brewing centre in Britain is Burton, a small and rather scruffy town between the West Midlands city of Birmingham and the East Midlands cities of Derby and Nottingham. Burton originally became a brewing centre because of the qualities of its water, and its renown grew when its brewers were the most active in the popularization of pale ales.

Burton Ale★★ →★★★ (1047.5) is a full-bodied premium Bitter, with the fruitiness that typifies the town's brews. It is produced by Allied's brewery in Burton. Another member of the Big Six, Bass, has a brewery — its original and most famous — in Burton. Within the premises is a museum of brewing (☎0283-45301). **Draught Bass★★★** (1044) is regarded among today's draught pale ales as being the original. Its distinctive fruitiness is slightly sour and its body gentle for the gravity, yet these negative-sounding features make for a unique character, irresistible to its admirers. The sedimented **Worthington White Shield★★★ →★★★★** (1052) is its bottled counterpart. The brewery has sought to retain the character of these two products, though the yeast is no longer bred and trained in the old circulatory system of linked wooden barrels, known as Burton Unions.

The Marston brewery does to some extent use Burton Unions, and its **Pedigree★★★★** (1043) is surely today the classic English draught pale ale (or "best" Bitter). It has the Burton fruitiness but also a balancing maltiness, the two blending into a nutty finish. Marston also has a soft, complex dark ale at the same gravity, **Merrie Monk★★ →★★★**, and a rich strong ale, **Owd Roger★★ →★★★** (1080).

The old Everards brewery in Burton is being restored as the Heritage Museum, and in that guise will continue to produce ale. The somewhat newer Burton Bridge boutique produces ales very much in the town's tradition. **Bridge Bitter★★ →★★★** (1042) has a big, plummy aroma and a fruitiness that carries right through to its soft finish.

Away from Burton, palates and styles change. In the West Midlands, both dark and pale milds are traditional and there is often little to distinguish the latter from the region's characteristically sweet "bitters". The area also has no fewer than three out of the four original brewpubs in Britain (that is to say, the old ones that had continued to operate before the new wave).

Not far from the Welsh border, in the Shropshire village of Bishop's Castle, is the Three Tuns (☎0588-638797), a pub with its own traditional tower brewery. Also in Shropshire, near the town of Telford, at Madeley, is Mrs Lewis's All Nations (☎0952-585747). Yet more urban is Ma Pardoe's Old Swan (☎0384-53075), at Netherton, near Dudley. This brewpub, nothing short of an institution, was recently threatened with demise, and saved with the help of CAMRA, The Campaign for Real Ale.

An eight-pub brewery may be small, but it has to be regarded as a free-standing independent. In nearby Brierley Hill, behind its Vine pub (locally known as the Bull and Bladder), is Batham's, a classic small Midlands brewery. Its **Bitter★★ →★★★** (1043) has a subtly balanced Midland maltiness in palate and body with a light hoppiness in the finish. Its local rival in Dudley is Holden's, not a great deal bigger, with a characteristically malty range.

The regional giant, Wolverhampton and Dudley Breweries, enjoys considerable success with its ales, and is noted for the medium-dark Hanson's and Banks' **Milds★★**. Davenport's dark **Mild★★** and soft **Bitter★★** have the light, sweetish maltiness that is so characteristic of the West Midlands, and it is to be hoped that this character will be retained after a recent takeover by Greenhall Whitley. Bass has a West Midlands brewery making only Mild. On these grounds, its fruity **Highgate Mild★★★** should surely be regarded as a classic (it has a gravity of 1036; most of its local rivals are just under, or around, this figure). Oddly, one of its favoured local rivals, Ansell's **Mild★★ →★★★** (with a coffeeish aroma and palate), is now brewed outside the area. Several of Ansell's former workers started the excellent Aston Manor boutique, in Birmingham.

In the East Midlands, the city of Leicester has a working beer museum at Hoskins (133 Beaumanor Rd, ☎0533-661122), which was England's smallest brewery before the boutiques began. Hoskins produces excellent, firm-bodied ales, with a nutty start and a hoppy finish. The brewery's founding family left to form a new company, also in Leicester, producing a couple of hoppy Bitters under the name Hoskins and Oldfield.

The East Midlands' other big city, Nottingham, has no fewer than three old-established breweries: one, with the curious name of Home, produces notably well-rounded ales; Hardy and Hanson's sweetish ales are unexceptional; Shipstone's are still enjoyable and hoppy, though less so since the brewery was acquired by Greenall Whitley. Nottinghamshire also has the Mansfield brewery, a recent convert to "real ale", although in export markets its lager beers are easier to find.

The outstanding brewery of the East Midlands is away from the cities, on the coast: Bateman's, of Wainfleet, near Skegness, in Lincolnshire. Its "best" Bitter, **XXXB★★ →★★★** (1048), is full of hops in aroma and finish, with a mighty draught of malt to keep them apart. Sad to say, the brewery's future has been clouded by family difficulties and takeover prospects.

WALES

The Welsh seem to have been known for their mead before they brewed ale. They even used honey to spice their ale in Saxon times (another antecedent for the sweet character of ales on the Celtic fringe?). They no longer do that, nor do they have their own distinctive style of brewing. They once had a style of ale called *cwrwf*, but no one else in the world could pronounce it, so nobody ever established what it was. It is equally hard today to dragoon a pronunciation out of Felinfoel, a Welsh brewery that nonetheless exports to the US.

Admirers of the writing of Dylan Thomas might find themselves in the area of Swansea, near which is Llanelli, famous for Rugby Union and the manufacture of tinplate. Britain's first canned beer was made here, by Felinfoel. Today the brewery is known for good-quality ales, including a very fruity **Bitter★ →★★** (1038) and a nuttier "best",

Double Dragon★★ (1040). Felinfoel is part-owned by Buckley, which is in the same town. Buckley has a lightly fruity **Best Bitter**★ →★★ (1036), with both malt and hop coming through in the palate. There is a fruitiness, too, in Crown ales, notably its **Special Best Bitter**★ →★★ (1036). Brain's ales, however, are distinctively malty. Brain's "best" Bitter called **S.A.**★★ →★★★, is a delicious ale from a classic brewer in the centre of Cardiff, capital of Wales.

Bass has Welsh Brewers, producing pleasant ales under the Hancock's brand. Whitbread and Allied have breweries whose products are of no special interest. At the opposite end of the scale, one or two boutiques have opened. In the border town of Monmouth, the Queen's Head Hotel, in St James' Street, has its own boutique, whose products include a strong ale called Brain Damage. In Central Wales, the Samuel Powell boutique is in Newtown, Powys.

THE WEST COUNTRY

The most westerly brewery in Britain is also one of the oddest. It is the Bird in Hand brewpub, in Paradise Park, at Hayle, Cornwall. The name derives from the fact that Paradise Park is a garden in which rare birds are bred. It supports itself by attracting visitors – and by selling them three hearty ales in its pub.

An earlier brewpub, in fact one of the original four, is also a popular stopping place for visitors to Cornwall: the Blue Anchor, in Helston, produces a range of strong ales under the name **Spingo**★★ →★★★. Cornwall also has the old-established independent St Austell brewery, with a very full-flavoured and well-balanced ale called **Tinners' Bitter**★★ (1038), after the local mining industry.

The centralized big brewers have found distribution difficult along the craggy coasts and hilly countryside of the thinly populated West, so brewpubs and boutiques bristle through Devon and Somerset, around Bath and Bristol, and into Gloucestershire. There are too many to visit on a single tour, and they are as prolific and fragile as mushrooms.

In Totnes, the Blackawton Brewery, founded in 1977, is now Devon's oldest. Among the older-established examples in Somerset, and producing excellent ales, are Golden Hill and Cotleigh (both in Wiveliscombe), and the Miners' Arms (Britain's first new brewpub, except that it was actually a restaurant; now in Westbury-sub-Mendip). In the county of Avon, Butcombe and Smiles were both pioneers. Pubs specializing in boutique brews include the Masons' Arms, in Taunton; the Star (23 Vineyards); King William (Thomas St) and Bladud Arms (Lower Swainswick), all in Bath.

An ale-tour on this route might continue to arc north through Gloucestershire (more boutiques: like Three Counties, Cirencester, and Uley) to the Cotswold Hills. There, the prettiest brewery in Britain is to be found: Donnington, at Stow-in-the-Wold, producing malt-accented ales of great subtlety. Still in Cotswold country, but no longer in the West, Hook Norton, at Banbury, has a magnificently traditional tower brewery and some delicious, dry ales.

An alternative route (or the southern half of a round-trip) would sample the ales of the four old-established, independent, country breweries in Dorset: Palmer's of Bridport (very pretty, with lightly hoppy ales); Devenish of eymouth (light, dry ales); Hall and Woodhouse, of andford Forum (lightly fruity) and Eldridge Pope of orchester (with several well-known specialities). There uld then be a sampling of the ales from the classic utique of Ringwood (in the New Forest) and the old-ablished independents Gibbs Mew (Salisbury), Wadworth evizes) and Arkell (Swindon). Among several boutiques in iltshire, the drinker would most certainly not miss cher's (also Swindon).

ourage

is member of the national Big Six has its principal oduction of cask-conditioned ales in the West, in Bristol. s **Directors' Bitter**★★→★★★ (1046) is a British classic: a sk-conditioned "super-premium", with a firm, medium--full body, a malty palate with fruity undertones, but ost notable for its dry-hopped quality. Courage's Bristol ewery laid down a new stock of **Imperial Russian out**★★★★ (1104) in 1986. The company's brewery near eading produces **Bulldog**★★★, a warm-conditioned, bottled le ale that is a minor classic.

ldridge Pope

itain's most potent bottled brew, **Thomas Hardy's Ale** ★★, is produced by this old-established company in orchester. Much of Hardy's work was based in and around e town, and he wrote lyrically of the local beer. For a ardy festival in the 1960s, the brewery produced a lebration ale, and has continued to do so ever since. iomas Hardy's Ale is produced in numbered, limited itions. It is a bottle-conditioned dark ale of 1125.8; 9.98; .48. When young, it is very sweet, but it dries with age: a nt of oloroso sherry? Perhaps this is suggested by the fact at Eldridge Pope has its own soleras in Jerez, producing its vn range of sherries. It also uses the sherry casks for the aturation of Scotch whisky.
The company is also known in Britain for a super-emium Bitter called **Royal Oak**★★ (1048), with a notably ft, fresh, fruity character. Although this product is dry-pped, with Goldings, their character is more evident in ipe's 1880**★★ (1041), a premium, bottled ale.

ingwood

1e godfather of boutique breweries in many parts of the orld is Peter Austin, founder of Ringwood. After leaving an tablished brewery, he has set up his own, in the New Forest, 1d as a consultant has since helped many others to do the me thing. His ales all have a firm body, a dry maltiness, 1d plenty of hop character. Ringwood **Fortyniner**★★ (1049) 1d **Old Thumper**★★ (1060) are both widely admired.

Wadworth

assic country brewery that has quietly won the respect of e-lovers everywhere. Its **Henry Wadworth IPA**★★ (1034) is a hoppy acidity; its **6X**★★ (1040), often served from the ood, is bigger than its gravity would suggest, with a more vious fruitiness. In the darker **Farmer's Glory**★★→★★★ 046), the two elements reach a hefty balance: the hoppi-ss in the start is almost herbal, and there is a rich fruitiness the finish.

IRELAND

The land of dry stout, the style of beer famously typified ▌Guinness. While the best-known dry stouts of Ireland a▌produced by Guinness, of Dublin, there are also fi▌examples from two other brewers, Murphy and Beamis▌both in Cork, the second city of the Republic.

It is commonly held that the Guinness in Ireland is bett▌than that sold elsewhere. This is true of the draught produ▌in so far as the fast turnover encourages the brewery not▌pasteurize. **Draught Guinness★★★ → ★★★★** in Irelar▌therefore has a freshness, and perhaps a softer characte▌than its counterpart in other countries. In both Ireland ar▌Britain, the bottled product is supplied in pubs (but n▌necessarily in other outlets) in unpasteurized form, und▌the designation **Guinness Extra Stout★★★★**. It may be f▌less creamy, but the yeasty liveliness imparted by bott▌conditioning, and the lack of any pasteurization, frees th▌full, hoppy intensity that characterizes Guinness.

Despite their fullness of both flavour and body, dry stou▌tend to have fairly standard gravities in Ireland: arour▌1037-40, with an alcohol content in the region of 3.5 ▌weight, 4.3 by volume. The same is true in Britain, but th▌various American and Continental markets offer their stou▌at anything from 1048 to 1060-plus. Tropical countries hav▌the version of Guinness known, rather quaintly, as **Foreig▌Extra Stout★★★ → ★★★★**, at 1073. This highly distinctiv▌extra-strong stout is first slightly soured in its conditionin▌then pasteurized for stability. It thus has a hint of sharpne▌to balance its immense weight.

Murphy and Beamish are both excellent dry stouts, eac▌with their own distinctive characters. **Murphy's Stout★★★**▌firm-bodied, with a roasty character. **Beamish★★★** is ver▌creamy, only medium-dry, with some chocolate notes. Th▌Murphy brewery has recently received considerable inves▌ment from its owners, Heineken. Beamish is also owned by▌large brewing company, Carling O'Keefe of Canada. (It▌coincidental that the original O'Keefe came from Cork

Ales are a minor category in Ireland, although the numbe▌of brands has increased in recent years. Guinness, togethe▌with Allied Breweries of Britain, has a company called Iris▌Ale Breweries. They have breweries in Dundalk and Kilk▌enny. Irish ales are generally full in colour (often reddish▌full-bodied, sweet, sometimes with hints of butterines▌While this last characteristic would be unacceptable in▌lager, it is a distinguishing feature of some ales. Irish Al▌Breweries' products are, in ascending order of sweetnes▌**Macardle's★ → ★★** and **Phoenix★ → ★★**; **Perry's★ → ★**▌**Smithwick's★★**; and the newer **Twyford's★★**. There is also▌**Smithwick's Barley Wine★★★**.

The most Irish-tasting ale is arguably **Dempsey's★★**▌from a boutique brewery in Dublin. This is available cask▌conditioned in its local market, although "real ale" is no▌widely understood in Ireland. In the North, cask-con▌ditioned ales have been produced by boutique breweries o▌brewpubs like the Down Royal, near Lisburn, Count▌Antrim; the Hilden Brewery, also near Lisburn; Herald, a▌Coleraine; and Maiden Oak, in Derry.

Among lagers **Harp★ → ★★** is native Irish, but withou▌any specifically Hibernian character.

he fastest-growing consumption of beer in Europe is in Italy, where the bright young things of prosperous northern cities like Milan gard wine as a drink for their parents. Brewers in her European countries have poured their most phisticated beers into the Italian market, and now al companies are responding with their own ecialities.

Such influences reached their peak in 1985, when a ver of English ales started to produce one in a ewpub in Sorrento (The English Inn ☎0818- 3684). This is the tiniest brewery in Italy, but veral others remain in private ownership, ranging om the very small Menabrea through the middle- ed and well-respected Forst to Peroni, the coun- y's largest (its **Nastro Azzuro**★→★★ and the very milar **Raffo**★→★★ are well-balanced Pilseners).

A classic family-owned brewery (with its "mousta- ioed man" trademark) is Moretti of Udine, north of enice. In winter, the adjoining restaurant serves a astily unfiltered version (ordered as *integrale*, eaning "whole") of the basic **Moretti**★★ beer, which its normal form is a clean and lightly spritzy lsener. Moretti is also very proud of its export-style ns Souci★★ (15 Plato; 1060; 4.5; 5.6), which has a wery hop aroma and a smooth, malty finish. The ewery also has a higher-gravity (16; 1064; 5; 6.25), l-malt version of a Munchener dark, called **Bruna**★★ ★★★. Its most specialized beer, however, is the deep d **La Rossa**★★★ (18; 1072; 6; 7.5), that is also all-malt, evidenced by its rich aroma and palate.

A beer in the style of a "red ale", **McFarland**★★→★★★ 3.5; 1054; 4.4; 5.5) is made by Dreher (now owned Heineken). The most exotic speciality, a deeper pper-red in colour, is **Splügen Fumée**★★★, made with edium-smoked Franconian malts, by Poretti (in hich United Breweries of Copenhagen has a share). Elsewhere in Southern Europe, Spain has some easantly dry Pilseners and a good few double *Bock* ers (at around 17; 1068; 6; 7.5). On Malta, the top- rmenting specialities of the **Farsons**★★★ brewery are l worthy of attention: a genuine **Milk Stout** (1045); a rkish mild ale, **Blue Label** (1039); a very pale, dry ale lled **Hop Leaf** (1040); and a darker, fuller-bodied ale, ewer's Choice (1050). Greece has, for reasons no one n remember, a German-style law insisting upon all- alt beers. Yugoslavia, on the other hand, is a hop- owing country, so that ingredient tends to be nphasized by its brewers. Some, like Karlovačko, so have a bottom-fermenting **Porter**★★★ (1064).

CANADA

Against an easily conjured backdrop of m
tains, forests, wildlife and lakes, the brew
Canada have in recent years won attention
beyond their own country. Romance must take s
of the credit. By far the greatest part of Cana
brewing takes place where the people live: in ci
and not far from the border. The major Cana
breweries do equally well in their home market
producing under licence heavily advertised bra
from across the same border.

For the beer-drinker in search of true variety
individuality, a much more interesting inspiration
recent years has been manifested by the emergen
"boutique" (or, in Canada, sometimes "cotta
breweries. The French word may be coy, but su
less so than the English-language designation, ev
these new breweries are concentrated in Anglop
Canada. In the mid-1980s, new boutiques and b
pubs were opening more frequently in Canada t
anywhere in the world.

Since the everyday beers of Canada are slig
higher in both original gravity and alcohol con
than their cross-border counterparts, they do in t
respects manifest a slightly fuller flavour. Howe
the difference in alcohol content is exaggerated by
Canadians' sensible use of the volume system.
principal Canadian brews have an alcohol conter
5 percent by volume, amounting to 4 in the
weight" system used across the border. Their
counterparts have between 3.9 and 3.2 by weigl

The fullness of flavour also derives from
huskiness of six-row barley, which is widely used
against this is the lightening and sweetening effe
large proportions of corn, often in the form of syr
and modest hopping rates. Although they are b
means alone in this, Canadian brewers have a
siderable propensity for advertising beers as b
"smooth" when "bland" might be more honest.

A more interesting feature of Canadian brewir
the extent to which ales survive, in Ontario a
especially – Quebec. The major breweries' ales
golden in colour, usually made with "top" yeasts
fermented at notably warm temperatures, produ
a subtle but distinctive fruitiness. As ales go, they
lightly hopped, even in comparison with some of t
US counterparts. The "Canadian taste" – a full
that is not altogether of flavour but also of textu
is even more apparent in the ales. There are
one or two half-hearted porters and stouts f
the major brewers. Much more assertive specia

oducts are being made by some of the boutiques.
The most unusual range – including a *Weissbier*, an
lt and a brew in the style of California's Anchor
eam Beer – was proposed in 1985 by an embryonic
·mpany in Vaudreuil, near Montreal. At the same
·me, it was announced that a new brewery was to be
·ilt in Prince Edward Island, the only Canadian
·rovince without one.
Thus influences go full circle. The boutique brewery
·naissance began in Britain, crossed to the USA, and
·ogressed from California through the Pacific North-
·est into British Columbia before beginning to move
·ross Canada to some notably English-sounding
·aces (Windsor, Ontario, being another prospective
·te). As the various Canadian provinces relaxed their
·ws to make this possible, there was also a loosening
· restrictions on the availability of imported beers.
·eer-drinking in Canada was becoming a great deal
·ore interesting.

·here to drink

· brewpub revolution promises to liberate Canadians from
·e grip of tied taverns and state-monopoly liquor stores. It
·gan in 1982, at the Troller Pub, in Horseshoe Bay, a yacht
·arina and ferry terminal linking the city of Vancouver
·ith the island of the same name. That year, the Troller
·gan serving its own ales, albeit brewed (in accordance with
·e law of the time) at a separate premises – less than 100
·etres away. Since then, there have been periodic changes
·th in the range of products and their character, but the
·sis has been all-malt ales and porters; hopped with
·ossoms; primed, fined and cask-conditioned, but served
·der pressure, at around 10°C (50°F). The house **Bay**
·le★★★ is an impressive, copper-coloured bitter, with lots of
·orth American hop in its bouquet, palate and finish. **Royal**
·le★★★, an excellent "best" bitter, is still hoppy but with a
·gger, more malty, body. **Bay Gold**★★ is paler and drier.
The Troller offered the first cask-conditioned ale in North
·merica, and was within 100 metres of being the first
·ewpub. A couple of years later, one of its principals, John
·itchell, crossed to Vancouver Island, where he was allowed
·y a change of law to found an undisguised brewpub. The
·ub is called Spinnakers, and is in the island's principal
·wn, Victoria (308 Catherine Street). Despite being a town
· only about 70,000 people, Victoria is the provincial
·pital of British Columbia. The pub serves an outstanding
·nge of top-fermenting, naturally conditioned brews, some
·y gravity from the cask, others by hand-pump for cellar
·nks. **Spinnaker Ale**★★★, at an original gravity of 1042,
·as a straw colour, a hoppy nose, a dry, very smooth pal-
·e and a slightly acidic finish. Mitchell's **Extra Special**
·itter**★★★ →★★★★**, at 1049/50, has a copper colour, with a
·vely balance of malt, hop and yeasty fruitiness. There is a
·ry full hop flavour in the finish. **Mount Tolmie Dark**★★★,
· 1047, has a tawny colour and a rich, chocolatey dry-
·ess. **Empress Stout**★★★ →★★★★, at 1052, is extremely
·y, and smooth.

Spinnakers was soon sharing its thinly populated is
with more brewpubs: the Prairie Inn at Saanich;
Terminal Hotel at Nanaimo; and the Leeward at Como
passed up the opportunity to add to the variety, and se
for lagers of the type brewed to perfection by the ma
The Prairie Inn's "Black Malt Steam Beer" turned
merely to be a thin-bodied dark lager.

Both on the island and the British Columbia mainla
number of free-standing boutique breweries were es
lished. In 1985, Alberta introduced a bill to app
brewpubs, and there were hopes that the same would
happen in Saskatchewan. In Manitoba, the Noble
Brewing Company started to produce Canadian-style
and dark ales of no special character for a disco-pub c
Friday's, in the Travelodge Hotel in Winnipeg; eve
Canadian standards, this conjunction must strain
patience of the beer-lover. Enthusiasts in Ontario were
lobbying for brewpubs long after the first free-stan
boutiques there had been established. Quebec was slo
the mark, too, though its laws on drink are in general
most liberal in Canada. The nation's extremities seem t
best lubricated: another early brewpub was Ginger's Ta
on Hollis Street, Halifax, Nova Scotia. Ginger's serv
Best★★★ ale inspired by the Ringwood products in Engl
Also British-inspired, though wholly independent, is
vigorous CAMRA Canada, in the vanguard of the revolu

Amstel

This Dutch *alter ego* of Heineken has acquired the bre
formerly owned by Henninger, of Germany, as a N
American outpost. Amstel and Henninger brands
produced by the brewery, in Hamilton, Ontario – along
the more Canadian-sounding **Grizzly**★, which is swe
and slightly fruity.

Brick

Sizable boutique, in Waterloo, Ontario. Produces a pleas
all-malt beer called **Brick's Premium Lager**★★. Malt ac
ted, but with a hop balance.

Bryant's

Boutique at Maple Ridge, British Columbia. Products
varied, but have included a pale, hoppy, and rather a
Bitter★★, available only locally.

Campbell River

Boutique, Vancouver Island, British Columbia. Too
to rate.

Carling

"Black Label" is still an international brand, bu
Canadian parent has long settled for being one of the
Three" in its home country. **Carling Black Label**★ h
smaller sale in Canada than the company's misnamed
Vienna★, which is slightly less dry. By Canadian standa
the Carling products are in general dry and rather thin.
full name of the company is Carling O'Keefe, the la
identifying its principal ale. **O'Keefe Ale**★ is carbonic
fruity, but there is a little more hop character in **Buc
Ontario Special Ale**★→★★. Like its competitors, Car

'Keefe has a wide range, and branch breweries have some
cal labels. The company is part of the international
othman group, which is based in South Africa.

Conner's

boutique ale-brewery on the edge of Toronto. Too early
rate.

Granville Island

he "island" is a trendy and touristy shopping area in a
stored neighbourhood of the city of Vancouver. The
ewery is a sizable boutique, producing well-made beers
cording to the *Reinheitsgebot*. **Island Lager**★★ →★★★ has a
ft, malty body and a dry, hoppy finish. **Island Bock**★★★
as a tawny colour, a dense head, a malty aroma, and a
alancing dryness in the finish.

Island Pacific

more truly insular boutique – on Vancouver Island. Its
old Stream Local Lager★ →★★ is an all-malt brew, but
rly samples have been unbalanced toward fruitiness, and
ghtly harsh.

Labatt

ggest of Canada's brewers in recent years; controlled by a
linter of the Bronfman (Seagram's whisky) family. Its
ers lean toward a perfumey sweetness, most evident in its
g-selling, Pilsener-style **Labatt's "Blue"**★. A new
emium, **Labatt's Classic**★ →★★, is disappointing, despite
eing an all-malt, kräusened beer. The principal ale, **Labatt**
★, is agreeably aromatic but unexceptional. Its **IPA**★★★ is
y far its most distinctive brew. This ale has a conventional
olden colour, a little hop in the aroma, and a firm body,
ith a honeyish malty sweetness in the finish. **Labatt's**
elvet Cream Porter★ →★★ is closer to being a sweet stout.

Molson

ldest-established of the Big Three, and still controlled by
e Molson family. Of the three giants, it offers perhaps the
ost characterful products overall. In recent years, the
allertau hop character in some products seems to have
minished, accenting their softness and fruitiness. The
mpany's basic lager, **Molson Canadian**★, has some hop in
e nose, and a yeastily fruity palate. Its basic ale, **Molson**
olden★, is light and rather bland. Its **Export**, also
arketed as **Molson Ale**★ →★★, has slightly more hop
aracter and considerably more of the fruitiness of warm
rmentation. **Molson Stock Ale**★★ has a more definite hop
aracter, and malty body. An ale counterpart to a malt
quor, originally styled Brassée d'Or, but compounded to
e ugly **Brador**★★★, has an alcohol content of 5 percent by
eight, 6.25 by volume, and represents an interesting
ariation. Molson also offers Canada's best example of a
orter★★★, from its brewery in Barrie, Ontario.

Moosehead

zable regional brewing company, with plants in Nova
cotia and New Brunswick, though its frontier image is more
parent in the American market. Moosehead's beers have a
licacy of hop character, with a hint of Saaz, a firm body,

and a grassy yeastiness. Its local brew, **Alpine★→★★**, has little more character than **Moosehead Canadian Lager** which is marketed in the USA. **Moosehead Export★** is sweetish ale. **Moosehead Pale Ale★→★★** is drier. **Ten Penn Stock Ale★★** is slightly darker and more characterful, an fractionally stronger.

Mountain Ales

The mountains are on the border, whence it is a sho distance to this boutique brewery in Surrey, an outer subur of Vancouver. Several ales have been produced. Some hav been outstanding, but consistency has been a problem especially when they have had to travel any distance. At i best, **Mountain Premium★★→★★★**, a copper-coloured al has a fruity nose; a very soft, malty palate; and a light hoppy finish. **Mountain Malt★★→★★★** is a darker, tawny a with a smooth palate, hoppier than its English inspiratio Newcastle Brown. Both are all-malt.

Northern Breweries

Former Carling breweries sold to the employees throug the unions. A positive notion, but uninteresting beers.

Old Fort

Regional independent, formerly owned by the entrepreneu "Uncle Ben" Ginter, in Prince George, British Columbi Produces several Pilsener-type beers, including the robus **Pacific Gold★** and the more mellow **Yukon Gold★**.

Rocky Mountain

Another former Ginter brewery, in Red Deer, Alberta. It premium product, **Gold Peak★**, is a Pilsener-style lager wit a fresh, light aroma.

Upper Canada

Sizable boutique, in Toronto. Its unusual **Upper Canad Ale★★★** has a full, tawny colour; a pronouncedly fruit aroma (pears in cream, perhaps?); a rounded body; and a ric roasty, malt character; and a late bitterness from Hallerta aroma hops. Its **Upper Canada Lager★★★** has a very tast malt character, again balanced by a hoppy finish. It is a ver assertive and well-balanced beer. Both are *Reinheitsgeb* brews, naturally carbonated and unpasteurized. Th brewery has shareholding links with Granville Island.

Victoria Brewing

Boutique in Victoria on Vancouver Island. First produc is a sweetish, thin-tasting amber lager. Too early to rate.

Wellington County

Cask-conditioned ales, hopped with Fuggles and East Ken Goldings, and boutique-brewed in the town of Guelph Ontario. One of the founders of the town was a member o the Arkell family, who own a brewery in Swindon, Wiltshire England. In his honour, the Guelph brewery calls its "best" bitter **Arkell★★★**. This has an original gravity of 1038; a dry malty start; a nutty palate, with refreshingly fruity under tones; and a hoppy finish. The brewery's "super-premium" **Wellington County★★★**, has a gravity of 1052, an aromati fruitiness; and a hearty smack of hops from start to finish

THE UNITED STATES

t is widely believed that there are fewer brewing
companies in the United States than there were
four or five years ago; in fact, the number has been
creasing since the early 1980s. Closures have been
utstripped by openings, albeit of tiny, "boutique"
reweries.

It is assumed that there is a lesser choice of beers
rewed in the United States; perhaps surprisingly,
day's selection (although not universally accessible)
broader than it has been since Prohibition. It is
cognized that, in volume, there has been a growth in
e production of lighter, blander beers; it is not so
adily grasped that, in numbers of products, there
as been a far greater growth in speciality beers: not
ly "super-premium" Pilseners but also lagers in the
ienna and Munich styles; ales and stouts; even the
ld *Altbier* and several wheat beers.

The lightness of body and palate in mainstream
merican beers leads some consumers to believe that
ey are especially low in alcohol. This is not so. Some
ates stipulate that anything labelled "beer" (as
pposed to "malt liquor" or "ale") must not exceed
2 percent, but that figure represents alcohol by
eight. In volume terms, this amounts to 4 percent, a

level not unknown in other parts of the world. A "light" or low-price beer might be around this level in whatever state it is bought. A premium or super premium beer has, though, in most states an alcohol content of between 3.6 and 3.9 by weight (4.5–4.8) from a gravity of 10.75–11.25 Plato (1043–1045). Most American ales have an alcohol content of around 4.25–4.75 by weight (5.3–5.9), 12.25–12.5 Plato (around 1050). Malt liquors may have a similar alcohol content, or may go up to around 6.5 (8).

The mainstream American beers are a derivation from the Pilsener style. What makes them characteristically American is their lightness of both body and palate. When, not satisfied with this, American brewing companies developed the category "light beer", it was like Volkswagen announcing that it would extend its range by starting to build small cars.

Although one or two "super-premium" brands of American-style Pilsener beer are made from all-malt mashes, the lightness of body is usually achieved by the use of other grains, often in proportions as high as 40 percent. One or two premiums use rice, but corn (maize) is more common, in the form of flakes or grits or (especially in cheap brands) as a syrup. The lightness of palate is achieved by low hopping rates, with units of bitterness often as low as 13 and rarely higher than 17.

It is the skill of the big American brewers to produce beers in this way while also seeking a clean, lightly crisp, taste. In so doing, they walk a faint line between delicacy and blandness.

THE EAST

The renaissance of traditional beer styles in the United States has a special relevance for the East. Having been the first part of the country to be settled, the East has the oldest brewing tradition, rooted in Colonial times, and still with an inclination toward ale. This has now been given a new life by boutiques like the Manhattan Brewing Company, New Amsterdam and Newman's, upstate in Albany. While these breweries have the assertiveness of youth, a more restrained approach to ale is offered by large independents like Genesee (of Rochester, New York) and, with its McSorley's label, among others, Schmidt (of Philadelphia). Pennsylvania, better known for its German tradition, is still one of the states best blessed with independent breweries. It has half a dozen, most of them very small.

Where to drink

"The biggest selection of beers in the United States" is a claim that has in recent years been offered by several bars and restaurants in the United States, but the consistent leader has been the Brickskeller (1522 22nd Street NW) in fashionable Georgetown in the heart of Washington, DC. Underneath a hotel, this brick-lined cellar stores many

ndreds of beers (the number increases all the time), even
the extent of admitting that the age of some "endangered
ecies" may render them of less interest to drinkers than to
an collectors. In much the same spirit, genuine buffalo stew
s been known to feature on the menu.

Despite its being an institution, New York City's most
mous pub P.J.Clarke's (915 3rd Ave and 55th St) has no
eat claims in respect of beer; surprisingly, its branch in
acy's department store seems more interested. The biggest
election of beers in a bar is at the Peculier [*sic*] Pub (182 W
th St, between 6th and 7th Avenues), in Greenwich Village;
a weekdays, owner Tommy Chou does not open until 4
clock in the afternoon. For beer-lovers, another man-
atory call – in the East Village – is McSorley's Ale House
5 E 7th St, between 2nd Avenue and Cooper Square).
though it was founded in 1854, McSorley's attracts a
oung crowd to drink its house pale and dark brews
roduced by Schmidt's). For more interesting beer, the bar-
staurants of the Manhattan and New Amsterdam
eweries should not be missed. The biggest selection of
ers in a store is in the Village at the Waverley Deli (327 6th
ve, between 3rd and 4th Streets). Many other stores have
od selections, and beers are well represented at the famous
urmet food shop of Dean & DeLuca (121 Prince Street) in
Ho.

Boston's most celebrated old tavern is Jacob Wirth's,
868, 31 Stuart and Eliot); its "famous dark beer" has been
pplied by more than one brewery over the years, and
cent samplings have been rather thin, soft and fruity. On
arvard Square, Cambridge, the old-established Wursthaus
ar and restaurant has a large beer-list, though not as
xtensive as is claimed.

Boston Beer Company

he Bostonian revolutionary politician Samuel Adams may
ave known more about tea parties, but his name has been
ppropriated by a fine, new beer, created by this small
rewing company based in his home town. **Samuel Adams'
oston Lager**★★★ first appeared in 1985, and was judged
est-of-show at that year's Great American Beer Festival, in
enver. On the day, it had more Pilsener character than any
her beer in America. It is an all-malt beer, brewed from the
latively high gravity of 12.5 but to a conventional alcohol
ntent of around 3.5 percent by weight, with kräusening
d dry-hopping. It has a dense head, a huge hop aroma – its
itstanding characteristic – and a big body. The Boston
eer Company is established by a young entrepreneur,
d the product is made to his specifications in an old-
tablished East Coast brewery.

Champale

alt liquor specialist in Trenton, New Jersey. Its **Champale**
mes in versions flavoured with citrus fruits and grenadine,
at owes more to novelty than tradition.

Chesbay

outique, whose full name is Chesapeake Bay Brewing.
hesbay Gold★ → ★★ is Pilsener with a dry fruitiness. **Ches-
ay Amber**★ is a medium-dark beer with a rather light body.
he brewery is at Virginia Beach, Virginia.

Eastern Brewing

Specialist in low-price and supermarket brands. Brewery i
Hammonton, New Jersey.

Geary

Boutique ale-brewery announced for Westbrook, Maine.

Genesee

The biggest specialist brewer of American-style ales, and
major regional independent, in Rochester, New York. I
ales are the principal examples of their styles, but it would b
hard to rate such diffident brews as classics. **Twelve-Hors**
Ale★★ →★★★ is golden in colour, with a fleeting fruitiness
aroma and palate, and a very lightly creamy texture.
proportion of this top-fermented brew is blended with
lager to produce **Genesee Cream Ale**★★ →★★★. Both hav
an underlying sweetness. Genesee now produces the Fre
Koch brands, including the malty **Jubilee Porter**★★.

Iron City

The brand is better known than its parent, the Pittsburg
Brewing Company. **Iron City**★ has lost some of its charact
in recent years. **Iron City Dark**★ →★★ is, however, one of th
more full-flavoured examples of a Munich-style America
beer. The brewery has also produced many novelty brand
aimed at can collectors.

Jones

Small brewery founded in 1907 by a Welsh family i
Smithton, Pennsylvania, and still owned by them. Produc
the clean-tasting **Stoney's Beer**★ →★★, proclaimed to co
tain no additives, and the light **Old Shay Cream Ale**★.

Latrobe

Small, beautifully equipped brewery in Latrobe, Penn
sylvania, making only **Rolling Rock**★★, a very clean-tastin
beer that has a cult following in the East. Rolling Rock ha
some rice adjunct, is brewed with spring water, and blossom
hopped with American varieties.

Lion

Small, old-established, brewery in Wilkes-Barre, Penn
sylvania, noted for the (bottom-fermented) **Stegmaie**
Porter★ →★★, with its pronounced licorice character.

Manhattan Brewing Company

Despite a great beer tradition, and much-bruited civic prid
New York City lived for almost a decade without a brewer
until this boutique was established in the mid 1980s. Th
Manhattan Brewing Company is in SoHo, on Thompson S
at Broome, between 6th Avenue and W Broadway. A brew
kettle decorates the outside of the building, and other
embellish the bar and seafood restaurant. The company als
has drayhorses fit to cause heart attacks among New Yor
cabbies. The splendid products are all top-fermenting, an
are tank-conditioned and fined for serving at the brewer
under pressure. The principal brews are a pale, **Golden Ligh**
Ale★★ →★★★ (1044), lively and dry, with a hoppy finish; a
aromatic, fruity, but beautifully balanced **Royal Amber**★★
(1048); and a smooth, dry **Special Porter**★★★ (1056).

F.X.Matt

The present Francis Xavier Matt is the third generation of his family to run this small brewery in Utica, New York. Its products, which tend toward a creamy softness, include: a full and fruity Pilsener-type beer called **Matt's Premium →★★**; **Maximus Super★★**, a malt liquor of 5.25–5.5 percent alcohol by weight; the top-fermenting **Utica Club Cream Ale★★**; and a new super-premium Pilsener, **Saranac 1888★★**, which is an all-malt, exclusively two-row, brew, hopped with Cascades and Hallertaus, and kräusened.

New Amsterdam

The first revivalist beer of New York, though initially production time was rented upstate at the Utica brewery. New Amsterdam's own brewery and tap room opened its doors in 1985, in the city's Chelsea neighbourhood, at 235 11th Avenue and 26th Street. **New Amsterdam Amber Beer★★ →★★★** has an appropriately full colour (perhaps it should have been called New Vienna?) and a pleasant Hallertau and Cascade hop character, but with warm fermentation providing a degree of ale-like fruitiness. Having started with this gently different beer, the parent Old New York Brewing Company has since added a dry-hopped version, which is described as **New Amsterdam Ale ★ →★★★**. The brewery can be seen from the Tap Room, which serves a cosmopolitan range of snack meals.

Newman's

The first boutique brewery anywhere in the East, but Newman's has never had the credit it deserves. Its misfortune is to be in Albany, which may be the state capital but is an unimaginable distance – about 140 miles (225 km) – from downtown Manhattan. Those miles are along the stately Hudson valley, and Albany – an elegant city that was once the centre of ale-brewing in America – is worth a visit to sample the Newman's products in their draught form. In this form, they are fined in the cask, then stabilized by cold conditioning. They have in general a soft, tasty character. The local specialities are **Albany Amber Ale★★ →★★★** (1042), malty and spicy; a **Pale Ale★★★** (1045) with a copper colour and a lot of floral hop character; and a seasonal **Winter Ale★★★** (1050), dark and chocolatey but dry.

The brewery also has a product in a paler copper colour, at 1036, which is top-fermenting but described nonetheless simply as being Newman's "beer". This fruity but well-balanced brew is available in a good many states, in the bottle, as **Albany Amber Beer★★**.

Schmidt

Major regional brewer, with a lovely, old plant in Philadelphia, interesting yeasts and one or two colourful specialities. These brews are cherished by beer-lovers, but Schmidt's attitude toward its position as their provider is not always clear.

The regular **Schmidt's★ →★★** and the similar **Rheingold →★★**, its New York brand, are slightly fruity and fairly full-bodied. The company also produces the golden-coloured **McSorley's Cream Ale★★**, bottom-fermented but with a degree of hop in the nose and palate. There is a similar character to **Prior Double Dark★★**, which seems to have lost

something of its fullness. Recent sightings of **Tiger Head**★
a top-fermenting, golden-coloured ale, have been rare.

Straub

Very small, old-established brewery in St Mary's, Penn
sylvania. **Straub Beer**★ → ★★ is a fairly light-bodied lager
with a longish, dry finish.

Yuengling

The oldest brewery in the United States. Yuengling, foun
ded in 1829 and still family owned, is best known for it
"Celebrated Pottsville Porter"★★, which has a soft, mediun
to full body, a mild hopping, but a dash of roasty dryness i
the finish. The brewery, in Pottsville, Pennsylvania, also ha
Lord Chesterfield Ale★ → ★★, English-sounding but
American in style, with a flowery hop aroma and a golden
colour. Both are actually bottom-fermented. There are
several other products, all pleasant but none exceptional

THE MIDWEST

Most Americans would identify their nation's greatest
brewing region as the Midwest, but that is no longer true
except in Germanic tradition. From its business base in
Detroit, Stroh's is a growing brewery company, but it no
longer produces beer in its home city. Chicago has, at least
for the moment, no brewery; in St Louis, Anheuser-Busch
prospers but Falstaff has long gone; worst of all is the plight
of Milwaukee, supposedly the brewing capital of the United
States. Of its three famous names, Miller is now in the hand
not only of tobacconists but also of grocers (a situation no
unique to American breweries). Pabst is a shadow of its tra
ditions; and Schlitz no longer brews in the city it claims to
have made famous. Despite the cluster of breweries in Wis
consin, no Midwestern state makes as much beer as California

One giant set to restore some tradition is Heileman (of La
Crosse, Wisconsin), which is building a boutique brewery
(though it will no doubt avoid such a California-sounding
description) in Milwaukee. The Milwaukee area is, indeed
gaining several boutiques. Meanwhile, several old-estab
lished small breweries have begun to give more emphasis to
speciality beers. Some have done so under new ownership
and new names, notably Hibernia (formerly Walters of Eau
Claire, Wisconsin) and Rhömberg (formerly Pickett's of
Dubuque Star in Iowa).

Where to drink

The workaday cities of the Midwest are not the best places in
the United States in which to find a fancy selection of beers
though Chicago is notable for the survival of German tastes
It is the only city where these vestiges of the past form a
bridgehead to the new awareness of beer. The most famous
beer tavern in Chicago, in The Loop, is The Berghoff (17 W
Adams St), founded in 1898. The Berghoff has its own beer
(brewed by Huber, and similar to Augsburger), an 80ft
stand-up bar, and a lunch counter that becomes an oyster
bar in the evening, and a restaurant. Also in Chicago, the
Weinkeller, in Roosevelt Road, Berwyn, is a liquor store and
tavern with a wide selection of beers. The German bar Resi's
on Irving Park Road, west of Lincoln, is appropriately

hauvinistic. Milwaukee has two famous beer taverns: Karl
atzsch's (320 E Mason) and Mader's (1037 N 3rd Ave).

Anheuser-Busch

he world's biggest brewing company, headquartered in St
ouis, Missouri (the gateway city to Middle America), and
roducing between 60–70 million barrels a year, its capacity
nared between ten of its own plants across the nation.
nheuser and Busch were related by marriage, and the
ompany – formed in 1865 – is still controlled by the family.
ddly, the family name is appropriated to a low-price brand
f beer, **Busch**★, this having originally been the local brew
r St Louis. The Royal Court brewery of Bohemia inspired
ne name **Budweiser**★ →★★ for the world's first consciously
ass-marketed (ie national "premium") beer. A Bohemian
rewing town also inspired America's first "super-premium"
eer, **Michelob**★★, from the same company. The delicacy of
nese two beers was developed over the years from four
rincipal influences: the use of a proportion of rice
raditionally 30 percent in Budweiser and 25 in the fuller-
odied Michelob) to provide lightness and "snappiness"; a
omplex hop blend of more than eight varieties (notably
regon Fuggles), in at least three additions, to impart
omplexity of aroma and palate; a house yeast that confers a
ery subtle, apple-like fruitiness; and fining over beechwood
hips, to ensure a clean character. Recently, the company
as re-emphasized, under the Michelob brand, its **Classic
ark**★, but this has less character than it promises.

Ballantine

nce East Coast classics, these top-fermenting ales are now
roduced in Fort Wayne. The basic **Ballantine Ale**★★ is in
he American golden style. The dry-hopped, wood-aged
allantine IPA** (India*n*a Pale Ale?)★★★ has a copper-colour.
lthough it has lost some of its character over the years, it
emains an interesting brew. It has a gravity of 1076 and 5.6
ercent alcohol by weight (7 by volume). **Narragansett
orter**★★ is dry but rather thin.

Capital

Iew boutique at Middleton, Wisconsin. Producing lager
eers with a German accent. Too early to rate.

Cold Spring

ery old small brewery in Cold Spring, Minnesota. "Super-
remium" **Cold Spring Export**★★ is a little fuller-bodied
han most beers of its type, with some Cascade aroma.

Geyer

he smallest of the old-established breweries in the United
tates and the one with the most antiquated plant. Geyer, in
rankenmuth, Michigan, is unusual in that its principal
roduct is a copper-coloured "dark" beer. Despite its colour,
rankenmuth Bavarian Dark**★★ has a light, dry palate.

Heileman

)ften thought of as a regional brewery, perhaps because its
lagship products have anonymous names. In part by
cquisition of companies whose own leading brands have
een sensibly retained, Heileman is now fourth among the

six brewing groups that dominate the United States. Its ba
brewery is in La Crosse, Wisconsin, and it plans to oper
boutique under the old Blatz name downstate in Milwauke
Heileman makes a point of kräusening. This is, however, le
evident in its rather limp **Old Style★** than its spritzy **Spec**
Export★★. Subsidiaries include Blitz-Weinhard and Raini

Hibernia

A new company, established by an American Irishm
(hence the name) at the old Walter brewery, in Eau Clai
Wisconsin. Hibernia's emphasis is on speciality beers
excellent quality. Its year-round speciality is a pale lag
called **Eau Claire All Malt★★ →★★★**, smooth and tasty b
surprisingly dry. It does, however, also make a point of
seasonal brews. These include a bronze-coloured, hop-acce
ted, top-fermenting **Winterbräu★★**; a fresh, soft, soothi
Dunkelweizen★★★ →★★★★ (a dark wheat beer, for summe
with hints of chocolate and vanilla before a refreshi
acidity in the finish; and a copper-coloured, malt-accent
but well-balanced **Oktoberfest★★★**. Some of the Walte
range are still produced.

Huber

Old-established brewery in Monroe, Wisconsin. Recent
acquired by new owners. Known for its **Augsburger★**
which is a Pilsener-style beer with a touch more he
bitterness than most of its competitors. It is a well-ma
example of an American beer. The same can be said f
Augsburger Dark★★ and **Huber/Augsburger/Rhineland**
Bock★★ →★★★ (4.6 by weight; 5.75 by volume).

Hudepohl

One of two old-established small breweries in Cincinnati. I
speciality is a malty super-premium lager called **Christia**
Moerlein★★★, after an early brewer in the city. This is
Reinheitsgebot brew, with plenty of body and a full, smoo
finish. The brewery made a malty, copper-coloured brew
considerable character to celebrate its Jubilee; perhaps th
should be substituted for the rather thin **Hudepo**
Oktoberfest★ →★★. The original brewery was known
Buckeye (see page 27) because it was on Buckeye Stre
(now East Clifton Avenue).

Kalamazoo

Home-brew boutique in Michigan. Too early to rate.

Leinenkugel

Old-established small brewery in Chippewa Falls, Wisco
sin. Has won a cult following for its light, flowery premiu
beer, known simply as **Leinenkugel★ →★★** (by devotees,
"Leiny"). Also a pleasantly malty, tawny **Bock★★** (5; 6.25

Miller

Owned by Philip Morris, and with marketing skills to matc
Known for **Miller Lite★**. Its new "Genuine Draft" version
Miller Highlife★ is lightly malty and dry. **Plank Road★** als
new (and taking its curious name from a brewery address
has a similar character but with a faintly more perfum
palate. Though lack of pasteurization is a bonus, the produ
itself is not of great interest.

Mill Stream

Boutique in the "Colonies" of the Amana sect, in Minnesota. Lager beers. Too early to rate.

Pabst

Long ago, **Pabst Blue Ribbon★** was a classic premium beer. Perhaps its slightly savoury character, and hint of chewiness, has led some of today's Americans to see it as a smokestack beer. The image has not been dispelled by a new owner.

Point

Old-established small brewery in Stevens Point, Wisconsin. Unlike many of its contemporaries, this brewery has nurtured strong local support; its **Point Special★★** also emerged as top beer in a tasting organized by the feisty Chicago columnist Mike Royko. It is a full-bodied, and well-balanced, beer. A well-made **Bock★★** is also produced.

Rhömberg

Original name, now restored, of the former Pickett's brewery, in Dubuque, Iowa. Under new but still fairly local (Milwaukee) management, this brewery is now producing a beautifully balanced beer, with a pale copper colour, that is broadly in the Vienna style. It has the typical maltiness of aroma, and of palate (emerging more clearly with every sip) but it is never sweet, and has a definitely hoppy finish. Although this product is called simply **Rhömberg All Malt★★ → ★★★**, it is best identified by its blue label. While most breweries give a special designation to their dark beers, Rhömberg does so with its **Classic Pale★★** (brown label), which has an aromatic nose, a full texture, and some sweetness in the finish.

Schell

Old-established small brewery that has enlivened its range with the lightly aromatic, dry, firm-bodied, all-malt, kräusened and well-matured **August Schell Pilsner★★**; a fruity, almost liqueur-ish **Weiss★★★**; and a nicely dark and rich but rather sweet **Ulmer Braun★★**. The brewery, in New Ulm, Minnesota, has a small deer park.

Schoenling

Smaller of the two old-established small breweries in Cincinnati. Schoenling specializes in the sweetish, mellow **Little King's Cream Ale★★ → ★★★**. A taste of Americana.

Sprecher

The first new brewery in Milwaukee since 1947. A boutique making pale and dark lagers. Too early to rate.

Stroh

A fast-spreading brand-name since this Detroit-based company went national by acquiring Schlitz and Schaefer. Stroh makes a point of using direct flame to fire its kettles. This traditionalist technique of "fire-brewing" pre-dates the more common use of steam-heating. The flames create hot spots in the kettle, and the swirling brew has the briefest of flirtations with caramelization, thus acquiring a tinge of sweetness to be found in **Stroh's★ → ★★**, which is otherwise

unexceptional. The same character is more evident in th
fuller-bodied super-premium **Signature**★★. The old Schli
super-premium **Erlanger**★★ is a firm-bodied all-malt brew
but of no great distinction. The label describes it as
Märzenbier but it bears no relation to the German style.

Vienna

The Austrian capital has inspired many beers over the year
but the latest is an outstanding example. A talented youn
brewer in Milwaukee founded Vienna Brewing Inc, and als
uses the city's name to identify his product. **Vienna All Ma
Lager Beer**★★★ is an assertive but beautifully balance
brew. It is true to the Viennese style in its colour an
maltiness, but also has a great deal of hoppy dryness. It i
produced for its creator by a small brewery in Wisconsin

THE WEST

The principal areas for the cultivation of both the win
grape and the hop in the United States were originally th
northeast and are now the northwest. The grape command
the valleys of northern California, and has spread int
Oregon and Washington State. The hop has moved mor
decisively, gradually deserting northern California for th
two states beyond. Oregon and Washington (especially th
latter, in its Yakima Valley) are hop-growing areas c
international standing.

Although the success of boutique wineries created
precedent for the new brewers, they do not like th
soubriquet. They dislike it precisely because it may mak
them sound fashionable and therefore ephemeral. It doe
though, explain them to the consumer: a boutique makes, o
a small scale, a hand-crafted product of individuality an
personality; it does not seek to compete with the mass
produced goods (however well-made and competitivel
priced) of the department store. The new generation prefe
the term "micro-brewer". Perhaps that has a ring of Silico
Valley, but it could as well evoke the computer consoles o
the giant breweries, nationally owned, in which the pros
perous, populous, West is now also the leader.

Where to drink

The West is the land of outdoor drinking: at the mountain
the cookout, the beach, the boat. Nonetheless, it also ha
many restaurants and bars that boast very large selection
of beers. Distinguished voices have praised, for example, th
range at the Old Chicago pizza restaurants in Denver an
nearby Rocky Mountain towns. (This is also the country o
the Great American Beer Festival, by far the bigges
sampling of US brews, on Memorial Day weekend, at th
beginning of June.) Throughout the West, a deft hand i
employed by Restaurants Unlimited, in its eclectic an
stylish establishments: a good example, favoured by Wes
Side folk in Los Angeles, is Cutters in Santa Monica.

San Francisco has a famously eccentric beer bar calle
Tommy's Joynt at Geary and Van Ness; a more restraine
selection of beers at the pub in the St Francis Hotel; and a
few vintage taverns and restaurants (like Schroeders o
Front Street); probably the best retail selection of beers i
the United States is at the gourmet food store in The

annery; and the KQED international beer festival is in
rly July. In nearby San Mateo, there is also a good
lection at the Prince of Wales pub (16 E 25th Avenue).

The first brewpubs in the United States were established
northern California in 1983–84. One, appropriately, is in
old hop-growing area (now known for its wines). This is
e Mendocino Brewing Company, in the town of Hopland,
out 100 miles (160km) north of San Francisco on Highway
)1, which heads on to the Redwood National Park and the
regon state line. Tourists stop to buy champagne magnums
led with the fruity **Red Tail Ale★★**, or to sample the
ocolatey **Black Hawk Stout★★**. East of San Francisco,
ward the white wine country of the Livermore Valley,
uffalo Bill's (1082 B Street, Hayward) offers a fluffy yeasty
ger that defies rating. The Redwood brewpub produces
p-fermenting beers in Petaluma, close to the wine country
Sonoma Valley.

Portland, Oregon, already lauded for Henry Weinhard's
rivate Reserve, has become a very interesting brewing
wn with the addition of three boutiques (the closure of
eneral Brewing, across the river, was no great loss to beer-
vers). Old-established sampling spots include Produce
ow (204 SE Oak) and the Horse Brass Pub (4534 SE
elmont). Four pubs specializing in draught are run by beer-
eak Mike McMenamin, whose Hillsdale (1505 SW Sunset
oulevard) produces its own flippant specialities.

Seattle, too, has become an American beer capital. Local
outique brews are heavily featured at J.C. Fox (2307
astlake Avenue E., near Lake Union), Murphy's (2110 N
5th Street, near the university) and Cooper's, with a
artling array of local draughts (8065 Lake City Way).
here are smaller, but well-chosen, beer selections at the
'estin Hotel; the Mark Toby, a hangout for cafe society (90
adison Street); Place Pigalle, with a bistro ambience (81
ke Street); and another Cutters, with an imaginative and
aried menu of light meals (Pike Place Market). Near the
ingdome sports stadium F.X. McRory is a tavern-style
staurant with a wide range of beers and Bourbons.

Seattle has many more attractions for the beer-lover, but
or should such an enthusiast leave the state without taking
ae drive – about 120 miles (193km), over mountains and
esert – to the hop-growing town of Yakima, to visit Grant's
rewery and pub.

Anchor Steam

he renown of this small San Francisco brewery has
adually spread across the nation, though its particular
aim to fame is not always understood. The point is that its
rincipal product, **Anchor Steam Beer★★★★**, is made by a
rocess unique to the United States (and, for more than 60
ears, to this brewery). Anchor Steam Beer is thus not only a
rand but also the sole example of a style. It is also a wholly
riginal way of brewing, and not a dilution of a European
yle (as are such minor categories as cream ales, malt liquors
d light beers). Anchor Steam Beer is produced by bottom-
rmentation but at high temperatures and in unusually
ide, shallow vessels, in a method once typical of the Bay
rea. This technique marries some of the roundness of a
ger with the fruitiness of an ale. Irrespective of the
chnique, Anchor Steam Beer also has a firm body and

plenty of hop character, both in the aroma and the fini

The brewery also makes a number of top-fermenti styles: a rich, creamy **Anchor Porter★★**; a very aromatic a bitter, dry-hopped **Liberty Ale★★★**; a light, delicate int pretation of a **Wheat Beer★★ → ★★★**; and an occasional **O Foghorn Barley Wine★★★ → ★★★★** (7 percent alcohol weight; 8.75 by volume) that is surprisingly lively for weight, with an intense interplay of malt, hop and yeas fruitiness. From Thanksgiving each year, a Christmas Ale available. Each "vintage" has a deliberately differe character, and these brews are not to be missed. The Anch brews are all produced to a very high quality, natura carbonated, and only flash-pasteurized. Being an old-esta lished brewery (though "rescued" in more recent times), a having grown beyond being tiny to being merely sm (about 40,000 barrels a year), Anchor is not a boutiqu though its example has inspired many.

Blitz-Weinhard

Best known for its super-premium **Henry Weinhar Private Reserve★★ → ★★★**. When this product was launche in what were for American beer-drinkers the bland 197 the brewery took the revolutionary step of admitting that employed hops. Even more daringly, the hops were perm ted to announce themselves with a bouquet. Such extrove behaviour is less noticeable in today's climate of boutique but, among super-premium Pilseners, Henry's is still one the more aromatic, and in the light style that is charact istic of western examples. The same lightness of charac underlies the dry **Henry Weinhard Dark★ → ★★** and t gently fruity **Blue Boar Ale★ → ★★**, described as "Irelan style", a claim as valid as its grammar. Blitz-Weinha with its brewery in Portland, Oregon, is owned by Heilema

Boulder

Barely a boutique, if that term could ever have been appli to a brewery that began in a goat-shed. Now, it is not much a micro as a macro, with a purpose-built brewery th is architecturally reminiscent of a modern church. **Bould Extra Pale Ale★★ → ★★★** has a fruity aroma, a soft palate a an assertively hoppy finish. **Boulder Porter★★ → ★★★** ha hint of licorice in the aroma, a firm body, a dry, roas palate, and a rather quick finish. An intense **Bould Stout★★★** is occasionally produced. The brewery is Boulder, Colorado.

Bridgeport

Boutique in Portland, Oregon, producing the character **Bridgeport Ale★★ → ★★★**, notably sweet, but with smo undertones, a soft, full body and an attractive ruby colo The brewery also has the well-balanced **Bridgeport Stout → ★★★**. Although the name Bridgeport is more familiar local beer-lovers, the company is called Columbia Riv Brewing. It was founded by the Ponzi family, owners o well-known Oregon winery. A pub is planned.

Coors

The biggest single brewery plant in the world, despite remote Rocky Mountain location in Golden, Colorado. Fr the outside, it looks like an atomic power station; inside, i ne of the world's most beautiful, and remarkable, reweries. Its pristine, tiled brewing halls are lined with rows ' traditional copper vessels — a tub of blossom hops by every ettle — capable of producing 25 million barrels a year. The aditionalism of the Coors family extends to a dislike of asteurization, instead of which the beer is filtered to an nusual degree. From the seeding of its own barley to the roduction of its own packaging, Coors takes astonishing are over its product. The best of brewers guard their beers s though they were their children; perhaps Coors is extra-rotective because its beer is so innocent. The basic **Coors**★★ ust surely be the lightest and cleanest premium beer in the orld, with just a hint of maltiness to remind the drinker aat this is not pure Rocky Mountain spring water. In recent ears, Coors has experimented with a considerable number ' further brands. The unlikely sounding **George Killian's**★★ arted out as a licensed re-creation of an Irish Red Ale, but s character has diminished. The brewery's latest product, r a separate company formed by Coors, Molson and altenberg, is a beer called **Masters**★, aromatic, smooth, ghtly fruity, and designed for a mass audience.

Excelsior

outique lager brewery in Santa Rosa, California. Too early rate.

Grant's

op Country boutique producing some of the most distinc-ve brews in America. With a long background in both the op-growing and brewing industries, Bert Grant makes ssertive products to his own taste, and sells them in his own ab in Yakima and elsewhere throughout the northwest, here they enjoy a dedicated following. Grant spent the first vo years of his life in Dundee, on the strength of which he alled his first product **Scottish Ale**★★★. Despite its full body nd malty firmness, this is less Scottish than American, with s Cascade hop accent in both its huge aroma and its mphatic bitterness (1050–55; around 4.5 by weight, 5.6 by olume). This was followed by an appropriately more ttenuated **IPA**★★★, at just under 1050, with an immense op character, especially in its long finish. Among a number ' more idiosyncratic brews, Grant's has won special ttention for its "Russian" **Imperial Stout**★★★ → ★★★★ (at round 7, 8.5), in which the typical "Christmas pudding" alate is underpinned by a dash of honey and dried, again, y hefty hopping. Since their launch, some of these products em to have diminished slightly in their richness, and it is to e hoped that standards can be maintained.

Hale's Ales

Vell-made, unfiltered, English-style ales from a boutique rewery in the remote town of Colville, in eastern Washing-n. These products can sometimes be found in Idaho and regon, too. All of them have a good head, a malty start, a ean palate and a hoppy finish. Among the hops used are an laho-grown strain of the aroma Hallertau. Hale's merican Pale Ale★★ → ★★★ (1040; 3.9, 4.8) has a lush, straw ɔlour; a malty dryness; and some light, hoppy acidity in the nish. The tasty **Special Bitter**★★ → ★★★ (1045; 4.3, 5.4) has deeper colour, a subtle amber; a warm aroma; a bigger

body; and a depth of hop bitterness. The **Celebrati**
Porter★★ → ★★★ (1050) is lightly chewy, with a hint of w
cherry, and a roasty dryness in the finish.

Kemper

Boutique producing what it describes as a Munich style
lager, but with a distinctively fruity palate. The fruitines
so emphatic as to hint at blueberries. **Thomas Kemp**
Lager is so eccentric as to be hard to rate. The brewery is
Bainbridge Island, near Seattle.

Kessler

A most interesting and well-made range of bottom-fermer
ing beers from a boutique in an unlikely location: near L
Chance Gulch, in Helena, Montana, in the wilds of t
Rockies. This new boutique revives the name of a lor
defunct local brewery. Its beers in general have a complex
of hop aroma and flavour, but are malt accented. T
regular, Pilsener-style **Kessler Beer★★** is aromatic and s
big-bodied, with a clean sweetness. **Kessler Wheat Be**
★★ → ★★★ is broadly a *Dunkelweizen*, with a tawny-r
colour, some iron-like tones in the nose, and a dry, ma
palate; it needs a slice of lemon. The brewery's **Oktoberfe**
★★★, at 13 to 14 Plato, has a fine reddish colour and plenty
malt in the aroma and palate, with a gentle dryness of hop
the finish; an outstanding example of its style. A dry-hopp
Holiday Beer★★★, for Christmas, has a medium amb
colour; a rich, fruity aroma; a malty palate; and a love
lingering bitterness in the finish. A **Bock★★★**, marketed
March and April, has a subtle, tawny colour; a firm, ma
body; and again plenty of hop, both in aroma and finis

Küfnerbräu

The only bottle-conditioned, bottom-fermenting beer in
United States, from a brewery that is not so much boutiq
as back-room. After its bottle-conditioning, the beer
pasteurized. The result is too eccentric to rate. The brewe
is in Monroe, not far from Seattle, and is run by an Americ
German. With its yeasty fruitiness – almost cidery – **Küfn**
bräu Gemütlichkeit Old Bavarian Style could just ha
been made in a Franconian farmhouse.

Olympia

Once chic for their classically western lightness, **Olympi**
beers were overtaken in the mass market by more su
footed local rivals, and among more demanding drinkers
the billowing of boutiques. The brewery, in Tumwat
Olympia, is now owned by Pabst.

Palo Alto

English-style naturally conditioned draught ales, the first
be served in the United States by a hand-pumped be
"engine". Brewed not only for expatriates but also
cosmopolitan tastes, in Silicon Valley. The brewery is
Mountain View, near Palo Alto, on San Francisco Bay.
was founded by a computer entrepreneur, who sold out to
employees in 1985. Initial products were modelled on t
ales of Brakspear, in England. Palo Alto uses malt extra
from Edme, Hereford Fuggles and East Kent Goldings, wi
dry-hopping. Early brews were a 1035 **Drake's Gold**

e★★ → ★★★ and a 1042 **London Real Ale**★★ → ★★★, both
th a hoppy, yeasty, fruitiness, and with hints of oak,
ough an interesting Bourbon-wood character no doubt
me from an odd barrel.

ortland Brewing Co

ew boutique and brewpub in Portland, Oregon, with its
vn ale, and licensed versions of the Grant's products. Too
rly to rate.

yramid

efinitively New Western ales from the small Hart boutique
Kalama – in Washington State but not far from Portland,
regon. The combination of a clean, soft but dry fullness
th an intense hop character – notably in aroma as well as
tterness – renders **Pyramid Pale Ale**★★★ such a good
ample. Various seasonal specialities have included a
mmer wheat beer. With the curious name **Wheaten
le**★★ → ★★★, this combines a surprisingly full hop character
th citric tones – almost grapefruit, though without the
tterness; acceptable, perhaps, in a wheat beer.

ainier

efore the boutiques, Rainier was famous among brew-
vers throughout the West for its ale. Perhaps the north-
est's new enthusiasm for the brewing of ales was en-
uraged by the example of Rainier. Even among today's
lourful contemporaries, the copper-coloured **Rainier
le**★★★ in its full-strength version (around 5.8 by weight;
25 by volume, where state laws permit; popularly known,
ter its potency and label colour, as "The Green Death")
mains a force with which to be reckoned. It is bottom-
rmented but with its own yeast and at high temperatures.
he boutique ales are more authentic, but Rainier has a far
eater character than its mass-market counterparts in
anada, whence it originated. There is also a firm-bodied
ger called **Rainier Beer**★. The brewery is in Seattle, with
ount Rainier as a backdrop. It is owned by Heileman.

ed Hook

ell-established boutique in Seattle, founded by people
ith backgrounds in the wine and coffee businesses. **Red
ook Ale**★★★, although less rampant than it once was,
mains the fruitiest in America. Initially, its fruitiness
otably from banana esters) was a *cause célèbre* in Seattle,
inning admirers and critics of equal ferocity. It would
robably have been more widely appreciated in Belgium.
lack Hook Porter**★★ → ★★★ is very dry but soft and
oothing. **Ballard Bitter**★★ → ★★★ is, contrary to its name, on
e sweet side, lightly malty and nutty.

axon

ome-brewer gone legal, in the Sierra Nevada foothills at
hico, California. Too early to rate.

ierra Nevada

lassic boutique. Established in the early days of the
ovement, it has grown quickly, not only in size but also in
e esteem of knowledgeable beer-lovers far beyond its little
ome-town of Chico (in northern California, close to the

Sierra Nevada range). The brewery's **Pale Ale**★★★ has bot
the floweriness of Cascade hops and the citric fruitiness o
the yeast in its bouquet, and is beautifully balanced, with
clean, fresh character. Its **Porter**★★★ is among the bes
brewed anywhere; firmly dry, but with a gently coffee-is
finish. Its **Stout**★★★ is well-balanced and full of flavour. It
Big Foot Barley Wine★★★ → ★★★★, with a huge hoppiness i
its earthy aroma and chewy palate, is the strongest beer i
the United States (1095; 24.5 Plato; 8.48 percent alcohol b
weight; 10.6 by volume).

Smith and Riley

"Honest beer", its creators call it. **Smith and Riley**★ → ★★ is
firm-bodied, Pilsener-style beer, with some hop flavour i
the finish. Devised by a couple of beer-lovers in Vancouve
(the US town in Washington State, not the one nearby i
Canada). Produced for them by a commercial brewery.

Snake River

A hop-farming family owns this small boutique, in Caldwel
west of Boise, Idaho. A hop field surrounds the brewery, an
the family also grow their own malting barley. Surprisingly
there is only a light – albeit very fresh – hop character i
Snake River Premium Lager★ → ★★, which is on the swee
side. There is also an emphatically sweet and malty **Ambe
Lager**★★. Yet more surprisingly for a boutique, and especial
ly one that grows its own barley, this brewery uses
proportion of adjunct: rice in this case.

Stanislaus

The *Altbier* launched in 1984 by Stanislaus was the first to b
produced in the United States since at least the time o
Prohibition. This boutique takes its name from its locatio
east of San Francisco, in Stanislaus County, at Modesto,
major winery town of the Central Valley of California. I
launching a style unfamiliar to the United States, "S
Stan's" further complicated matters by having two ver
sions, **Amber**★★★ and **Dark**★★★. Although these are mor
than creditable, most *Altbier* is made in just one colou
somewhere between the two. Perhaps St Stan could no
decide whether to be inspired, among the Düsseldor
originals, by Schumacher or Zum Uerige.

Thousand Oaks

A home brewery gone commercial, in Berkeley, California. A
wide range of rather yeasty products, somewhat eccentric
but with a local following.

Widmer

Second *Altbier* brewery in the US, in 1985. Brewer Kur
Widmer, a second-generation American based in Portland
Oregon, has family connections in Düsseldorf, and was freel
advised by a (perhaps incredulous) Zum Uerige. His **Wid
mer Alt**★★★ is brewed from four malts, with step infusion
and hopped twice, with American-grown Perle and Tett
nang blossoms. It is a fine example of the style, with a dens
head; a deep, burnished-copper colour; both malt and hop
in the nose; and a very hoppy palate. Widmer has als
turned its attention to other German-style specialities
including a very hoppy **Weizenbier**★★ → ★★★.

THE SOUTH

ocial geography is not always what might be expected of it.
n the United States the drinker had best go to San
rancisco or Seattle, perhaps Chicago or New York, to find a
eally good selection of Kentucky whiskeys. Gastronomic
nterest in drink has yet to make much impression on the
outh, certainly in relation to whiskey – its native tradition
and scarcely more in respect of beer.

Serious interest in beer in the United States began in the
West, took three or four years to vault to the East, and is
till in its early stages in Middle America. As for the South,
ome of the more cosmopolitan cities are beginning to take
n interest, but even a bustling place like Atlanta has little
o offer. In some states, notably Alabama and the Carolinas,
he number of dry counties means that the drinker is
rateful for whatever can be provided.

Where to drink

he one gastronomically famous city of the South, New
Orleans, has probably the best-known spot for devotees of
eer: Cooter Brown's (509 S Carrollton). New Orleans also
as its own independent brewery, Dixie, which shows signs
f revival under a new ownership.

Gastronomically inclined visitors to the "Third Coast"
night also discover something to enjoy in Houston – and at
425 Alabama they will find the Ale House. One of the best
etail selections of beer in the South is in Dallas, at the
Bluebonnet grocery store (2106 Lower Greenville Avenue).
Dallas also has its own boutique, with the unlikely (but
ustifiable) name of Reinheitsgebot Brewing. Even more
ncongruously, the state capital of Texas – Austin – has a
Belgian speciality beer bar, called Gambrinus, in its main
treet. There are also good selections of beer in several of the
ars along Austin's nightlife strip of 6th Street, notably
Maggie Mae's.

The Arkansas Brewing Company (originally Riley Lyon), in
Little Rock, is also a boutique, if such an effete term may
e used there. Boutiques are planned elsewhere in the south,
nd no doubt selections of beers are growing in several cities,
ut too often the message is: "Coldest beer in town". Or:
"Last beer before dry county". In either case, what is on
ffer is probably a popsicle made from Schlitz.

Arkansas Brewing Co

This boutique was originally called Riley-Lyon, after its
ounders. The first product was **Riley's Red Lion**★★★, a well-
nade, copper-coloured pale ale, with a fresh, fruity acidity
n the finish. This proved too challenging for some local
alates, and emphasis has subsequently been given to the
nore orthodox **White Tail Lager**★ →★★, which is only lightly
opped, quite full in body, with a rather quick finish.

Dixie

The beer called simply **Dixie**★ is very light and sweetish.
However southern, the name hardly captures the spirit of
New Orleans, Louisiana, where the brewery resides. Perhaps
Cajun beer will emerge in due course.

When this old-established brewery was rescued by a dis-
ributor called Coy, a "super-premium" product was added.

This is called **Coy International Private Reserve★ →★★**, an
is markedly full in body, with slightly more colour and a hi
of hop.

Duncan

This former supermarket brewery in Auburndale, Florid
has recently been producing an all-malt, bronze lage
Hatuey★★, on behalf of Bacardi, for the Hispanic marke

Lone Star

Chauvinistic Texans swear by the crisp, dry **Lone Sta
★ →★★**. It is a pleasant enough beer, but in no wa
exceptional. The brewery, in San Antonio, is owned b
Heileman.

Pearl

Also in San Antonio, this brewery is owned by the sam
group as Pabst. **Pearl★** is a light, sweetish beer.

Reinheitsgebot Brewing Co

The name is an allusion to the German Beer Purity Law, th
inspiration and credo of this boutique, which is in th
community of Plano, in Collin County, on the edge of Dalla
Its principal product is **Collin County Pure Gold★★★**, a ful
bodied, all-malt, Pilsener-style beer, with a hearty, dry
hopped, bouquet. More products are planned.

Shiner

A "Spanish mission" building in a tiny town in the middle o
nowhere, about 70 miles (112km) south of Austin, an
slightly farther from San Antonio. It is a wonderfull
romantic brewery, serving a scatter of old and seemingl
incongruous Bohemian and Bavarian settlements, but it
principal product, **Shiner Premium★**, is an undistinguishe
product. **Shiner Bock★ →★★** has something of a followin
among young drinkers in Austin. This is a dark beer, bu
sadly a *Bock* is not allowed to be of high strength unde
Texas law.

THE CARIBBEAN

Emigrants from the Caribbean have helped spread th
popularity of several beers from the region. The best-know
internationally is **Red Stripe★**, a light-tasting, soft-bodie
lager from Jamaica. Other examples include the maltier an
fruitier **Banks Lager★**, from Barbados; and the malty, bu
drier, **Carib Lager★ →★★**, from Trinidad. Gravities ar
typically in the classical Pilsener range of 11.5–12 Plat
(1046–48); units of bitterness low (15–19); and lagerin
times short (two weeks is common).

Several Caribbean breweries also have sweet or medium
dry stouts, often bottom-fermented, and usually a
"tropical" gravities: in the range of 15–20 Plat
(1060–1080), with alcohol contents of between 4.5 and
percent by weight; 5.75–7.5 by volume.

Colonists introduced beer-brewing to the Caribbean, an
many European links remain, though there are also compan
ies under local control. At least ten islands currently hav
their own breweries (sometimes more than one), as do mos
countries on the Central American mainland.

LATIN AMERICA

From Mexico through Central and South America, the Latin countries of the New World all have breweries, and most are excitably proud of their beers: from **Cerveza Panama★** (dry, spritzy, quenching) to **Colombian Gold★→★★** (which tastes noticeably of hops, rather than their cousin cannabis), the beer trail stretches to Chile (where drinkers order beer by the square metre, to fill a table) and Brazil the biggest brewing nation in Latin America, boasting even the odd top-fermenting beer, like **Brahma Porter★★★**, at 17.5 Plato; 1070; 6.7; 8.6).

Mexico is also a major brewing nation in volume, and the biggest exporter from Latin America, with its industry in the hands of three large companies: Cuauhtemoc and Moctezuma are separate enterprises under one holding company; Modelo is family-owned. These three companies own 17 breweries, subject to current rationalization. Although all of the beers are bottom-fermenting, they are more varied, and interesting, than is commonly appreciated.

Cuauhtemoc

Second-largest of the Mexican brewing companies. Also owns Cruz Blanca. The products of Cuauhtemoc are lightened by a high proportion of corn, and tend to have a dry, slightly tannic, finish. A typically Mexican range includes a *bière ordinaire*, perilously bottled in clear glass, **Chihuahua★**; a dry, crisp quencher, **Tecate★**, customarily served with a pinch of salt and a slice of lime or lemon; a mainstream beer, **Carta Blanca★** (which in the US market has a notably smooth **Dark★★** version); a pleasantly hoppy, Pilsener-type, **Bohemia★→★★**, which has a higher than normal gravity (13; 1052; 4.2; 5.4); Vienna-type beer, **Indio Oscura★**, rather thin and dry for the style; and a dark, strong Christmas beer, **Commemorativa★★** (14.3; 1057; 4.3; 5.6). There is also a low-cal beer, **Brisa★**.

Moctezuma

Biggest exporter, but smallest in the Mexican market. Uses a lower proportion of adjuncts and makes a point that they include rice. Its beers tend to be relatively smooth, with a spritzy finish: kräusening is another point of policy. **Sol★** is its clear-glass beer; a very dry, light brew called **Hussong's★** is a newcomer to the range; **Superior★→★★** is a lightly fragrant, spritzy, Pilsener-type (11.5; 1046; 3.6; 4.5). Then comes the rather confusing Équis range. **Tres Equis★→★★** is a marginally fuller Pilsener-type. **Dos Equis Lager Especial ★→★★** is fractionally fuller again (12; 1048; 3.7; 4.6). The best-known version, simply called **Dos Equis★★★**, is amber-red in colour, and is the closest example among such Mexican beers to the traditional Vienna style. It, too, has a gravity of 12 Plato, and its palate achieves a teasing balance of malt and hop. **Tres Equis Oscura★★** is slightly darker in colour, and fuller-bodied (with a lovely malty finish) despite

being brewed from a slightly lower gravity. The dark brow
Noche Buena★★★ Christmas Beer (15; 1060; 4.2; 5.4) is ver
full-bodied, with both malt and hop in its long finish.

Modelo

Biggest of the Mexican brewing companies, also ownin
Yucatan. Its most noteworthy product is the **Negr
Modelo★★**, on the dark side for a Vienna-style beer, cream
in body, with a hint of chocolate (just the thing with chicke
molé). The Yucatan brands include a similar beer, the tasty
hoppier, **Negra Leon★★**. The group's other product
embrace the clear-glass **Corona★**, dry, firm and fruity; an
the carbonic **Victoria★**, a favourite with the working man i
Mexico. Some kräusening is done.

ASIA

When the United States sent Commodor
Perry to "open up" Japan in 1853, the ide
of beer-brewing was seeded, and soon grew
Outside the United States, the biggest brewin
company in a domestic market is Kirin, of Japan. Th
basic **Kirin Lager Beer★→★★** has the fullest bod
among the Japanese Pilseners, with Hallertau an
Saaz hops in both aroma and flavour. Among severa
excellent specialities, **Kirin Stout★★★** (18 Plato; 1072
6.4; 8) is especially notable. It is bottom-fermenting
but full of "burnt treacle toffee" flavour.

Sapporo Black Beer★★★ represents a Japanese
speciality (which seems originally to have been base
on the Kulmbach beers). This dry, dark lager, wit
licorice tones, can best be tasted in the beer garden i
the Victorian part of the brewery in Sapporo. Thi
company also has an unpasteurized (micro-filtered)
all-malt premium Pilsener called **Yebisu★★**, very
fruity, with some hop bitterness in the finish. Asahi'
beers tend to be dry and fruity, but with a weak finish
Suntory produces unpasteurized beers that are nota
bly clean and mild, though dry. This company'
speciality is the all-malt **Suntory Märzenbier★★★**.
slightly paler than those of Bavaria, with a drier.
firmer palate and a wonderfully fresh Saaz hoppiness
in both its bouquet and finish.

When Germany enjoyed a colonial "concession" in
Shantung, China, a brewery was established in the
resort town of Tsingtao. This is now one of China's
major exporters, and **Tsingtao Beer★→★★**, a hoppy
Pilsener, is a popular accompaniment to its national
cuisine in New York and San Francisco. The very
sweet **Tsingtao Porter★** is harder to find in the West

rews from other towns, such as **Tientan**★, a smooth,
alty Pilsener from Beijing, are exported in a small
ay, but China's economic growth means that
emand for beer cannot be met, despite every major
wn already having at least one brewery (several
ave two). More are planned, with technical help from
Vestern and Japanese brewers, and from at least one
British boutique-owner.

German technical help was used in 1934 to set up
he Boon Rawd Brewery, which produces the out-
tandingly hoppy **Singha Lager**★★★ (13.8 Plato; 1055;
.8; 6; and a hearty 40 units of bitterness) in Thailand.
The local rival **Amarit**★→★★ is milder.)

While the Singha is a mythical creature resembling
 lion, Tiger Beer is a legend in its own lunchtime,
erhaps because it entered literature through the pen
f Anthony Burgess. **Tiger Lager Beer**★→★★ is a
oppier cousin to Heineken. The same brewery has in
ts range the creamy, roasty, medium-dry **ABC Extra
tout**★★→★★★ (18.2; 1073; 6.5; 8.1). These products are
nade in Singapore and Malaysia.

India had 14 breweries in Colonial days, four by
ndependence, and now has no fewer than 32. United
Breweries, of Bangalore, is active in export markets
vith its dry, well-balanced **Kingfisher**★ lager and a
lightly hoppier, and smoother, premium Pilsener
variously called **Jubilee** and **Flying Horse**★→★★. The
ompany also makes a roasty, bottom-fermenting
London Stout★★ (1046). In Sri Lanka, McCallum makes
n all-malt **Three Coins Pilsener**★★ and a smooth,
hocolatey, bottom-fermenting **Sando Stout**★★→★★★
15; 1060). The rival Ceylon Breweries has the fruitier,
op-fermenting (in wood) **Lion Stout** ★★★, also all-malt,
it a similar gravity, producing 5 percent alcohol by
veight; 6.3 by volume. Astonishingly, Ceylon
Breweries' lager and stout are available, unpas-
eurized, from wooden casks, drawn by hand-pump,
it The Beer Shop, in the brewery's home town of
Nuwara Eliya, and at U.K.D. Silva, in the holy city of
Kandy.

Except in fundamentalist Muslim countries,
almost every corner of Asia has breweries. In a
eversal of Colonial roles, Spain's San Miguel
reweries have their parent company in The Philip-
ines. In addition to the light, smooth, dry **San
 iguel**★→★★, a pale Pilsener, the Filipinos also enjoy
Gold Eagle★→★★, lower in gravity but fuller in colour,
nd the stronger (14; 1056; 5.5; 6.8) **Red Horse**★★, soft-
odied, with some fruity notes. **San Miguel Dark
Beer**★★ also has an above-average gravity (13.5; 1054;
.1; 5.2) and a good toasted-malt character. The new
ival Asia Brewery is notable for its all-malt **Max
** →★★ (11.2; 1045; 4.5; 5.6).

AUSTRALASIA

For the lover of distinctive beers, the establish
ment of boutique breweries in Western Aus
tralia (Anchor and Matilda Bay) and on th
South Island of New Zealand (Mac's) during the earl
1980s represented a tiny hope of better things t
come. So did the glimmerings of a greater apprecia
tion for Cooper's ales and stouts, once widely regarde
with puzzlement even in their native South Australia

The provincialism of the Australian beer-drinke
has long rung as hollow as an empty schooner. Even i
the days when breweries like Carlton (in Victoria
emphasized the scope of their range, the difference
between most of the beers was not great. Nor wer
there huge distinctions between the beers of one stat
and another, contrary to the chauvinistic insistence o
their respective drinkers.

Such sensibilities were flouted when Carlton bega
to promote one of its products, Foster's, as a nationa
brand, on the way acquiring Tooth's Brewery (of New
South Wales), the two companies then being sub
sumed into the agricultural group Elders IXL, whic
then turned its attention to international markets
While this grouping was soon claiming almost 5
percent of the Australian market, a further 40 percen
was coalescing into a rival power bloc, embracin
Swan (of Western Australia), Castlemaine (of Queens
land) and Toohey's (of New South Wales).

All of these mergers took place between 1983 an
1985. These were breathless years in the Australia
brewing industry, but the excitement dwelt little o
its heritage, or the individuality of any product
involved (such as the dark ale **Toohey's Old**★★★ or th
characterful **Sheaf Stout**★★★). Beer had become
commodity for the financial pages, with attentio
focused on the swashbuckling entrepreneurs: fo
Elders, chairman and chief executive John Elliott; fo
the rival group, Alan Bond, the British-born Aus
tralian who was at the same time helping his countr
seize the America's Cup.

Meanwhile, in New Zealand, Lion swallowe
Leopard. This feline act left the country with only tw
major brewing companies, the other being Dominion

If there is a national character to the brews of eithe
country, it might be argued that Australia's lager
have traditionally been quite full-bodied, firm and o
the sweet side (sometimes using cane sugar as a
adjunct); New Zealand has some extremely swee
beers (often copper in colour, an inherited memory o
British ales, though bottom-fermenting), as well as
number of Pilseners in a more international style.

Anchor

irst revivalist pub brewery in Australia, at the "Sail and
nchor" (locally known by its previous name "The
reemason"; ☎335 8433), in Fremantle. In a beautifully
stored 1850s pub, hand-pumps are used to serve a selection
f very traditional, top-fermenting ales. Early examples
ave included a sweetish pale **Mild**★★★ (1035) similar to
ose found in the West Midlands of England; a Burton-
yle, cask-conditioned **Traditional Bitter**★★★ (1050), also
vailable in chilled draught form as "Best", bottle-con-
itioned as "Anchor Real Ale" and in a more carbonated
ariation as "Steam Beer"; a dark, strong ale called
ogbolter★★★ (1080); and a sweet **Milk Stout**★★★ (1065). All
erit attention, not least for their rarity. The same com-
any's Matilda Bay boutique specializes in bottom-fermen-
ation. Initial products have all been all-malt (for which
raise is deserved) lagers of 1055. They include a fairly
oppy, "Czech-style" **Pilsener**★★→★★★; a slightly milder,
Danish-style" **Light**★★ (the name refers to colour rather
an body) and a "Bavarian-style" **Dark**★★→★★★.

Carlton

he basic **Carlton Draught**★→★★ is a firm-bodied lager with
medium bitterness and full, golden colour. **Melbourne
itter**★→★★ is a little drier; **Victoria Bitter**★ lighter in
avour, darker in colour; **Foster's**★ full-bodied and sweetish.

Cascade

asmanian brewery. Its **Cascade Draught**★→★★ has a
ightly lower gravity and alcohol content (10.2; 1041; 3.7;
.6), but a fuller colour and more flavour, than its **Special
ager**★→★★ (10.8; 1043; 3.8; 4.8). While these typically
ustralian products have bitterness units in the range of 20,
bottom-fermenting **Sparkling Pale Ale**★★ (11.7; 1047; 4.1;
2) has 25 B.U. **Cascade Export Stout**★★ (15; 1060; 4.9; 6.1)
as 29 B.U. Cascade, in Hobart, and Boag's, of Launceston,
re under the same ownership. Boag's Export Stout is
narginally lower in gravity and alcohol content, and less
itter, but fuller in colour. Boag's range includes a fairly full-
odied and dry **Lager**★★ (11.5; 1046; 4.3; 5.4).

Castlemaine

Known for its "Fourex" probably since the days when the
nark XXXX was branded on to wooden barrels to identify
premium product. **Castlemaine XXXX**★★ is the most
haracterful of Australia's mass-market lagers, firm-bodied,
weetish but with a definite hop flavour. Blossoms are used.
Gold Lager★★ is slightly higher in gravity, drier, clean and
mooth. The company still makes its full-bodied, tangy
Carbine Stout★★→★★★ (13–14; 1055; 4.03; 5.10).

Cooper

Classic brewery that must seem wildly incongruous in
Australia. Cooper's is the only established Australian
rewery to retain top-fermenting ales and stouts as its
rinciple products. As if that were not enough to distinguish
t, Cooper's also uses wooden tuns for maturation. Better
till, it bottle-conditions. It is hard to say whether this
levotion to tradition resulted originally from principle or
leepiness. Now that Cooper's products are beginning to be

appreciated, it is to be hoped that tradition is not dilute
The characteristically cloudy, "real" **Ale★★★ → ★★★★** (iro
ically, labelled in some markets as "sparkling") is alread
paler than it once was. It is nonetheless a characterful bre
(with an alcohol content of 4.6; 5.75), full of fruitiness a
hop bitterness. Likewise the earthy, dryish **Extra Sto**
★★★★ (5.4; 6.8).

Dominion

The dubious achievement of having developed the conti
uous-fermentation method is accorded to this New Zealar
brewing company. **Dominion Bitter★** is its main produc

Leopard

Despite its having been taken over by Lion, this Ne
Zealand company still operates its Hastings brewer
producing **Leopard DeLuxe★ → ★★**, a premium Pilsen
using yeast from Heineken (former part-owners). It is
lightly fruity beer with some hop character.

Lion

Formerly known as New Zealand Breweries. Its **Lic**
Red★ → ★★ has a pale copper colour, a gravity of 9 Pla
(1036; 2.95; 3.7), and is malty, sweet and bottom-fermen
ing. A pale lager called **Rheineck★** is marginally strong
(9.8; 1039; 3.05; 3.85), again very sweet, but with son
fruitiness. **Steinlager★★** is a mildly dry premium Pilsen
produced at slightly different gravities depending upo
the market.

Mac's

Boutique brewery in New Zealand, near Nelson, at Stok
Founder Terry McCashin buys hops and barley grown in th
locality, and has his own maltings. His products, thoug
suggest caution either on his part or that of the consume
Mac's Real Ale★★ is actually produced with a lager yea
and, in its bottled form, pasteurized. It is intended to hav
ale characteristics but is really a malty, full-flavoure
bronze lager. **Black Mac★★** is a dark (deeply coppe
coloured) lager. **Mac's Gold★★ → ★★★** is a pale lager, wel
hopped and smooth. **Southop★ → ★★** is a sweet lager in th
style typical of New Zealand.

South Australian

Adelaide brewery whose products include the dryish **We**
End Draught★ → ★★ (9.9; 1040; 3.6; 4.5); the perfumy, b
maltier, **Southwark Premium★ → ★★** (12; 1048; 4.4; 5.5); an
the sweetish **Old Southwark Stout★★ → ★★★** (16.3; 1065; 5.
7.4). An export lager recalling the old **Broken Hill★ → ★**
brewery has earthy hoppiness in the nose and a spritzy body

South Pacific

The well-made **South Pacific Export Lager★ → ★★** is a light
fruity and dry, refreshing beer with a family resemblance t
its parent Heineken. The brewery is in Papua New Guine

Swan

West Australian giant, producing beers that are, by nation
standards, dryish and fairly light-bodied. Recently succes
ful with a low-alcohol **Swan Special Light★**.

AFRICA

The continent of Africa might claim to have had some of the first brewers, as the ancient Egyptians produced beer in at least 3000BC.

These beers were brewed from barley that was "malted" by a process of being germinated and then baked into a bread-like condition. This was then fermented, and must have produced something like the *kvass* that is still widely consumed in Russia. The unfiltered beer may have resembled the turbid, porridge-like traditional brews that are still made in Africa, from millet, cassava flour, plantains, or whatever is locally available.

However, all except the most fundamentalist Muslim countries of Africa have their own breweries producing modern beers. Most of these beers are of the Pilsener type, though the odd Bock can occasionally be found – and there are one or two ales (in South Africa) and stouts (in several countries, notably Nigeria). The stouts are usually dry, and sometimes of considerable strength (the tropical version of Guinness, at more than 18 Plato and 1070; around 8 percent alcohol by volume is typical).

Household names in most western European nations have established breweries in Africa, or contracted or licensed their products to be made there. Or they have acted as consultants or partners to local breweries, often with participation from national governments. In all, there are about 175 breweries in Africa, in at least 45 countries. By far the most heavily-breweried country is Nigeria, with more than 50, most of them built in the last two decades. Zaire and South Africa are also significant brewing nations in terms of volume. However, some very well-made beers are brewed in very small countries, like Gambia, Togo and the Seychelles.

Africa's first boutique brewery went into operation in 1984, in Knysna, Cape Province. The brewery began with an all-malt draught lager, then began to experiment with seasonal ales and stouts, cask-conditioned. Knysna is on the south coast, between Cape Town and Port Elizabeth. The owner of this remarkable enterprise, Lex Mitchell, formerly worked for South African Breweries, who otherwise enjoy a monopoly.

Having imported a taste for European beer, Africa is now flexing its muscles in export markets. Two early contenders are the slightly woody-tasting Ngoma Castel, from Kinshasa, and the smooth, sweetish Mamba, from Ivory Coast. Both are full-bodied and robust – lusty, emergent beers.